Out in the World

An LGBTQIA+ (and friends!) travel guide to more than 120 destinations around the world

AMY B. SCHER & MARK JASON WILLIAMS

NATIONAL GEOGRAPHIC

WASHINGTON, D.C.

Contents

Introduction 13

1 ✿ Our Favorite Small Towns With Big Pride 16

2 ✿ Boozy Trips and Trails 40

3 ✿ Can't-Miss Coastal Spots 70

4 ✿ Where No One Gets Hangry 98

5 ✿ Romantic Rendezvous 122

6 ✿ Holiday Season Escapes and Where to Escape the Holidays 146

7 ✿ Walk on the Wild Side 172

8 ✿ Get Your Theme On 194

9 ✿ Fun Haunts and Spooky Spirits 212

10 ✿ Nature and Nurture 232

11 ✿ Rainbows That Get Left Off the List 250

12 ✿ Classic Cities With Something for Everyone 270

Acknowledgments 292

Illustrations Credits 293

Index 295

INTRODUCTION
Join Us Out in the World

As passionate travelers who've spent decades trekking the globe, we're always up for new adventures—and we love helping others plan their journeys, too. But in researching destinations and experiences to explore, we've been disappointed with the significant lack of LGBTQIA+ content available.

Though some travel guides have small queer-focused sections, almost all of them stop after a few listings for LGBTQIA+ bars and typical hot spots. We do love a good drink, as well as lively drag shows and Pride parades, but we also want to go beyond the obvious to discover cute small towns, safari adventures, and pockets around the world that offer more well-rounded experiences—while still being able to be our true selves.

That's what led us to write this book. We wanted to create our own ultimate guide that supports LGBTQIA+ travelers, and our allies, in meaningful ways—including queer-owned and welcoming businesses, exciting destinations, and memorable activities where everyone feels like part of a community. And so, we're guiding you to more than 120 destinations that are LGBTQIA+ (and ally!) friendly.

We believe that travelers should never feel limited. When trips are thoughtfully planned, LGBTQIA+ travelers and our allies can enjoy many of the same places around the world. We can also rediscover the joys of travel with renewed energy and possibilities—together.

Some of the destinations we feature in these pages are not historically known for being LGBTQIA+ friendly (but are making progress). We still think they're worth a visit—with precautions—to truly discover what the world has to offer and to encourage these places to continue to leave old laws and views behind (see Africa's Seychelles, page 88). We've also included destinations that pleasantly surprised us for being more inclusive than we imagined (hello Fairhope, Alabama, page 256).

Most important, we only shared destinations we feel comfortable visiting ourselves (as both solo travelers and with our spouses). Although we are excited to share these with you, we of course support you in making travel choices within your own comfort zone.

Join us as we journey to exciting destinations and create opportunities for unforgettable memories with your partner, old friends and new, your entire family, or on your own—not just *around* the world, but *out* in the world.

Explore Venice via the water on a canal tour. PAGES *2–3*: Grampians National Park, Victoria, Australia PAGES *4–5*: Pride decorations at the Siam Paragon shopping center, Thailand PAGES *6–7*: Côte d'Or Beach, Seychelles PAGES *8–9*: The New York City skyline during Pride month

MEET YOUR TRAVEL GUIDES: AMY AND MARK

Amy B. Scher

I've always loved to travel, especially as a kid in our family's VW bus named Bernie, making stops along the way before unpacking at hotels with fluffy beds and mounds of pillows. Then, in 2007, when I was in my late 20s, travel took on a new meaning: life or death. After struggling for almost a decade with an incurable illness (chronic Lyme disease and serious complications), I took a leap of faith and raised the funds to go to Delhi, India, to pursue an experimental treatment I hoped would save my life. The entire trip, including the unexpected love story of meeting my future wife there, became my life's biggest plot twist—and led to my ultimate healing. Slightly more than 10 years later, I got to tell the world about it in my memoir, *This Is How I Save My Life*.

Grateful for my complete recovery, I now use my experiences to share how travel and well-being can intersect, and how exploring our neighborhoods and destinations around the world helps us discover and become who we really are. I hope this guide helps more people feel like their truest and brightest selves, no matter where they go in the world.

Mark Jason Williams

I first dreamed of journeying around the world when I was five years old, but as a kid with leukemia, I wasn't sure I'd have the chance. I felt sad that my friends went to Walt Disney World while I was left behind, but my parents lifted my spirits by bringing issues of *National Geographic* into my hospital room. Flipping through the pages inspired me to keep dreaming.

Sixteen years later, I embarked on my first big trip: a study abroad program in Florence. I worked multiple jobs and took out student loans to pay for it, but walking across the Ponte Vecchio was magical and made it worthwhile. While exploring the city, I felt more cultured and confident than ever before, which helped me come to terms with my sexuality and become proud to be a gay man.

Today, I love experiencing the world with my husband (my favorite travel partner). Together, we've achieved my lifelong dream of making it to seven continents. I feel fortunate each time I visit a new place, no matter how near or far. And that more of the world is welcoming to queer travelers like us.

OUR INCLUSIVE APPROACH

All the hotels, restaurants, stores, and other businesses we've listed are known as either queer-owned or LGBTQIA+ welcoming. On some occasions, we've called out specific bars, inns, or other establishments that might cater to a specific group (for example, gay men). This is to help you navigate where you might feel most comfortable as you explore our many suggestions.

In the cases of major hotel brands (such as Hilton, Axel, and Marriott), we chose those we appreciate, love, and respect for their inclusivity and equitable treatment of the LGBTQIA+ community. They are brands that make us feel at home around the world.

HOW TO USE THIS BOOK

Though typical travel books tend to be organized geographically, *Out in the World* helps you plan your vacations more intuitively—organized into quirky and fun chapters based on vibes, experiences, and themes. We'll help you find the best (and most welcoming) places to fill your travel bucket lists and discover destinations that may not be on your radar yet.

The recommendations for each destination are designed to inspire but never overwhelm you. Though we provide plenty of details to help you build your itinerary, we encourage you to go at your own pace and choose your own adventures, too.

We start every entry with the LGBTQIA+ Lowdown, which provides info on laws, community groups, and other aspects of inclusion in the area. You'll also find helpful sidebars with suggestions on when to go (including the times for Pride and other not-to-miss LGBTQIA+ events), where to stay (our favorite hotels and inns), and what to know (which includes close side trips or special information to consider).

As for how to read this book, we suggest front to back to discover all the possibilities. Or skip around to meet your mood as you plan your next weekend outing or the trip of a lifetime. Either way, we'll be there for it.

BE AN ALLY OUT IN THE WORLD

♦ This may feel obvious, but it's so essential we're adding it to the top of our list: Support queer-owned businesses (while traveling, that means tour companies, restaurants, and hotels in particular) and/or those known to champion the queer community.

♦ Join your LGBTQIA+ travel partners at the bars and clubs . . . but respect their space if they'd prefer you don't.

♦ Show your Pride beyond the parades and seek out other LGBTQIA+ events to attend or local groups to support.

♦ Remember your trans and nonbinary loved ones when planning a day at the pool or beach, and try to find facilities like gender-neutral changing rooms.

♦ Learn and respect someone's pronouns. It's totally OK to ask but best to never assume.

♦ When traveling with others, have an honest, judgment-free conversation about your travel companions' wants, needs, and comfort levels—and be open to altering plans if need be.

CHAPTER 1

Our Favorite SMALL TOWNS — With — BIG PRIDE

We love big cities for their LGBTQIA+ visibility and inclusion. But many small towns (and smaller cities with a real village vibe) also come with a whole lot of Pride. Places such as Provincetown in Massachusetts, a longtime LGBTQIA+ favorite escape, and Thessaloniki in Greece, host of EuroPride 2024, enthusiastically wave the welcoming rainbow flag, support queer-owned businesses, and embrace queer residents and visitors as part of their communities. Read on to discover how our favorite small towns deliver the perks of larger destinations with more space and relaxing vibes, so you can enjoy your time and travel just as you are.

ESCAPE TO A MAGICAL MOUNTAIN SHANGRI-LA.
Ojai, California, U.S.A.

Try a "Moon Face" chocolate sculpture at Beato Chocolates.

THE LGBTQIA+ LOWDOWN Tucked away in the idyllic Topatopa Mountains between Los Angeles and Santa Barbara, this town is so LGBTQIA+ friendly that residents say, "Everyone is just out, everywhere."

With its laid-back vibes, stunning natural habitats, farm-fresh food, and heart-centered gathering places, Ojai is the perfect place to relax, nourish yourself, and just be.

Take in stunning valley views at the International Garden of Peace at Meditation Mount, a nonprofit organization with flower-filled grounds (make sure to preregister). Go right before sunset to see Ojai's famous "pink moment": when the valley lights up in a pink-and-reddish glow. For more time outside, drive into the valley to Rose Valley Falls, a one-mile (1.6 km) hike through the trees to a waterfall, doable for most fitness levels.

For culture and community, there's no better fix than grabbing a coffee downtown and browsing through the queer women–owned Beato Chocolates for bite-size sculptures created from iconic Ojai artist Beatrice "Beato" Wood's pottery molds and chocolate bars wrapped in packaging that

features reproductions of her hand-colored etchings. No trip to Ojai is complete without perusing Bart's Books, the world's largest outdoor bookstore, founded in 1964. Bart's carries mostly used books, including many queer titles and those on gender and sexuality.

Have a meal at Rôtie, a farmer-driven Lebanese French picnic spot with rotisserie chicken and handmade sourdough, plus local wine and beer. Or try family-owned Boccali's Pizza and Pasta with its vineyard views and famous strawberry shortcake. For an Instagram-worthy hangout, head to Tipple & Ramble, a female-owned business with wine, cheese, and a yard with twinkling string lights and retro furniture. Zaidee's, located on Soule Park Golf Course, has a *Cheers*-like vibe and breathtaking views of the mountains. Enjoy an afternoon at the iconic Ojai Deer Lodge, the oldest tavern in Ojai, with a really fun vibe and live music and drinks that flow freely.

◆ WHEN TO GO

Ojai has mostly temperate weather, except for heat waves in July and August that are best to avoid. June offers the Ojai Music Festival, a four-day classical music celebration.

◆ WHERE TO STAY

The Ojai Valley Inn for a splurge, set in Mission-style buildings, has scenic mountain views, tennis courts, golf, and great pools. For something less hotel-y, Caravan Outpost has luxe Airstreams or tiny wooden houses. Or just a short walk to town, Emerald Iguana Inn was designed with the surrealist architect Gaudí in mind. You'll find warm wood tones and Barcelona vibes plus a cozy pool with lush surroundings.

◆ WHAT TO KNOW

Just 20 minutes south of Ojai, Ventura makes for a great day trip. You'll find some of the best thrifting in Southern California (along downtown's Main Street), and Surfers Point is a fantastic place to perch and watch the waves. From "the point," as locals call it, walk the boardwalk until you hit the Pier, a filming location for *Little Miss Sunshine*. Stop by Paddy's Bar + Lounge, an LGBTQIA+ institution with karaoke, drag shows, and drinks all night. Or consider heading 30 miles (48 km) north of Ojai to the weekend Santa Barbara Arts & Crafts Show, which stretches along the beach with more than 150 artisan vendors at Chase Palm Park.

The Peace Portal, constructed from a 1,200-year-old Douglas fir, invites visitors into the International Peace Garden.

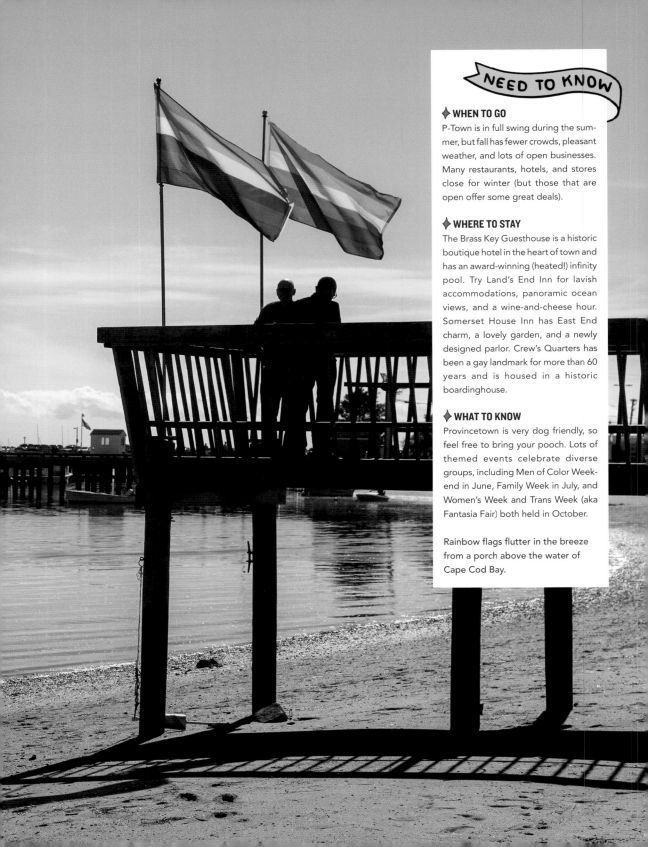

NEED TO KNOW

◆ WHEN TO GO
P-Town is in full swing during the summer, but fall has fewer crowds, pleasant weather, and lots of open businesses. Many restaurants, hotels, and stores close for winter (but those that are open offer some great deals).

◆ WHERE TO STAY
The Brass Key Guesthouse is a historic boutique hotel in the heart of town and has an award-winning (heated!) infinity pool. Try Land's End Inn for lavish accommodations, panoramic ocean views, and a wine-and-cheese hour. Somerset House Inn has East End charm, a lovely garden, and a newly designed parlor. Crew's Quarters has been a gay landmark for more than 60 years and is housed in a historic boardinghouse.

◆ WHAT TO KNOW
Provincetown is very dog friendly, so feel free to bring your pooch. Lots of themed events celebrate diverse groups, including Men of Color Weekend in June, Family Week in July, and Women's Week and Trans Week (aka Fantasia Fair) both held in October.

Rainbow flags flutter in the breeze from a porch above the water of Cape Cod Bay.

GET SWEPT AWAY BY SEASIDE CHARMS AND A THRIVING QUEER COMMUNITY.

Provincetown, Massachusetts, U.S.A.

THE LGBTQIA+ LOWDOWN Provincetown is a longtime haven for the LGBTQIA+ community with many queer-owned businesses and the largest number of same-sex households in the U.S. per capita.

On the northern tip of Cape Cod and an easy drive (or ferry) from Boston, Provincetown (or P-Town, if you please) is a relaxed waterfront destination with art galleries, pretty beaches, scenic bike paths, and many inclusive bars and restaurants.

Start on Commercial Street. After people- (and puppy-) watching to your heart's content, visit the 252-foot (77 m) Pilgrim Monument (spectacular views await), Provincetown Public Library (look for the half-scale model of the celebrated schooner *Rose Dorothea),* and Provincetown Art Association and Museum, featuring more than 4,000 works by 900-plus artists.

With so many cool shops on Commercial Street, favorites include lesbian-owned Womencrafts, promoting female artisans, authors, and musicians since 1976; Adam's Nest, a gay-owned and gay-operated clothing store that strives to "create some social change and look f*&kin' fabulous while doing it"; and Toys of Eros, a queer, female-owned adult shop and museum with sex-positive products and messaging for everyone, including those who are trans, nonbinary, or genderqueer. Over on the East End, stop at AMP (Art Market Provincetown), Bowersock Gallery, and East End Books, which is right on the beach and has a wide selection of LGBTQIA+ titles. All are queer owned.

Next, hit the beach! Herring Cove is popular with gay men and offers a nudist section and spectacular sunsets. Race Point has big waves and impressive dunes (get a closer look with Art's Dune Tours). Look for whales with the Dolphin Fleet of Provincetown, led by naturalists since 1975. Or enjoy a bike ride on the Province Lands Bike Trail, which connects Herring Cove and Race Point.

The "birthplace of U.S. theater," P-Town offers great live entertainment, too. Catch a Broadway star in concert at the Provincetown Art House or see a play at the historic Provincetown Theater.

When you're hungry, get in line for *malasadas* (Portuguese fried dough) at the Provincetown Portuguese Bakery, founded in 1900. Or enjoy lobster eggs Benedict at Liz's Café, Anybody's Bar. Seafood lovers, check out the Canteen or the Lobster Pot. Italian is on the menu at Strangers and Saints and Mistralino, both gay owned and gay operated. Quench your thirst at Crown and Anchor, Atlantic House (one of the oldest queer bars in the United States), Provincetown Brewing Co., or the Shipwreck Lounge. In warmer months, don't miss the famous tea dance at the Boatslip Resort and Beach Club, a nearly 50-year-old tradition where P-Town gathers for a spirited outdoor dance party.

A group of mermen saunter across downtown's bustling Commercial Street.

EXPERIENCE SOUTHERN HOSPITALITY SERVED WITH PRIDE.
Eureka Springs, Arkansas, U.S.A.

THE LGBTQIA+ LOWDOWN Nicknamed the "gay capital of the Ozarks," Eureka Springs has long advocated for equality. Before the United States legalized same-sex marriage in 2015, Eureka Springs residents formed domestic partnership registries, and the town enacted laws banning discrimination based on sexual orientation or gender expression.

An Arkansas mountain town famous for its mineral springs and Victorian architecture, Eureka Springs may not be the first place you think of as a queer-friendly destination, but with more than 30 percent of its population identifying as LGBTQIA+, the town is a leader in southern hospitality.

Millions come for the Great Passion Play, "Christ of the Ozarks" statue, and Thorncrown Chapel, an architectural gem with 425 windows—more than 6,000 square feet (557 m²) of glass. According to architect E. Fay Jones, it's a place to "think your best thoughts."

Downtown Eureka Springs is a fun-filled labyrinth. Stroll the Historic Loop, a 3.5-mile (5.6 km) walking tour with 300 gorgeous Victorian-era buildings. Don't miss the rainbow steps on North Main Street for a Pride photo spot. Though we prefer seeing the sights on foot, be warned some of these streets are steep. An enjoyable alternative is the Eureka Springs Trolley: an 85-minute tour of the historic highlights. While downtown, support queer-owned businesses, including nuJava Coffee Company for ethically sourced artisan brews and Sugar & Spite for candies and glass-bottle sodas, plus games, house swag, and gifts.

Follow the town's Natural Springs Trail to Grotto Spring, Sweet Spring, and the popular Basin Spring Park, a great place to listen to live music. For a full-body experience, pamper yourself with a warm mineral bath at the Palace Hotel & Bath House.

Outside of the city, Turpentine Creek Wildlife Refuge focuses on big cat rescue. Accredited by the Global Federation of Animal Sanctuaries, the 459-acre (186 ha) property is home to tigers, lions, leopards, cougars, and more. There's also a cool tree house with a panoramic view of the Arkansas landscape.

You can also go for a swim, hike, and picnic at Beaver Lake, take a subterranean tour at Onyx Cave Park, go back in time at Blue Spring Heritage Center, or visit Quigley's Castle, known as the Ozarks' "strangest dwelling," for loads of tropical plants and eccentric collections.

Eat your way around town: Try gay-owned Nibbles Eatery for gourmet salads, Le Stick Nouveau for fine dining, and the Stone House for meats, cheese, and wine. Then continue the fun at Missy's White Rabbit Lounge for drinks and live music, Rowdy Beaver Den (try the fried pickle chips), and queer-owned Eureka Live for the biggest party in town, complete with fantastic drag shows and dancing.

The Eureka Springs Wanderoo Lodge first opened as a campground called Camp Joy.

⬧ **WHEN TO GO**

Spring brings temperatures that hover in the 60s and less humidity.

⬧ **WHERE TO STAY**

The 1886 Crescent Hotel & Spa, a lavish accommodation, is allegedly the most haunted hotel in the United States. Gay-owned options include Magnetic Valley Resort, an all-male (including trans men) retreat in a serene setting, and the pet-friendly Wanderoo Lodge, which has a bar, restaurant, and the town's largest swimming pool.

⬧ **WHAT TO KNOW**

Generally, Arkansas is conservative. Use caution if visiting other destinations in the state.

The rainbow-covered "Cash and Boardman Mural" staircase in historic downtown Eureka Springs

NEED TO KNOW

◆ WHEN TO GO
Spring and fall have comfortable temperatures, blooming flowers, and changing leaves.

◆ WHERE TO STAY
Check out Pineapple Hill Inn B&B for period antiques, a wraparound porch, and a koi pond. Try Wishing Well B&B for its character, cozy fireplaces, and historic well. Both properties are gay owned. The River House at Odette's has amazing riverfront views, luxurious rooms, a great restaurant, and hosts Pride and other LGBTQIA+ events.

◆ WHAT TO KNOW
While in New Hope, visit the equally charming Lambertville, New Jersey, via a quick stroll over the aptly named New Hope–Lambertville Bridge.

The Bucks County Playhouse operates out of a late 18th-century gristmill.

EXPERIENCE THE BEST KIND OF DRAMA IN BUCOLIC BUCKS COUNTY.

New Hope, Pennsylvania, U.S.A.

THE LGBTQIA+ LOWDOWN New Hope has welcomed the LGBTQIA+ community for decades with its inclusive hotels, restaurants, and stores. In May, New Hope PrideFest brings the town together for dance parties, art exhibits, educational events, and a parade complete with floats, marching bands, and a 25-foot (8 m) rainbow flag.

Just an hour from Philadelphia and 90 minutes from Manhattan, New Hope is a total charmer, complete with a vibrant arts scene, pretty scenery, and renowned theater.

Don't miss a chance to visit Bucks County Playhouse, a historic theater that has entertained audiences since 1939 and premiered plays by celebrated playwrights such as Terrence McNally and Neil Simon. Stars have also graced its stage, including legends like Angela Lansbury and Audra McDonald.

We're also fans of New Hope Arts, a place for local artists to showcase visual, written, and performance pieces. From exhibitions to film festivals and salons, New Hope Arts always has something cool happening.

Main Street is where you'll find everything from luxury bath products at the Soap Opera Company to Gothic art at the Creeper Gallery. Grab your next great read at Farley's Bookshop, an independent bookstore that's been open since 1967. Or find unique crafts at Heart of the Home and just about anything else at Love Saves the Day, packed from floor to ceiling with vintage magazines, toys, clothes, and more. Then check out Peddler's Village, a ridiculously cute

18th-century-style complex with specialty stores, an inn, restaurants, and special events. There are also lots of places for antiquing, including Hobensack & Keller and America Antiques and Design.

Get outside on the Delaware Canal towpath (part of Delaware Canal State Park), which offers 60 miles (97 km) of flat land to walk, bike, or even cross-country ski in winter months. At Washington Crossing Historic Park, see where George Washington led troops across the river in 1776 (and marked a turning point in the Revolutionary War) and tour gardens and historic homes. Or head to Bowman's Hill Wildflower Preserve, which has more than 700 native plant species and almost five miles (8 km) of trails through forests and meadows. For a scenic ride, hop on the New Hope Railroad and journey through Bucks County's bucolic woods and farmlands.

Head to the Ferry Market, a complex with vendors offering everything from Peruvian empanadas to garlic-knot potato tots, plus outposts for coffee, wine, and beer. Other excellent dining choices include the Salt House, a gastropub housed inside a stone building dating back to 1751, and Karla's, a longtime LGBTQIA+ community favorite with an excellent brunch and a lovely covered porch.

Main Street is a popular destination for eclectic shopping and local eats.

MAKE WAVES IN THIS LOBSTER-LOVING TOWN.
Ogunquit, Maine, U.S.A.

Bring your four-legged friends along for a day at the beach in Ogunquit, Maine.

THE LGBTQIA+ LOWDOWN If any place could be called *the* LGBTQIA+ spot in Maine, it would be this town. Queer welcoming, and with its own large LGBTQIA+ resident community, Ogunquit was one of the first towns to pass a nondiscrimination ordinance to protect LGBTQIA+ people.

Its name translates to "beautiful place by the sea" in the Abenaki language, and Ogunquit lives up to the hype both in place and heart. Seventy-five miles (121 km) from Boston, this charming seaside resort town with a narrow peninsula is consistently named one of the best beaches in the United States.

Take the winding cliffside coastal trail, Marginal Way, through the dunes to Perkins Cove, a postcard-worthy fishing village at Ogunquit's south end. Beach Plum Farm is also a great spot to soak up nature. With 22 acres (9 ha), Beach Plum is the last remaining saltwater farm in Ogunquit. Take the half-mile (0.8 km) trail through a meadow with views of the Ogunquit River, dunes, and the Atlantic Ocean. And because Maine loves its lighthouses, go see Cape Neddick's Nubble Lighthouse, built in 1879, with its vibrant red roof. It's not open to the public, but you can get great views from Sohier Park. For a scenic tour, ride the Ogunquit Trolley, which has been running through town since 1981.

There's also great theater at the world-class Ogunquit Playhouse. Listed on the National Register of Historic Places, the playhouse has made uplifting artists and administrators of color, all genders, and varying disabilities part of its mission.

Productions range from Broadway shows to big-screen adaptations, with choices for all ages.

Visit the Ogunquit Museum of American Art for contemporary and modern art dating back to the 1800s. The Ogunquit Heritage Museum, housed in an 18th-century residence and devoted to Native American history, is also on the National Register of Historic Places.

Hungry travelers should try Jonathan's, owned by Jonathan West who converted his family home into the restaurant in 1976. West sources ingredients from his 12-acre (5 ha) organic farm and prioritizes sustainable seafood. Or get a table at the Front Porch, an award-winning restaurant open for more than 40 years. You'll find a diverse menu and a popular sing-along piano bar. The Old Village Inn restaurant is LGBTQIA+ friendly and a popular mainstay that serves New England chowder, fish-and-chips, baked haddock, and other favorites. For a more casual option, try Footbridge Lobster, a little red shack in the center of Perkins Cove (its owner sails out each day for his catch), or Barnacle Billy's, a neighborhood institution. With Maine's lobster industry widely recognized as one of the most sustainable in the world, you can feel good about what you eat. Mainestreet is a happening LGBTQIA+ nightclub with dancing, drag shows, karaoke, and an outdoor deck.

❖ NEED TO KNOW

❖ WHEN TO GO
It's a seasonal beach destination, so avoid the winter months when many things are closed. May, June, and September are best for those who tend to shy away from crowds.

❖ WHERE TO STAY
The Norseman Resort is the only beachfront hotel on Ogunquit Beach. Anchorage by the Sea offers direct access to Marginal Way. The 2 Village Square Inn Ogunquit is a B&B in a renovated Victorian home from 1886 and has ocean views, a pool, and a porch with rockers.

❖ WHAT TO KNOW
Kennebunkport is a historic fishing village about 10 miles (16 km) from Ogunquit. It has both a charming downtown and a rural vibe, plus nice coastal inlets for boating, fishing, and more.

Cape Neddick's Nubble Lighthouse, operating since 1879

PERKINS COVE

Small-town charm is on full display in Ogunquit's Perkins Cove, situated smack-dab between the harbor and the Atlantic Ocean. Formerly a fishing village and a colony for artists, "The Cove"—as locals call it—now bustles with artisan shops selling everything from handcrafted chocolates to original, multimedia artwork. You can also sample Maine's famous lobster, chowder, and other fresh catches at great eateries, including local favorite Barnacle Billy's. And did we mention the amazing ocean views and sea breezes? Stroll the Marginal Way, or catch a boat for fishing excursions or scenic cocktail cruises.

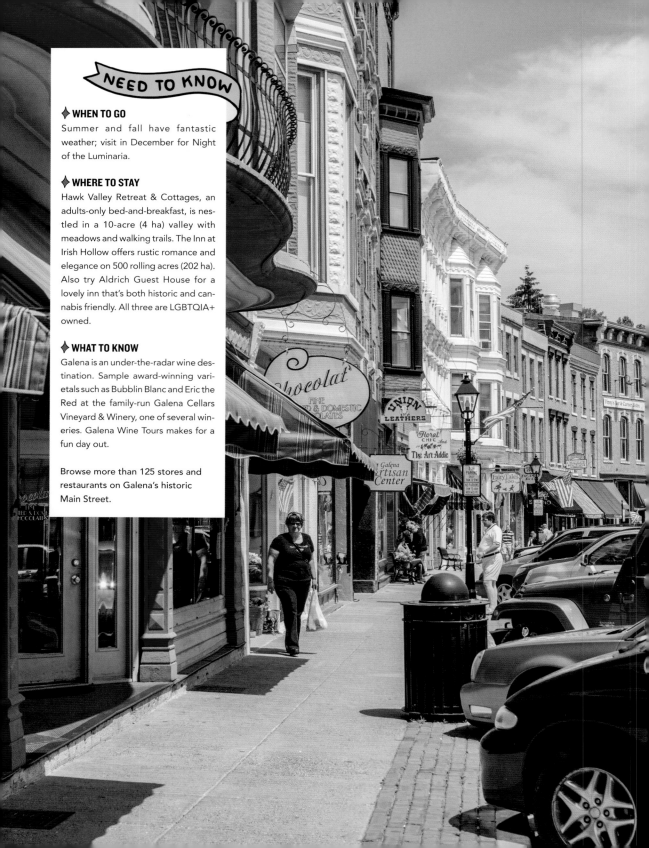

NEED TO KNOW

◆ WHEN TO GO

Summer and fall have fantastic weather; visit in December for Night of the Luminaria.

◆ WHERE TO STAY

Hawk Valley Retreat & Cottages, an adults-only bed-and-breakfast, is nestled in a 10-acre (4 ha) valley with meadows and walking trails. The Inn at Irish Hollow offers rustic romance and elegance on 500 rolling acres (202 ha). Also try Aldrich Guest House for a lovely inn that's both historic and cannabis friendly. All three are LGBTQIA+ owned.

◆ WHAT TO KNOW

Galena is an under-the-radar wine destination. Sample award-winning varietals such as Bubblin Blanc and Eric the Red at the family-run Galena Cellars Vineyard & Winery, one of several wineries. Galena Wine Tours makes for a fun day out.

Browse more than 125 stores and restaurants on Galena's historic Main Street.

WALK ONE OF THE BEST MAIN STREETS IN THE U.S.
Galena, Illinois, U.S.A.

THE LGBTQIA+ LOWDOWN Galena is one of the most queer-friendly towns in the Midwest, known for treating its residents and visitors with equality and respect. It may be small, but the town is big on queer-owned inns, restaurants, and shops to explore.

Just three hours from Chicago and Milwaukee, Galena is known for its remarkably preserved 19th-century architecture (more than 85 percent of the town's buildings are listed on the National Register of Historic Places), scenic countryside, and super-welcoming environment.

Main Street—dubbed the "Helluva Half Mile"—favors independently owned businesses for eating, drinking, and perusing. You'll find more than 125 locally owned businesses. Some top spots include the Galena Canning Company, stocked with sauces, marinades, and more, all made nearby and packed with character; Poopsie's, which has fun toys, books, and gifts; Galena's Kandy Kitchen, offering homemade sweet treats; and Peace of the Past for its humongous inventory of antiques, books, and treasures. During the holidays, experience Night of the Luminaria, when the entire town is illuminated by candlelight and storefronts feature festive window displays.

History buffs will want to tour the former home of U.S. president and Civil War general Ulysses S. Grant. This Italianate-style brick house features original furnishings and artifacts dating back to 1865, the year the town gifted the house to Grant after he returned from the war.

To take advantage of Galena's great outdoors, go to Casper Bluff Land and Water Reserve, a serene spot for birding and hiking with amazing views of the Mississippi River. This architecturally rich site contains centuries-old Native American mounds that were used for burials and other sacred rituals. For more nature, hike to a gorgeous waterfall at Thunder Bay Falls, enjoy year-round activities, including skiing and zip-lining at Chestnut Mountain Resort, or head to state parks such as Horseshoe Mound Preserve for more stunning views along hiking trails.

Save time to try Galena's restaurants and watering holes, too. Start your day at Otto's Place, serving French toast, lox on sourdough, and grilled ham and cheese. Next, get Wiener schnitzel and escargot at Fritz and Frites, which combines French and German cuisine. Fried Green Tomatoes has steaks, seafood, and an A-plus wine list (in a gorgeous exposed-brick dining room), and Durty Gurt's is known for juicy burgers and thick shakes. Raise a glass at Miss Kitty's Grape Escape, serving specialty martinis (plus a Bloody Mary buffet every Saturday), or the Blaum Bros. Distilling Co., a craft distillery producing premium whiskey, vodka, and gin.

Horseshoe Mound Preserve offers 200 acres (81 ha) of outdoor recreational opportunities.

(WATER)FALL IN LOVE WITH THIS VICTORIAN-ERA GEM.
Niagara-on-the-Lake, Ontario, Canada

Niagara Falls celebrates Pride with a rainbow light show at the iconic waterfalls.

THE LGBTQIA+ LOWDOWN Among the world's most welcoming countries, Canada enacted antidiscriminatory laws in 1996 and legalized same-sex marriage in 2005. The Niagara region is home to organizations such as OUTniagara, focusing on advocacy and community-building, and Pride Niagara, which sponsors Niagara Pride Week and other queer-focused events.

One of Canada's most picturesque towns, Niagara-on-the-Lake (as in Lake Ontario, one of the five "Great" ones) looks like something out of a 19th-century storybook, complete with an unmissable clock tower, immaculately preserved Victorian buildings, and ornate gardens. If you love waterfalls as much as us, Niagara Falls is a must-see. But with about 30 million people visiting every year, the area can get a little busy. Thank goodness that the utterly adorable Niagara-on-the-Lake is a welcome escape just 30 minutes from the famous falls with reasons to visit that are all its own.

A big draw is the Shaw Festival, an annual theater extravaganza running from May to December. Entertaining audiences since 1962, it's spread across three theaters—the Royal George, Festival, and Jackie Maxwell Studio—and features the works of famed playwright George Bernard Shaw, plus other plays, musicals, and events.

Take a stroll along the lake at Queen's Royal Park, where clear days show off the Toronto skyline, or cycle the Niagara River Parkway. You can also visit historic Fort George and walk down swoon-worthy Main Street for fun stores like Cool as a Moose and Old Tyme Candy Shoppe. Step back in time at Niagara Apothecary, a pharmacy museum with a mesmerizing collection of glass bottles containing paints, dyes, tobacco, and "miracle" potions pharmacists used 100 years ago.

If you like vino, you're in luck: The Niagara Peninsula is the largest wine region in Ontario with more than 30 wineries where you can sample Pinot Noir, Riesling, or the region's world-famous ice wine (a sweet wine created from grapes frozen on the vine). Canada produces more ice wine than all other countries combined, and the majority comes from the Niagara region. At Peller Estates, try their signature Ice Cuvée (made with sparkling wine and ice wine) while sitting in an igloo-like setting or next to a roaring fire. It also has an on-site restaurant.

Other notable spots include Pillitteri Estates Winery, which started as a small farmers market and grew into an award-winning winery, and Inniskillin, famous for being Canada's first estate winery (launched in 1975) and an international award–winning maker of ice wine. Visit the estate to enjoy a tasting in the historic Brae Burn Barn, or park yourself in a Muskoka chair and take in vineyard views.

Last, but certainly not least, head to Niagara Falls. When you're done staring at this marvel, consider a poncho-draped ride with Maid of the Mist—prepare to get wet.

NEED TO KNOW

◆ **WHEN TO GO**
Between May and October the weather
is most pleasant.

◆ **WHERE TO STAY**
The Prince of Wales offers luxury,
including antique furnishings and inlaid
floors. Queen's Landing is an opulent
Georgian mansion overlooking the
Niagara River. For dog-friendly comfort
in a lovely setting, go to the Harbour
House Hotel.

◆ **WHAT TO KNOW**
The area makes for a great couple's
getaway. Though there aren't
LGBTQIA+ bars or clubs, you'll find
plenty of options in nearby Buffalo (an
hour away) or Toronto (about 90 minutes away).

Step back in time at Fort George
National Historic Site.

◆ WHEN TO GO

Go during the annual ChillOut Festival (March), the largest queer festival in Australia since 1997. VicBears hosts the annual BearFEST, with dance parties as well as the Mr. VicBear competition, typically the last week of January.

◆ WHERE TO STAY

Hotel Frangos Daylesford is a super-LGBTQIA+-friendly home away from home, in a building from the 1800s (and with a great wine bar). Lake House Daylesford offers water views, gardens, and a cooking school. Another option, the Daylesford Hotel, is a 100-year-old building in the center of town where you can stroll to shops, cafés, and more. To be close to the ChillOut Festival, choose the Daylesford Art Motel, located close to all the action; suites feature work from local artists.

◆ WHAT TO KNOW

In Australia, the summer months of December, January, and February bring the warmest weather.

Look out over Mount Stapylton and the Wimmera Plains from Hollow Mountain in Grampians National Park.

THIS IS THE PLACE FOR WINE, WALKS, AND KOALA CUTENESS.

Daylesford, Victoria, Australia

Enjoy a warm evening with a meal on Vincent Street.

THE LGBTQIA+ LOWDOWN Daylesford is the queer capital of Victoria and the new home of Tinder's Big Rainbow Project, celebrating regional pride and inclusion. It's the first of more than 150 "Big Things" across Australia dedicated to the LGBTQIA+ community.

Located in the Macedon Ranges, Daylesford was a gold rush site in the mid-1800s, now known for the largest concentration of mineral springs in Australia, its scenic countryside, and great wineries.

Start at Wombat Hill Botanic Gardens, built on an inactive volcano. Wander the grounds to Convent Gallery, an iconic 19th-century mansion overlooking Daylesford. Then see Grampians National Park for its sandstone mountains, echidnas, and wallabies. Within the park, don't miss Brambuk: The National Park and Cultural Centre, where you can learn about local Aboriginal history and see rock art. Or take a trail to MacKenzie Falls, the only waterfall in the Grampians that flows year-round.

No trip to Daylesford is complete without koala sightings. Look for them at Tower Hill Wildlife Reserve, perched upon a volcanic crater, where you might also spot emus, kangaroos, koalas, and birds. To see koalas in the wild, look in the high forks of eucalyptus tree branches. For a sure thing, take the ferry to Raymond Island and hit the Koala Trail.

During January's lavender peak, visit the 100-acre (40 ha) Lavandula Swiss Italian Farm, an original homestead built in the 1850s. Explore the gardens and historic stone buildings, meet the farm animals, and, during warmer months, watch as gardeners harvest the crop by hand. Close by in Hepburn Springs, taste a variety of mineral formulations at Hepburn Mineral Springs Reserve; the first of its kind in Australia, it dates back to 1865. Go to Hepburn Bathhouse and Spa, run since 1895, for several bathing options, including a private session.

Come dinnertime, try the tasting menu at Sault, located on a 125-acre (51 ha) estate with lavender and sunflower fields, plus lake views. Or dine at Farmers Arms, a gastropub and beer garden that's been around for more than 165 years and showcases wild and farmed ingredients from around Daylesford and the extended region.

Wine lovers, try Daylesford Wine Tours—run by Labrador Maizy and her humans—which offers the chance to meet the makers and see inside the cellar doors, with tons of winery, cidery, beer, spirit, port, and liqueur stops. They run an annual tour called Wigs & Wine. Also hit up Daylesford Cider, which received the trophy for Best Traditional Cider in Show at the national Australian Cider Awards.

Don't leave town without tasting some of the area's famous Pinot Noir at Passing Clouds Winery (10 minutes away in Musk), a dog-friendly spot that was one of the first vineyards in the region.

GET YOUR GREEK ON WITH PRIDE AND PERFECT VIEWS.
Thessaloniki, Greece

The sun sets over the picturesque town of Thessaloniki and its old Byzantine castle (top right).

THE LGBTQIA+ LOWDOWN A port city on the glistening Aegean Sea, this town was chosen as the host of EuroPride 2024 and is home to the Thessaloniki International G.L.A.D. Film Festival.

Known as the cultural capital of Greece, Thessaloniki sits on the Thermaic Gulf of the Aegean Sea and draws visitors seeking culture, sun, and fun.

Museum lovers will be delighted, as Thessaloniki has something for almost everyone. For ancient Greek and Roman artifacts, visit the Archeological Museum of Thessaloniki. The Museum of Byzantine Culture features intricate mosaics and iconography. For more recent works, check out the Macedonian Museum of Contemporary Art. And for techies, the UYiLO Museum is the first technology museum in Greece and the second in the world. For even more fun, try the Museum of Illusions or Selfie Museum.

When you've had your fill of museums, make your way to two UNESCO World Heritage sites. First, the Church of Agios Demetrios honors St. Demetrios, the patron saint of Thessaloniki. Then, see the Byzantine Baths, one of the only remaining preserved baths from the 12th century.

For great views of the city, head to Eptapyrgio Castle (Yedi Kule in Turkish), a fortress and former prison from the Byzantine and Ottoman eras. *Eptapyrgio* means "seven towers," and the castle is a great way to see both the water and mountains surrounding the city. Another nice viewpoint is the observation deck at Trigonion Tower, a 15th-century armory and artillery tower. It's especially beautiful as the sun sets over the Thermaic Gulf and the historic center. Don't miss the White Tower of Thessaloniki, a mystical waterfront monument and museum in the Ano Poli district, a section of town where an old Byzantine wall remains. As you explore the tower's six levels, you'll experience Thessaloniki's history via interactive exhibits.

We also recommend Modiano Market, the hub of gastronomic culture in the city, which spans several blocks. Go here for cheese and olives sourced from all over Greece. Next door, you'll find Louloudadika, where you can grab a traditional Greek coffee (foam on top and grounds at the bottom). Then continue on to browse the flower shops that brighten this part of town. For more great fare, try Tiho-Tiho, a Greek tavern with a modern spin on traditional cuisine; Ouzou Melathron for meze; or Mia Feta for feta and other Greek cheeses (and a deli, too).

Pavlou Mela Street is a popular gathering place for the LGBTQIA+ community and has a significant lesbian presence. There, visit the inclusive Ánōthen Café Bar, Enola (known as Thessaloniki's gay bar), or Pastaflora Darling café for coffee, cocktails, and pies.

◆ WHEN TO GO

August to October brings the best weather. Beware of possible snow in the winter. Thessaloniki Pride, as well as the World Naked Bike Ride, is in June, and the G.L.A.D. Film Festival is in October.

◆ WHERE TO STAY

Consider the Modernist hotel, a building from the 1920s rebuilt to make a space where minimalist style meets mid-century. Or try Zeus Is Loose, a hostel with a hip location off one of the busiest squares in Thessaloniki.

◆ WHAT TO KNOW

Add another great Greek island to your vacation with a ferry from Thessaloniki to the Sporades, Cyclades, or North Aegean Islands. For flamingos, wild horses, and possibly water buffalo, drive 30 minutes west of town to Axios-Loudias-Aliakmonas National Park, one of the most important ecosystems in Greece. Kalochori village is easily reached by bus and has lagoons where you can spot flocks of flamingos in winter.

The intricate stone designs and architecture of the Church of Agios Demetrios

◆ WHEN TO GO

Winters are cold and stormy but still have plenty of open pubs and entertainment. Go in the summer for Pride (including the Trans Pride Parade), one of the biggest in the U.K. and held in Preston Park with arts, a film festival, dog show, and village party. At Brighton Festival, which unfolds across town in May, you can enjoy artist open houses. Brighton Fringe festival is held in tandem with other events, from comedy to art exhibitions and family art workshops.

◆ WHERE TO STAY

Try Blanch House, a historic Georgian terrace building just off the seafront in Kemptown, or New Steine Hotel, a fully refurbished five-story Georgian town house in the center of town with a popular bistro (both queer owned). The Charm Brighton Boutique Hotel and Spa is a luxurious stay with a great breakfast in a restored 200-year-old building in Kemptown.

◆ WHAT TO KNOW

To avoid a flood of bar-hopping groups that tend to be a bit rowdy, steer clear of West Street on weekend nights and stay away from Brighton Station and pubs on football nights.

The Royal Pavilion & Garden attracts butterflies, birds, bees, and other pollinators.

THIS TOWN HAS SEASIDE CHARM AND QUEER CHEER.
Brighton, England, U.K.

Performers during Brighton's annual Pride parade, the most popular Pride event in the country

THE LGBTQIA+ LOWDOWN Often referred to as the unofficial gay capital of the U.K., and host of its own Trans Pride Parade for more than a decade, Brighton is about as welcoming as it gets.

Once a fishing village, Brighton's East Sussex resort town is a 90-minute train ride from London and has a whole different vibe from the big city.

Start with its major landmark, the Brighton Palace Pier, built in the late 1800s. With its wooden plank pier and pebbly beach, you can have all the fun with rides, games, and people-watching. Or hit up the Lanes: narrow alleys with shops, restaurants, bars, and antiques stores. North Laine, a different area with a more modern vibe, is a trendy district with hundreds of shops crammed into quaint lanes.

The Royal Pavilion & Garden is a regency museum that lets visitors experience what was once George IV's (formerly Prince of Wales) palace. Monk's House, formerly Leonard and Virginia Woolf's 16th-century country retreat, is a must for lit lovers. Visit the lodge where Woolf wrote most of her major works and peruse the English cottage garden with views of the Sussex Downs. For more scenery, visit Devil's Dyke, a National Trust and beautiful woodlands area just five miles (8 km) north of town. Take the South Downs Way, a 100-mile (161 km) national hiking trail through the countryside. If weather permits, head to Black Rock Naturist Beach (a nude beach) just five minutes from Brighton.

Kemptown, named one of the coolest neighborhoods in the world by *TimeOut,* is the heart of Brighton's queer community. To drink it up, start at the Bulldog, a landmark LGBTQIA+ pub (the oldest in the city) known for lively karaoke nights; then head to Camelford Arms with its Moroccan-style patio, or the Marlborough Pub and Theatre, a historic venue associated with the queer community since the '70s. During summer, check out the in-progress boardwalk regeneration project with an open-water swimming center with sea lanes and a heated 164-foot (50 m) outdoor pool along the busy seafront.

You'll find food and fun at the Curzon, a cabaret bar, theater, and cinema. For a buzz, try UnBarred Brewery, where creativity and freedom are core ethos, and DaddyLonglegs for a welcoming feel and modern but informal food. The Dorset gastropub has served ale and fine foods since 1819. Roundhill restaurant does vegetarian small plates right. The Arcobaleno (meaning "rainbow" in Italian) is an LGBTQIA+ café and bar that hosts drag shows, burlesque, and quiz nights.

CHAPTER 2

BOOZY TRIPS
and trails

We're here to keep the drinks and good cheer flowing with gorgeous wine regions and backcountry booze trails. These spots offer the best places to enjoy a fine Pinot poolside or a cocktail by a roaring fire. Let's raise a glass together as we span the globe from the Finger Lakes in upstate New York to California's Sonoma County, which hosts Gay Wine Weekend to benefit LGBTQIA+ organizations. You'll also find off-the-beaten-path wineries in the Texas Hill Country and some of the world's best wine areas, including Stellenbosch in South Africa, Mendoza in Argentina, and Lyon in France.

Prefer spirits or brews? We've got you covered with the Kentucky Bourbon Trail; Boulder, Colorado's impressive number of breweries; and Santa Fe, New Mexico's Margarita Trail. We also provide a guide to sample Dublin's iconic beer and Scotland's famed whisky. Join us as we uncork an unforgettable adventure.

TASTE AWARD-WINNING RIESLING IN A "GORGES" LOCATION.
Finger Lakes, Upstate New York, U.S.A.

Red wine grapes are ready for harvest at a vineyard in the Finger Lakes.

THE LGBTQIA+ LOWDOWN Upstate New York is committed to equality. Several towns, including Auburn, Corning, Geneva, Ithaca (home to Cornell University), and Rochester have Pride celebrations, LGBTQIA+ history tours, and queer spaces, including bars and community centers. Auburn is also home to the New York State Equal Rights Heritage Center.

The Finger Lakes area in upstate New York is a collection of 11 long and narrow lakes formed from receded glaciers. Stretching 4,692 square miles (12,152 km²), the area hosts tons of award-winning wineries that prove East Coasters can make great wine, too. Famous for its Riesling, Chardonnay, and Cabernet Franc, the region boasts three distinct wine trails, several farm-to-table restaurants, inviting inns, and magnificent state parks. Some call the scenery absolutely "gorges"—and we agree.

On the Cayuga Lake Wine Trail (the first in the United States), we're fans of Buttonwood Grove Winery, Lucas Vineyards, and gay-owned Americana Vineyards (try the fudge!). The Keuka Lake Wine Trail has must-visits like Dr. Konstantin Frank Winery (a Finger Lakes pioneer and New York's most award-winning winery since 1962), Heron Hill Winery, and McGregor Vineyard. Highlights of the Seneca Lake Wine Trail include Hermann J. Wiemer Vineyard, Red Newt Cellars, and Wagner Vineyards, which also has its own craft brewery.

Enjoy the great outdoors at Cayuga, Keuka, and Seneca Lakes, where you can swim, boat, kayak, lounge on the beach, or catch a sunset cruise with Cayuga Lake Boat Tours or Mid-Lakes Navigation. Note: Traveling between each lake can be time-consuming and getting a rideshare or taxi isn't always easy, so having your own vehicle or sticking to one area is best.

Letchworth State Park, known as the "Grand Canyon of the East," has a nature trail designed for individuals on the autism spectrum, along with 66 miles (106 km) of hiking trails. Camp in rustic cabins, go horseback riding, or take an unforgettable hot-air balloon ride. Or visit Watkins Glen State Park for the spectacular Gorge Trail, which features a 400-foot-deep (122 m) gorge and waterfalls such as Central Cascade and Rainbow Falls. At Taughannock Falls State Park, you'll find the tallest waterfall in New York State (yes, even higher than Niagara Falls), which plunges 215 feet (66 m) against the picture-perfect backdrop of—you guessed it—another gorge.

Complement your wine and adventures with dinner at one of the region's top-notch restaurants. Try F.L.X. Table in Geneva for a gourmet dinner prepared in front of you in an intimate setting or Moosewood in nearby Ithaca with its renowned cookbooks and amazing vegetarian and vegan options. Save room for dessert at Great Escape Ice Cream Parlor in Watkins Glen.

NEED TO KNOW

✦ WHEN TO GO
May to October brings the best weather and Pride festivals (held in June).

✦ WHERE TO STAY
Chalet of Canandaigua is a luxury bed-and-breakfast in wooded hills. Or try Inn at Gothic Eves to relax in a prime location between Seneca and Cayuga Lakes. At Inns of Aurora, find historic charm, on-site activities like making s'mores around firepits, and waterfront views.

✦ WHAT TO KNOW
Rochester has the most options for LGBTQIA+ nightlife. Roar Rochester features drag shows and live bands. The city also hosts a queer film festival in April and is home to organizations such as Rochester Black Pride and Trans Rochester Speaks.

The Genesee River and Middle Falls in Letchworth State Park

NEED TO KNOW

◆ WHEN TO GO

The best weather is May to September. Special events include Pride in June and the Santa Fe Indian Market, which began in 1922 and is now the world's largest market of Native American art, including pottery, baskets, textiles, silverwork, and more, plus Native American dance performances, food, and a fashion show. Winter is great for skiing (Ski Santa Fe has 89 trails for all levels).

◆ WHERE TO STAY

El Farolito Bed & Breakfast Inn has beautifully appointed rooms and casitas tucked among gardens and intimate walled-in patios. Or try the pet-friendly Inn of the Turquoise Bear, which is an LGBTQIA+-owned B&B with gorgeous rooms and grounds. La Fonda on the Plaza is a historic and luxurious stay with a pool, great views, and an unbeatable location at the center of it all.

◆ WHAT TO KNOW

Consider extending your trip to visit queer-friendly Albuquerque (an hour away) or Taos (90 minutes). And if you can, take in a rodeo. Santa Fe is home to the New Mexico Gay Rodeo Association, a nonprofit (est. 1984) that fosters the western lifestyle within the LGBTQIA+ community and holds fundraisers for various charities.

La Plazuela restaurant at the celebrated La Fonda on the Plaza hotel

SIP MARGARITAS WHILE ENJOYING THE ARTS, SOUTHWEST STYLE.

Santa Fe, New Mexico, U.S.A.

THE LGBTQIA+ LOWDOWN With a historic arts scene and progressive nature, Santa Fe embodies an inclusive spirit and sense of belonging for all. The Santa Fe Human Rights Alliance sponsors Pride and other community events (including our favorite: drag bingo).

Santa Fe is known for its strong flavors, and we're not just talking about those world-famous green chilies. With dazzling desert scenery, a world-class art scene, and lovely pueblo-style buildings, you'll have loads to do between sipping some of the world's best margaritas.

According to legend, Santa Fe was the first place in (what's now) the United States to import tequila from Mexico, way back in the 1800s. Centuries later, the Santa Fe Margarita Trail was established in 2016. The trail has more than 45 restaurants and bars, each offering unique and creative spins on the cocktail. You can download the official Margarita Trail mobile app (for $3) or DIY your own experience.

Some of our picks include Del Charro for margaritas that are pomegranate flavored or infused with Hatch chilies. El Farol, which has been in business since 1835, offers classic margaritas as well as blood orange and prickly pear varieties. Try the Smoking Bull with Kimo Sabe Mezcal, cilantro, and a Chimayo red chili salt rim while taking in a flamenco show.

While in the area, go to Canyon Road, the epicenter of Santa Fe's arts scene, and browse more than 80 galleries and artisan shops selling everything from abstract paintings to handmade Southwestern and Native American crafts. Other fun things to do in Santa Fe include viewing the breathtaking work of Georgia O'Keeffe at her namesake museum, seeing the "miraculous" spiral staircase and stained glass windows at Loretto Chapel, and strolling through historic Santa Fe Plaza (including a stop at the Palace of the Governors and New Mexico History Museum). Save some time to catch a show at the Santa Fe Opera, or experience Meow Wolf's interactive art exhibits—great for the whole family. After a busy day, soak at Ten Thousand Waves, a relaxing spa and sanctuary inspired by Japanese hot springs resorts.

Pair food with your margaritas at Cowgirl BBQ, and try the Cadillac Margarita with reposado tequila, Grand Marnier, and sweet-and-sour mix alongside some award-winning bunkhouse brisket. Or try Maria's New Mexican Kitchen, which offers more than 150 margaritas made with 100 percent agave tequila. The green chili meatballs and tamales are worth a try, too!

As the sun sets, head to Bell Tower at La Fonda on the Plaza for drinks and stellar Santa Fe city views. Then continue the night at queer-popular spots such as the Matador, a classic dive bar; the Secreto Lounge, serving craft cocktails; or the piano bar at the Inn at Vanessie.

El Santuario de Chimayo, an adobe church built in 1813, attracts more than 300,000 pilgrims a year.

HERE, THE ROCKY MOUNTAINS TOWER AND THE BREWS IMPRESS.

Boulder, Colorado, U.S.A.

THE LGBTQIA+ LOWDOWN Boulder has been named one of *The Advocate* magazine's top 10 queerest cities in the country and one of *National Geographic*'s happiest cities in the U.S., and Boulder County was the first county in Colorado to issue a same-sex marriage license—and did so in 1975.

Just about 30 miles (48 km) from Denver, you'll find walkable Boulder, set against the iconic backdrop of the Flatirons—large red sandstone formations more than 300 million years old that line the west side of town. Explore the outdoors in 5,000 acres (2,023 ha) of Boulder's protected areas and head indoors for some of the country's best breweries.

At the base of the Flatirons, you'll find Chautauqua Park, part of a historic landmark since Boulder began preserving wildlands in 1898. The Chautauqua Trailhead is 40 miles (64 km) of hiking trails with wildflowers, rock climbing, and wildlife. After working up a sweat, cool off in Boulder Creek. Dip your feet or float the 30-plus-mile (48 km) creek by tube.

On pedestrian-only Pearl Street Mall, you'll find whimsical statues, craft breweries (like local favorite Mountain Sun Pub & Brewery), Art Mart with crafts and souvenirs, the three-story Boulder Book Store, and the colorful Boulder Dushanbe Tea House with hand-carved ceilings and hand-painted tables by more than 40 artisans from Tajikistan.

Just up from Pearl Street is University Hill (aka "the Hill"), where you can visit the Fiske Planetarium and Science Center, a public museum at the University of Colorado Boulder and the largest planetarium between Chicago and Los Angeles. It offers immersive shows in a dome and the chance to experience black holes, superstorms, and more.

But we're here for the beer. Boulder, with the highest concentration of breweries per capita in the country, is home to the Boulder Beer Trail, which winds through downtown. It includes Colorado's first microbrewery, Boulder Beer Company, started in a shed in 1979. Don't miss Post Chicken & Beer for a Howdy Western Pilsner and a bucket of crispy chicken. Enjoy some tasters with fries at Mountain Sun Pub & Brewery. Bohemian Biergarten has you covered for German-style beer and pretzels with hefty portions. Had your fill of beer? Attic Bar & Bistro calls itself the exclusive home of the Fat Albert and Chilly Albert cocktails. While you're downtown, check out DV8 Distillery, the best queer watering hole in Boulder.

Explore Boulder's restaurant scene at Little Tibet Restaurant & Bar, with popular authentic food, and Avanti, a food hall with seven restaurants. Or go to Jungle Tiki for its rum bar and burgers—and drag shows, live jazz, and Pride.

Autumn in the city of Boulder

◆ WHEN TO GO

Visit in March for the Winter Craft Beer Festival, which has more than 150 beers to taste; August for the Boulder Craft Beer Festival with food and brew tastings; and October for Boulder Burgundy Festival, an event for wine lovers.

◆ WHERE TO STAY

Try Hotel Boulderado for historic charm, a busy downtown location, and Victorian-inspired rooms. Basecamp Boulder, a stylish outdoor-themed boutique hotel, promises to help you explore like a local. The Nest B&B, a female-owned private cottage, prides itself on being a fit for independent women travelers.

◆ WHAT TO KNOW

In the winter, hit the slopes at Eldora Mountain Resort (20 miles/32 kilometers north of Boulder), known for having lower admission and rental fees than many other resorts, and for being a good choice for skiers of most abilities. In any season, visit Colorado Springs' stunning Garden of the Gods, a registered national historic site. Just 90 minutes from Boulder, it has huge red rock formations, climbing, jeep tours, and mesmerizing views.

Pearl Street Mall's crosswalk turns rainbow-hued during Pride month.

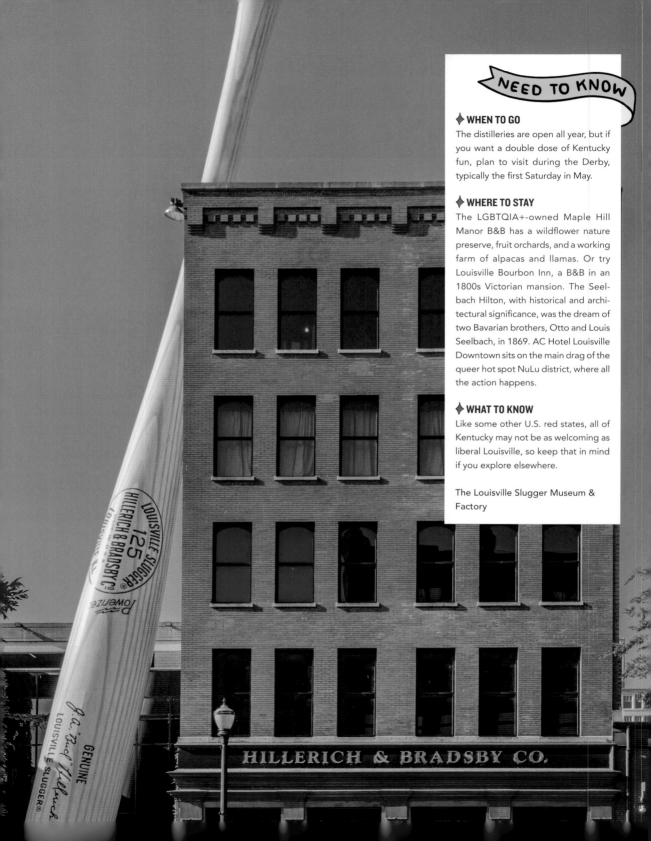

◆ WHEN TO GO

The distilleries are open all year, but if you want a double dose of Kentucky fun, plan to visit during the Derby, typically the first Saturday in May.

◆ WHERE TO STAY

The LGBTQIA+-owned Maple Hill Manor B&B has a wildflower nature preserve, fruit orchards, and a working farm of alpacas and llamas. Or try Louisville Bourbon Inn, a B&B in an 1800s Victorian mansion. The Seelbach Hilton, with historical and architectural significance, was the dream of two Bavarian brothers, Otto and Louis Seelbach, in 1869. AC Hotel Louisville Downtown sits on the main drag of the queer hot spot NuLu district, where all the action happens.

◆ WHAT TO KNOW

Like some other U.S. red states, all of Kentucky may not be as welcoming as liberal Louisville, so keep that in mind if you explore elsewhere.

The Louisville Slugger Museum & Factory

TAKE IN THE SPIRITS AND FOLLOW THE FAMED BOURBON TRAIL.
Louisville, Kentucky, U.S.A.

THE LGBTQIA+ LOWDOWN Louisville is the only city in Kentucky to earn a perfect score on the Human Rights Campaign's Municipal Equality Index (MEI). It also has a historic LGBT Center at the University of Louisville and is often praised as one of the best destinations for queer travelers, including families.

On the Ohio River, Louisville, the largest city in Kentucky, is known for its baseball and horse racing history—and some of the world's best bourbons. We love it for all that plus its culinary scene and numerous public parks.

Head to the Louisville Slugger Museum & Factory, which features the story of American baseball and Louisville Slugger baseball bats. Stop at the Kentucky Derby Museum to learn all about American Thoroughbred racing, then head to Churchill Downs (where the races happen).

Also around town, Whitehall Mansion includes the Arboretum, Specimen Garden, Formal Florentine Garden, and the Woodland Fern Garden. Speed Art Museum has a history of inclusion and curated exhibits to support LGBTQIA+ artists. Check out queer-owned Louabull, a boutique and gift shop with Pride tees, hats, and "cards for people who aren't uptight." BLōFISH is another great place to shop and has cool "Love Is Love" and Pride collections; a portion of every sale goes to the community. And Pandora Productions is a theater dedicated to telling LGBTQIA+ stories.

Louisville is known as the City of Parks. At Broad Run Park, see the Moss Gibbs Woodlands Garden and have a picnic in the Greensward, which honors the original name for New York's Central Park. The Louisville Loop, a still expanding 100-mile (161 km) trail system, is great for cycling.

Next, hit the Kentucky Bourbon Trail's Welcome Center, the gateway to the famous 42-distillery tour. For distilleries that are walkable to one another, go to Michter's Fort Nelson Distillery, Evan Williams Bourbon Experience, Old Forester Distilling Co., and Angel's Envy Distillery. With more time, visit the queer-friendly NuLu district and stop at Rabbit Hole Distillery and Bulleit Distilling Co. Twenty-five miles (40 km) outside the city is the famous James B. Beam Distilling Co. and the Green River Distilling Co.

After all that bourbon, you've probably worked up an appetite. Head to 610 Magnolia, where you can eat on the patio or in their rustic dining room. At Bistro Le Relais, in the historic airport terminal of Bowman Field, get views of the planes and 1940s art deco interior. Blue Dog Bakery & Café is a neighborhood joint serving fresh bread and pastries. Buck's Restaurant (located on the Bourbon Trail) is in the historic Mayflower Building with more than 50 drink selections. After dinner, have a fun night out at lesbian bar Purrswaytions.

Sip and cheers at any of the 42 whiskey and bourbon distilleries along the Kentucky Bourbon Trail.

TASTE ROBUST REDS AND CRISP WHITES AT MORE THAN 700 WINERIES.

Willamette Valley, Oregon, U.S.A.

Head outside of Salem for a tour and tasting of Pinot Noir at Willamette Valley Vineyards.

THE LGBTQIA+ LOWDOWN The Willamette Valley includes cities such as Portland, Eugene, and Salem, which consistently earn high marks for LGBTQIA+ equality and inclusion. Wine Country Pride, a nonprofit organization, sponsors drag shows, street fairs, and allyship events throughout the year.

The Willamette Valley, a 150-mile-long (241 km) stretch of land around the Willamette River, is known for its white-water rafting and some of the world's best Pinot Noir. With more than 700 wineries stretching across nearly 3.5 million acres (1.4 million ha), the choices are endless.

Many great wineries are centered around the areas of Dundee Hills and McMinnville, an inviting town with turn-of-the-century buildings, museums and galleries, and great restaurant and hotel choices. Sample delicious Italian varietals like Dolcetto and Sangiovese at Remy Wines, founded by queer winemaker Remy Drabkin (who also co-founded Wine Country Pride). Fans of whites should visit ROCO Winery, where Black, queer assistant winemaker Jarod Sleet and the ROCO team pour Chardonnay and sparkling wines such as RMS Brut. Meanwhile, at Quailhurst Vineyard Estate, you can enjoy your wine while visiting a five-acre (2 ha) Japanese garden overlooking Mount Hood.

McMinnville also offers the Evergreen Aviation & Space Museum (home of the *Spruce Goose*, an enormous, mostly wood aircraft) and the Erratic Rock State Natural Site, featuring a massive rock that floated in an iceberg more than 500 miles (805 km) from the Rocky Mountains during the Ice Age.

In the Salem area, Coria Estates is a Mexican American–owned and –operated winery known for Pinot Noir and Pinot Gris. Willamette Valley Vineyards offers tastings by cozy fireplaces or on their patio. Visit popular queer bar Southside Speakeasy, tour the State Capitol, and see waterfalls up close at Silver Falls State Park.

Around Eugene, King Estate serves up award-winning Pinot Gris. Sarver Winery has great Muscat and Gewürztraminer, and Sweet Cheeks Winery offers laid-back tastings.

When you're done, stop by the Cascades Raptor Center, which cares for more than 200 injured birds. Then check out cool cultural spaces like the Jordan Schnitzer Museum of Art. Or take in an opera at the Hult Center for the Performing Arts.

In Whiteaker, visit Spectrum, a queer space for food, drinks, and drag shows; grab a locally brewed beer at Sam Bond's Garage and Hop Valley Brewing, which supports LGBTQIA+ causes; or spend some time by the river at Maurie Jacobs Park.

NEED TO KNOW

◆ WHEN TO GO

May to September, weather is sunniest and the vineyards are spectacular. Visit in June for Wine Country Pride, which includes Queer Wine Fest, an outdoor tasting and celebration of queer winemakers, winery owners, and grape growers.

◆ WHERE TO STAY

Allison Inn & Spa in Newberg pampers on its beautiful 35-acre (14 ha) grounds, with one of the area's most extensive wine lists at Jory. Or consider the Lodge at Detroit Lake for log cabins, fireplaces, jetted tubs, and incredible stargazing. For something different, The Vintages Trailer Resort in Dayton offers luxury glamping in retro chic Airstreams with complimentary bicycles.

◆ WHAT TO KNOW

About 40 minutes from Salem, Dancing Oaks Nursery and Gardens is a lovely way to spend the day, and another fun out-of-town excursion is the 134-mile (216 km) Willamette Valley Scenic Bikeway, a cyclist's dream. Whether you attempt to tackle the whole route or take shorter rides on day trips, you can stop at wineries, coffee shops, restaurants, and more along the way. The ride from Albany to Shedd (42 miles/ 68 kilometers round-trip) is known to be flat and especially scenic.

Vines at Zenith Vineyard in the Eola-Amity Hills

◆ WHEN TO GO

Fall is the peak season for great weather. In October, Austin City Limits features an epic lineup of musicians with nine stages and more than 100 performances. The Austin International Drag Festival also takes place in October. The Pecan Street Spring Arts Festival, the longest-running arts and crafts festival in the nation, runs in spring and fall.

◆ WHERE TO STAY

In Austin, try W Austin Hotel or Austin Marriott Downtown for chic retreats with great locations near all the action. In the Hill Country, check into the Abundance Retreat (Wimberley) or the Swiss-inspired Barons CreekSide (Fredericksburg) on 26 tree-covered acres (11 ha) with log cabins—home to many LGBTQIA+ weddings.

◆ WHAT TO KNOW

When in the Hill Country, you're only about an hour from San Antonio, another great LGBTQIA+-welcoming destination worth your time. And a little more than 10 miles (16 km) from Austin is Hippie Hollow Park, a popular clothing-optional beach on Lake Travis.

The Colorado River cuts through downtown Austin.

DISCOVER THIS MUSIC MECCA WITH BARBECUE AND BOOZE GALORE.

Austin and Texas Hill Country, Texas, U.S.A.

Celebrators don rainbow balloons and tie-dye during the annual Austin Pride Parade.

THE LGBTQIA+ LOWDOWN Austin has a perfect score on the Human Rights Campaign's Municipal Equality Index and is widely known as a queer-welcoming destination. And following its influence, Texas Hill Country is spreading its Pride wings, too.

The state capital of Texas is a vibey college town known for its live music scene and an abundance of parks and lakes. But it's also popular for great BBQ, arts, and scenic countryside drives.

Start in lively South Congress for boutiques, restaurants, and the Continental Club music venue. Come sunset, be at Congress Avenue Bridge to watch Mexican free-tailed bats fly over the bridge in spectacular fashion (spring through fall).

Indoors, we love the Museum of the Weird (shrunken heads and Bigfoot-like creatures); Thinkery children's museum; BookWoman for queer literature; the Little Gay Shop for cards and gifts; and Casa Neverlandia, the whimsical home of artist James Talbot, with hidden passageways and a lookout tower (reservations required).

This is also a top-notch food town in Texas. Try lesbian-owned la Barbecue's grass-fed meat. Or hit the food trucks in dog-friendly Arbor Park and BYOB for a picnic. At Birdie's, you'll always find a line for the French- and Italian-inspired dishes. For dessert, get some gluten-free doughnuts at OMG Squee.

For queer bars, try Rain on 4th, Oilcan Harry's, the Iron Bear, and Cheer Up Charlies. WhichCraft Tap Room & Bottle Shop has rare beers, and East Austin's LoLo has natural wines and a nice patio. Or make your own wine tour by stopping at the Austin Winery, where you can sip your Pinot beside the barrels used to make it. Next, go to Meridian Hive for a modern take on the ancient beverage of honey wine (aka mead).

When you've had your Austin fill, head to Hill Country. Stop in Driftwood for Salt Lick BBQ, founded in 1967, with some of the best 'cue anywhere. Prepare for worth-the-wait lines. Salt Lick Cellars, on the same property with perfect views, serves Tempranillo, Sangiovese, farm-to-market blends, and its house BBQ Red and BBQ White wines.

Pause in the tiny hamlet of Luckenbach in Fredericksburg. It only has about a dozen residents but also an outdoor stage and saloon—brought to fame by Willie Nelson and Waylon Jennings. Grab a cold beer and enjoy the music.

Next, go to Gruene Hall, the oldest dance hall in Texas, running since 1878. Gruene Grove is a picturesque setting with an outdoor stage and a great selection of craft beers. Then visit Winery on the Gruene, a boutique winery that produces more than 30 vintages on-site.

In Wimberley, eat at Leaning Pear, the official brunch spot for Wimberley Pride. Visit the award-winning Limestone Terrace Vineyard for Texas-grown wines with incredible views.

POUR PINOT IN THE SUN AND FOREST BATHE IN THE REDWOODS.

Sonoma County and Russian River Valley, California, U.S.A.

Sonoma County's Gay Wine Weekend is a three-day LGBTQIA+ celebration run by Out in the Vineyard.

THE LGBTQIA+ LOWDOWN Once a best-kept secret for the Bay Area queer community looking to escape the fog and explore the abundance of wineries, Sonoma County is beloved for its dedicated Gay Wine Weekend and tons of queer-friendly spots.

More than 425 wineries dot Sonoma County, 45 miles (72 km) northeast of San Francisco. In addition to wine, you'll find a wonderland of eclectic shops and restaurants, backcountry trails, and serene vibes.

Begin your trip at the Armstrong Redwoods State Natural Reserve in Guerneville, an 805-acre (326 ha) preserve that's home to California's towering redwoods, including one that's more than 1,400 years old. Then explore the Russian River by kayak, dinghy, or inner tube. Or check out Sonoma Coast State Park for the famous Bodega Head (great for whale-watching) and Vista Point, which has a one-mile (1.6 km) loop with great views. Both are handicap accessible.

With a focus on conservation, the Safari West wildlife preserve is another great site, housing 1,000 wild animals native to Africa (you can stay overnight, too). The California Missions Museum houses built-to-scale models of 21 missions built in California between 1769 and 1833.

Pair a bit of history with wine at Korbel Champagne Cellars and sip the sparkling wine made with grapes from the valley; it's been served at presidential inaugurations since 1981. When you're ready for more, let the Sonoma Valley Wine Trolley take you to four wineries (including the historic Benziger Family Winery), then hop off and arrange a car service to discover Equality Vines (one of its co-founders, Jim Obergefell, was the lead plaintiff in the landmark Supreme Court case that legalized same-sex marriage across the United States), Muscardini Cellars, Viansa, Château St. Jean, Corner 103, La Crema, and Buena Vista Winery. For something different, head to Rainbow Cattle Company, a Western dive bar that's known as "Sonoma County's gay playground" and has been serving since 1979.

Of course, you can't have wine without cheese, so sample goat cheese, mozzarella, cheddar, and others from artisan cheesemakers on the California Cheese Trail—from Sonoma's Vella Cheese, Sebastopol's Joe Matos Cheese Factory, Ramini Mozzarella in Petaluma, and more.

Still hungry? Try Big Bottom Market for specialty biscuits, Boon Eat + Drink for a sustainable California bistro, the Girl & the Fig for country food with a French twist, and Glen Ellen Star for its wood-oven dishes. The Lost Church is a nonprofit that hosts jazz, blues, and more in a welcoming space.

✦ WHEN TO GO

Aim for June, when Out in the Vineyard hosts the annual Gay Wine Weekend with three days of queer-focused events, including winemaker dinners, winery tours, and more benefiting charities important to the LGBTQIA+ community.

✦ WHERE TO STAY

The Lodge at Sonoma, Autograph Collection is a fairy-tale oasis with a luxury spa set among beautiful vineyards. Or try El Dorado Hotel & Kitchen in the historic downtown square with a popular restaurant and heated pool. The queer-owned Sonoma Coast Villa is a romantic luxury resort in the countryside. For something more glampy, do AutoCamp Russian River, with its modern Airstream accommodations in the Sonoma redwoods. In Santa Rosa, the Sandman is a reimagined roadside lodge. If you want to camp, Bodega Dunes Campground has the most amenities.

✦ WHAT TO KNOW

Sonoma itself is a historic city, but the entire area is worthy of exploration, and jumping from town to town is all part of the fun. Take the scenic Bohemian Highway, a 10-mile (16 km) two-lane road that winds through redwoods, farmland, and vineyards of western Sonoma County, connecting the quaint communities of the area.

More than 425 wineries blanket Sonoma County's verdant hills.

SONOMA COUNTY

This LGBTQIA+ oasis boasts more than 50 miles (80 km) of coastline (including the Pacific Ocean and San Pablo Bay), three rivers (Russian, Petaluma, and Gualala), and a namesake lake. It's hard to resist sipping some of the world's finest vino, admiring redwoods, taking to the water, rejuvenating in hot springs and wellness centers, and visiting inclusive towns such as Healdsburg and Guerneville. We especially love Gay Wine Weekend, which pumps up the LGBTQIA+ spirit and raises funds for charities such as Face to Face, Sonoma County's HIV/AIDS network.

ENJOY SAUVIGNON WITH SWEEPING VIEWS.
Cape Winelands, South Africa

Try new wine varieties in the elegant tasting area of Steenberg Farm, open since 1682.

THE LGBTQIA+ LOWDOWN South Africa amended its constitution in 1996 to ban discrimination based on sexual orientation (the first country to do so) and legalized same-sex marriage in 2006. Still, there are ongoing incidents of racism and homophobia, so visit with caution.

In addition to hundreds of wineries (including some of the oldest outside of Europe), the Cape Winelands offers lush countryside, expansive estates, and historic towns an easy day trip from Cape Town, only an hour away. It's nice to spend a few days here sipping world-class Chenin Blanc and Pinotage, a South African original that mixes Pinot Noir and Cinsaut.

Start in Stellenbosch, South Africa's second oldest settlement, founded in 1679, with striking Cape Dutch architecture, tree-lined streets, and South Africa's first wine route. At Waterford Estate, pair Cabernet Franc with chocolate, or visit nearby Delaire Graff Estate, ranked as one of South Africa's best wineries. Sample an award-winning Sémillon/Sauvignon Blanc blend and browse an African art collection. Award-winning Cabernet Sauvignon, Chenin Blanc, and Pinotage are among the varietals at M'hudi Wines, the first entirely Black-owned wine tourism farm in South Africa.

Don't miss the daily duck parade at Vergenoegd Löw, a 300-year-old wine estate where thousands of Indian Runners strut their stuff. The ducks work on the estate as "natural pest control." Afterward, enjoy a glass of the aptly titled Runner Duck Range. We also like Tokara Wine Estate, a family-owned vineyard and olive grove where you can enjoy tasty Cabernet Sauvignon and Sauvignon Blanc (not to mention olive oil) while taking in the awe-inspiring sites of False Bay and Table Mountain.

After, take your pick of the area's many attractions, including the Rupert Museum, Stellenbosch Village Museum, Marzé Botha Art Gallery, Stellenbosch University Botanical Garden, and Dylan Lewis Sculpture Garden. Or head to the Jonkershoek Nature Reserve, a UNESCO World Heritage site stretching 27,181 acres (11,000 ha), to hike, swim, or mountain bike.

Another charming town, Franschhoek, is known for its French Huguenot heritage and Cap Classique bubbly. Head to Boschendal, where you can sip, shop, stay, and enjoy fun offerings like a drive-in cinema. Try the signature sparkling brut at Klein Goederust, a Black-owned winery on 16 acres (6 ha).

Cap off the trip with a tasty meal at Arkeste on Chamonix Wine Farm for seasonal dishes at the edge of a forest, or at La Petite Colombe in the vineyards of Leeu Estates, where the "Chef Experience" delivers a curated, multicourse meal with the backstory behind each dish.

While touring the wineries, let someone else do the driving with Vine Hopper (Stellenbosch) or the fun Franschhoek Wine Tram.

◆ WHEN TO GO

November through March are the warmest and driest months of the year.

◆ WHERE TO STAY

Maison Chablis Guest House offers a quaint and inviting country house, pool, and lovely grounds. Queer-owned Holden Manz Wine Estate is a hidden gem where you can enjoy some Merlot or Syrah, and wine and dine in the Franschhoek Kitchen. Also, Sugarbird Manor at Protea Heights Farm offers views and an amazing infinity pool in the vineyards.

◆ WHAT TO KNOW

Between Cape Town and the Cape Winelands area, don't miss Steenberg Farm, the first winery in South Africa to join the International LGBTQ+ Travel Association (IGLTA). Established in 1682, Steenberg Farm has some of the country's best views and Sauvignon Blanc, outstanding service, and a restaurant and hotel.

The Waterford Estate, nestled in the Blaauwklippen Valley beneath the Helderberg Mountains

The Andes rise above vineyards in Tupungato.

ENJOY MALBEC, MOUNTAINS, AND MOUTHWATERING STEAKS.
Mendoza Region, Argentina

Performers honor a drag queen beauty contest winner at Mendoza's Gay Vendimia Festival.

THE LGBTQIA+ LOWDOWN As a whole, Argentina is one of the most progressive countries in South America. Queer people can legally marry and change their gender, and they are protected by antidiscrimination laws. Mendoza, the provincial capital, is the second most queer-visited city in Argentina.

Famous for its top-notch Malbec, Mendoza is Argentina's largest wine region and is set at the base of Sierra de los Paramillos, part of the Andes Mountains. But it offers more than great wine, including outdoor adventures, delicious cuisine, and Gay Vendimia, an LGBTQIA+ wine festival.

Start in the Maipo Valley at Bodega Trapiche, one of Argentina's oldest wineries (founded in 1883). Then bike around Familia Zuccardi while learning about winemaking and sampling varietals created by Sebastían Zuccardi, one of the country's top winemakers.

Luján de Cuyo is about 40 minutes south of Mendoza and has some of the country's most prestigious wineries. Among them is Bodega Catena Zapata, known for its full-bodied Malbec and fruit-filled whites. Explore its Adrianna Vineyard (at almost 5,000 feet/1,524 meters in elevation), admire its Maya step pyramid design, and go on themed tours. Also in the area, visit Bodega Ruca Malen to learn about sustainable winemaking.

Mendoza's newest wine region, Valle de Uco, is about 75 minutes from the city but worth the drive. At 4,000 feet (1,219 m), Bodegas Salentein offers amazing mountain views plus an exclusive collection of Argentine art and a terrific restaurant. Domaine Bousquet is Argentina's leading organic winery and one of the country's most awarded.

Thrill seekers can enjoy spectacular natural sites such as Parque Provincial Aconcagua (especially great for climbing) and Cañon del Atuel for rafting, horseback riding, and more. If you prefer to relax, have a thermal soak at Cacheuta Thermal Spa.

Around the city, stop by San Martin Park, Plaza Independencia, and, of course, Museo Nacional del Vino.

Leave plenty of time for a hearty Mendoza meal. Head to 1884 Restaurante for *parrilla*, an Argentine classic. Taste delicious rib eye at Magnolia Restó, or sample vegetarian options at Calendula, located in a bright blue building with painted flower murals.

There's a small but spirited LGBTQIA+ nightlife scene at La Reserva (featuring concerts and drag shows), Antares with outdoor seating and tons of beers on tap, and Queen Disco (Mendoza's oldest queer club).

THE "ISLAND OF WINE" HAS SO MUCH MORE.
Waiheke Island, New Zealand

Come for the wine, stay for the ambience, at luxe Mudbrick.

THE LGBTQIA+ LOWDOWN Queer inclusion and equality are staples in New Zealand, one of the world's most welcoming countries. In 1999, Georgina Beyer became the world's first transgender person to be elected to parliament.

Nicknamed the "Island of Wine," Waiheke Island is an oasis of more than 30 wineries, olive groves, beaches, and an abundance of green spaces—and it's just a 40-minute boat ride from the bustling metropolis of Auckland, which has a vibrant queer scene.

Waiheke is an artisan wine paradise that includes bold reds such as Syrah and Cabernet. Discover local flavors at Mudbrick Vineyard and Restaurant, established in 1992 and known for its handpicking, hand-plunging, and gentle basket pressing of bespoke wines. While there, stroll the gardens and experience a seven-course pairing menu (with plant-based options available) at Mudbrick Restaurant with views of the Hauraki Gulf and Auckland. It's especially magical at sunset.

We also recommend Man O' War Vineyards and the Tantalus Estate, New Zealand's only beachfront wine-tasting experience. Try wines like Gravestone (Sauvignon Blanc) and Exiled (Pinot Gris). Then stay to explore the 4,500-acre (1,821 ha) family farm and beach via the comfy Man O' War Coach or a guided e-bike tour. Or head to the family-owned Tantalus Estate for 20 acres (8 ha) of vineyards, olive groves,

macadamia trees, beehives, and native wetlands in the Onetangi Valley. Note that many wineries require reservations.

Around the island, visit Oneroa Village, the main township for shopping, art galleries, and restaurants, while nearby Oneroa Beach is a prime spot for lounging on the sand. More beach options include Little Oneroa Beach, which has a great bay that's safe for swimming; Palm Beach (named for its Phoenix palm trees); and Onetangi Beach, which is the longest beach on the island and has waterfront cafés and bars. Or take the Matiatia Headland Path (about 90 minutes) for a scenic coastal path along the cliffs. Thrill seekers, try a flying fox zip line above vineyards and forests with EcoZip Adventures. Tip: The Waiheke hop-on hop-off bus connects you to the island's main attractions and wineries with stops at 17 locations, including shops, art galleries, beaches, and nature walks.

Many wineries offer on-site restaurants, but you'll also find good eats at Too Fat Buns gourmet burger bar and the Oyster Inn, an award-winning beachside bistro known for seafood (it's also one of our top hotel picks). Dragonfired in Little Oneroa Beach has tasty wood-fired pizza.

◆ WHEN TO GO

November through February have the warmest weather and sunniest skies.

◆ WHERE TO STAY

Te Whau Lodge has panoramic views of the island and bay, luxury suites with private balconies, and a cedar spa pool. Or the Oyster Inn for its boutique chic vibe, village location, and popular restaurant.

◆ WHAT TO KNOW

The Te Ara Hura trail is a scenic 53.7-mile (86.4 km) loop around the island. It's moderately challenging and takes about 24 hours to complete without stopping.

Oneroa's main street offers some of the finest shopping and dining on Waiheke Island.

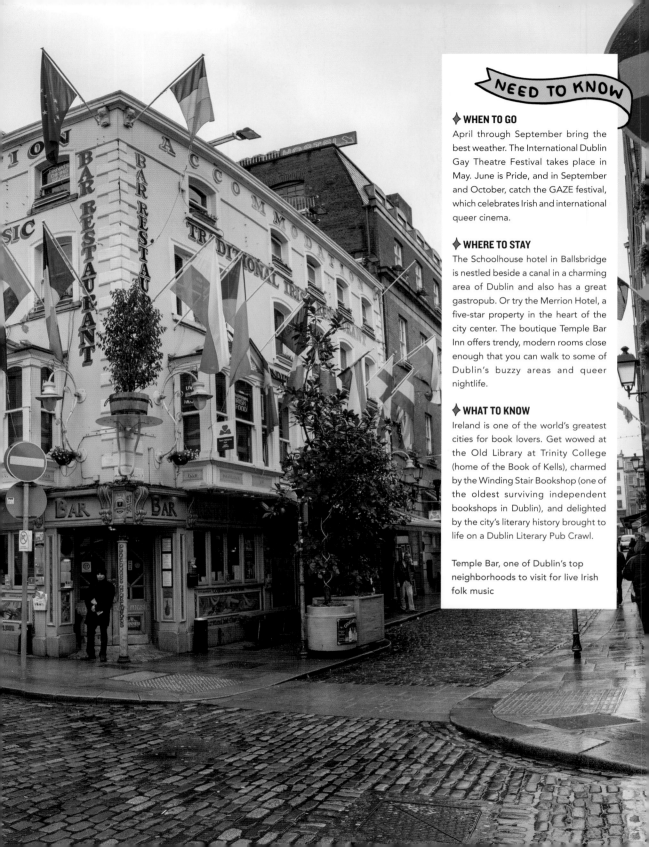

✦ WHEN TO GO

April through September bring the best weather. The International Dublin Gay Theatre Festival takes place in May. June is Pride, and in September and October, catch the GAZE festival, which celebrates Irish and international queer cinema.

✦ WHERE TO STAY

The Schoolhouse hotel in Ballsbridge is nestled beside a canal in a charming area of Dublin and also has a great gastropub. Or try the Merrion Hotel, a five-star property in the heart of the city center. The boutique Temple Bar Inn offers trendy, modern rooms close enough that you can walk to some of Dublin's buzzy areas and queer nightlife.

✦ WHAT TO KNOW

Ireland is one of the world's greatest cities for book lovers. Get wowed at the Old Library at Trinity College (home of the Book of Kells), charmed by the Winding Stair Bookshop (one of the oldest surviving independent bookshops in Dublin), and delighted by the city's literary history brought to life on a Dublin Literary Pub Crawl.

Temple Bar, one of Dublin's top neighborhoods to visit for live Irish folk music

HAVE A PINT OF GUINNESS AND ENJOY THE GREENERY.
Dublin, Ireland

Refuel with a pint of Guinness at the Merchant's Arch Bar & Restaurant.

THE LGBTQIA+ LOWDOWN Dublin has become one of the world's most welcoming spots for queer travelers. It's now home to Outhouse, a queer community space, café, and art gallery. Plus, you'll find several LGBTQIA+ outdoor groups like the Rainbow Swimmers and Out and About for hikers.

Dublin sports historic castles, city parks, museums, and, yes, lots of pubs, all with the backdrop of the River Liffey running through its center. It's the perfect place to share a pint with old friends or friendly strangers.

Before starting your pub crawls or whiskey tastings, learn about Ireland's journey to independence at Kilmainham Gaol, which once served as a prison and execution site. Or visit other great institutions like the Little Museum of Dublin, the Irish Emigration Museum, the National Gallery of Ireland, and the National Museum of Ireland–Archaeology. And St. Patrick's and Christ Church Cathedrals are worth seeing.

To take in (or should we say drink in) the history of Guinness, there's no better place than the Guinness Storehouse. While touring the brewery and exploring an interactive museum with tastings, classes, bars, and restaurants, you'll get the "history, heart, and soul of Ireland's most iconic beer." Visit the Gravity Bar for a 360-degree view of Dublin and grab your free pint that's included in the tour.

More into whiskey? Head to the Irish Whiskey Museum, Roe and Co. Distillery, and Jameson Distillery (still standing on the original site from 1790) for tours and tastings. But don't stop there. Dublin has nearly 800 watering holes, including the Brazen Head (the oldest pub in Dublin, established in 1198); the Palace Bar for more than 100 whiskeys, including their own; and Dingle Whiskey Bar to taste its single malt. For craft beer, try Porterhouse Brewing Company, Against the Grain, and the Brew Dock.

Hit up queer nightlife at the George, an iconic bar since 1985 that has dancing, drag shows, and karaoke. Another popular hangout is Pantibar, founded and run by LGBTQIA+ activist and Ireland's most famous drag queen, Panti Bliss. Street 66 Dublin and Mother Club are also worth visiting.

Grab a bite at Fish Shop for beer-battered fish along with great wine. Michelin-starred Variety Jones has a chef's choice tasting menu that gets huge raves (though not the best choice for those with dietary restrictions). Oscars Café Bar serves craft beers in a cool spot full of vintage furniture. It was founded by famous activist and drag queen Rory O'Neill. And try FIRE Steakhouse and Bar in a mansion built in 1710 for prawns, sirloin, and Irish classics.

DRINK ALL THE WHISKY AND TAKE IN THE ROLLING HILLS.
Speyside, Scotland, U.K.

See the swan-necked copper stills at Dufftown's Glenfiddich Distillery, open since the late 19th century.

THE LGBTQIA+ LOWDOWN Scotland is very welcoming, and this rural countryside three hours from Glasgow is no exception. Though there may not be a queer "scene" here, visitors will feel the inclusiveness of the country.

The Speyside area, which is part of the Northern Highlands in Scotland, is known as the heart of the malt whisky region for good reason: It's home to more than half of Scotland's malt whisky distilleries. But it's also charming, full of nature, and has a beloved coastline.

Hit the Speyside Way (66 miles/106 kilometers), designated as one of Scotland's Great Trails, and wind through mountains, moorlands, and more along the banks of the River Spey. For wildlife spotting, head to Spey Bay, a hot spot for bottlenose dolphins. Another great walk is along the Moray Coast Trail (approximately 50 miles/80 kilometers long), which has cliffs, caves, sheltered coves, and lively villages and towns.

For something unique, check out the Still art installation on the scenic routes of the SnowRoads, where leftover materials, such as gabion baskets (metal grids used to hold garden stone walls and fences in place), have been transformed into art among stunning landscapes.

When it's time to taste Scotland's famous spirits, Speyside's Malt Whisky Trail covers almost 75 miles (120 km) of ground and includes Glenfiddich Distillery, founded in 1886. There, you can make your own whisky and enjoy homemade ice cream. (They can accommodate mobility issues if you call ahead.) Glen Grant distillery, in the middle of the trail, has gardens and tasting rooms to relax in. The Speyside Cooperage is worth a visit to see how they make and fix more than 10,000 oak casks a year.

At the end of the whisky trail is Cairngorms National Park, the U.K.'s largest national park. It's home to 25 percent of the U.K.'s rare and endangered species and has hiking trails from which to look for ospreys, capercaillie, and Scottish wildcats.

When you're ready to eat (and drink some more), try Seven Stills, a family-run French restaurant and malt whisky lounge in the small town of Dufftown. Or visit Fiddichside Inn, a riverside pub just outside Speyside village, originally built as a "refreshment room" for the railway workers in 1842—it's a point of pride that very little has changed since. If you've got a sweet tooth, go to Walker's Shortbread for their famous cookies, in the same spot for more than 100 years!

◆ WHEN TO GO

May through October, the hills are full of color. The Spirit of Speyside Whisky Festival, held annually since 2000, takes place at the end of April or early May. Another Spirit of Speyside event, Distilled: Food & Drink, is typically held in early September.

◆ WHERE TO STAY

Eagle Brae is a village of luxury log cabins in the heart of the Scottish Highlands. At the Bunchrew House Hotel, all rooms have Loch Ness views. Also consider the family-run Dowans Hotel, set above the valley with views of the River Spey below and two bars stocked with more than 500 single malt whiskies.

◆ WHAT TO KNOW

While you're in this part of Scotland, visit Loch Ness, a 23-mile-long (37 km) lake by Inverness that's famous for being home to the legendary Nessie (aka the Loch Ness Monster).

Craigellachie Hotel, Scotland's oldest whisky hotel and home to a bar with 1,000 whisky options

✦ WHEN TO GO

The Fête des Lumières, a four-day light festival, takes place in December and is a magical display inspired by a tradition dating back to 1852. April sees Tigaly, an international LGBTQIA+ sports tournament. The Fête de la Musique in June offers free music performances throughout the city.

✦ WHERE TO STAY

Collège Hôtel is walkable from most of the city, earns positive ratings for its environmental footprint, and has a nostalgic "back to school" theme. Grand Hôtel des Terreaux is an art deco–inspired hotel that's one of the oldest in Lyon in the heart of the Presqu'île. We also love Hotel Silky by HappyCulture, housed in a historic building and praised for its environmental impact and use of organic and ecolabeled products. Also, consider the Mercure Lyon Centre Beaux Arts Hotel in a 19th-century building with great access to the city.

✦ WHAT TO KNOW

Most of central Lyon can be reached on foot, which you'll want to do because of the terrible traffic. This destination is extremely popular for foodies, so make sure you book ahead for any restaurants you have your heart set on.

Wine, hors d'oeuvres, and quintessential French countryside views in Lyon

WIND THROUGH WINERIES AND GET LOST AMONG LOVELY HILLS.
Lyon, France

Take a day trip from Lyon to Oingt, a charming village full of wine shops.

THE LGBTQIA+ LOWDOWN Widely considered to be one of France's most queer-friendly cities, Lyon draws foodies and wine lovers from all over the world.

Lyon is uniquely positioned at the confluence of the Rhône and Saône Rivers, helping to give this city that magical European feel. Although the city itself is a destination, greater Lyon, home to both the Beaujolais and Rhône Valley wine regions, can't be missed.

Start in the city and visit the Musée des Beaux-Arts de Lyon, France's largest fine art museum after the Louvre. Next, check out the Ancient Theatre of Fourvière, a Roman theater and UNESCO World Heritage site that sits on the hill of Fourvière and protects Lyon's historic city center. Wander through Vieux Lyon, the oldest quarter in Lyon, another UNESCO-designated site and one of the largest old quarters in Europe. There, you can explore the *traboules*, Lyon's secret covered renaissance passageways, once a way for workers of the 19th-century silk trade to travel from workshops to merchants.

The Presqu'île, the central part of the city, is known as the queer district. With pedestrian-friendly streets full of cafés, restaurants, and shops, it's home to many LGBTQIA+ bars and events, including Garçon Sauvage, a huge queer party. To hang at the most famous and oldest gay bar (for men), go to La Ruche, about a 10-minute walk from the Presqu'île.

To experience some of the food scene, head to the neighborhood of La Part-Dieu and famous Les Halles de Lyon, an indoor food market, for the freshest produce, bars, and restaurants. Chez les Garçons, a coffee shop that translates to "at the boys' place," has a fun feel for brunch. If you're overwhelmed by the options, book a guided crawl with Secret Food Tours.

Come wine o'clock, head out of the city to the Beaujolais Wine Route, which covers 80 miles (129 km) of vineyards, castles, and villages, including Oingt. This restored medieval village in Rhône is known as one of the most beautiful in France. The route extends from north of Lyon to Mâcon in the south of Burgundy.

Or consider these one-off stops in the region: Château de la Greffière, which has been producing wine since 1585, is now a winery and museum that's been in the family for four generations. Château de la Chaize, completed in 1676, is a castle, estate, and collection of vineyards that were entrusted to André Le Nôtre, the famous French gardener of King Louis XIV. Sample its Brouilly, one of the most renowned Beaujolais crus. Domaine de Corps de Loup dates back to A.D. 827; sample and buy wines from the Côte-Rôtie, Condrieu, and Saint-Joseph wine regions.

CHAPTER 3

Can't-Miss COASTAL SPOTS

In this chapter, we tour locations where you can enjoy the surf and sun but also explore plenty of other nature and cultural activities, too. With our top destinations, you'll find everything from festive pool parties and queer bars to laid-back clothing-optional beaches and quiet places to enjoy a sunset or a shore-line stroll with your loved ones. Some of our favorite welcoming and warm spots include Curaçao, with its bright blue water and a buzzing UNESCO-listed downtown; Sydney, New South Wales, Australia, for riding the waves at world-famous Bondi Beach and taking in the sounds of the Sydney Opera House; and St. Peters-burg, Florida, where you'll find inclusive beaches, colorful murals, lovely gardens, and the impressive Dalí Museum—perfect for an artsy date.

BEACHES, MURALS, AND MUSEUMS WILL LEAVE A LASTING IMPRESSION.
St. Petersburg, Florida, U.S.A.

The wide beaches of Treasure Island make it an ideal location for a beachfront wedding.

THE LGBTQIA+ LOWDOWN St. Petersburg has an LGBTQ Welcome Center, numerous queer-owned and LGBTQIA+-friendly businesses, and one of Florida's largest Pride celebrations. Popular queer areas include Historic Kenwood, Grand Central District, and the nearby towns of Dunedin and Gulfport, where a third of the population identifies as LGBTQIA+.

Located on the tip of the Tampa Bay peninsula, St. Petersburg is often called the "Sunshine City" but offers so much more, including world-class art institutions, buzzing cafés, and great beaches.

See colorful, inclusive murals throughout the city. Standouts include "Progressive Pride" (on Central Avenue and 25th Street), with 11 stripes to include people of color, and the Black Lives Matter mural (2240 9th Avenue South), created to honor Juneteenth and the BLM movement.

The area isn't lacking for beaches, either. Clearwater Beach is one of the best, with miles of soft sand and gentle clear water, plus a promenade with stores and cafés for when you need time in the shade. The 1,136-acre (460 ha) Fort De Soto Park also has a great beach plus nature trails. Sunset Beach on Treasure Island offers more of a party scene with tiki huts and beachside bars. It's popular with the queer community and is said to be among the places that inspired Jimmy Buffett's "Margaritaville."

Not a beach person? Chill in the 100-year-old Sunken Gardens with tropical flowers, waterfalls, hidden nooks, and more than 50,000 plants. Or visit the Boyd Hill Nature Preserve on Lake Maggiore for relaxing walks through woodlands and marshes, as well as opportunities to spot birds and butterflies.

Arts lovers should beeline to the (Salvador) Dalí Museum, housing an outstanding collection of oil paintings, drawings, and sculptures by the renowned artist. Then hop over to the St. Petersburg Museum of Fine Arts, which has 20,000 eclectic global works spanning more than 5,000 years.

While in town, find your next great read at the queer-owned Tombolo Books, which carries works by emerging and marginalized voices. Further support LGBTQIA+-owned businesses and have a great meal at Love Food Central (focusing on healthy foods, including vegan and gluten-free dishes) and Lingr (serving Nordic- and Asian-inspired cuisine with dishes like hamachi crudo and salt and pepper fish cakes). Top off your night with sundaes, floats, milkshakes, and malts at Let It Be Ice Cream and drinking, singing, and drag shows at queer bars Enigma, the Garage on Central, and Cocktail.

NEED TO KNOW

◆ WHEN TO GO
March through May bring the most comfortable weather, and June brings Pride celebrations.

◆ WHERE TO STAY
Postcard Inn on the Beach has tropical gardens and private balconies with an ocean breeze. Queer-owned Casa del Merman at GayStPete House greets you with a smiley face–clad Pride flag and has a clothing-optional pool and nightly beer and wine happy hour. The Hollander Hotel is a boutique property with a pool and an on-site restaurant.

◆ WHAT TO KNOW
Nearby Tampa (about 25 minutes) is home to the GaYbor District (in the west end of its historic Ybor City), a popular spot for queer bars, clubs, and drag shows.

The namesake clear waters and white sand of Clearwater Beach

♦ WHEN TO GO

Visit June through October for beach weather or autumn charm.

♦ WHERE TO STAY

The Dunes Resort offers nonstop fun. Or try Campit Outdoor Resort to sleep under the stars in a space reserved for the queer community, friends, and allies (it's also home to the Saugatuck LGBT Music Festival). The boutique Hidden Garden Cottages & Suites is in the heart of town and is great for couples.

♦ WHAT TO KNOW

LGBTQIA+-friendly Grand Rapids is just 40 minutes away. Visit to see the country's largest art competition, ArtPrize, or follow their Beer City Ale Trail to more than 80 microbreweries. For cocktails, head to Apartment Lounge, Michigan's oldest gay bar.

The roughly 3,000-acre (1,214 ha) Silver Lake Sand Dunes along the shores of Lake Michigan

SUPPORT THE ARTS, SWIM IN A GREAT LAKE, AND PARTY DUNES STYLE.
Saugatuck, Michigan, U.S.A.

THE LGBTQIA+ LOWDOWN Charming, artistic, and open-minded, Saugatuck has welcomed queer travelers for decades. It has more than 100 LGBTQIA+-owned businesses and a very friendly vibe.

Known as the "art coast of Lake Michigan," Saugatuck (and neighboring Douglas) are delightful towns where you can admire charming, centuries-old buildings, party it up at one of the Midwest's largest LGBTQIA+ resorts, or have a lazy day on a pristine beach.

Art lovers, take your pick of galleries galore, including Roan & Black, representing emerging and established artists and sculptors from across the country, and Amazwi Contemporary Art, a gallery that has been amplifying the voices of contemporary Africa since 2004. Or create your own masterpiece at the historic Ox-Bow School of Art and Artists' Residency, established more than 100 years ago, where you can try your hand at ceramics, glassblowing, painting, drawing, and more. For Broadway shows and indie films, don't miss the Saugatuck Center for the Arts, a "community spark plug bringing people together."

Saugatuck's perfect Lake Michigan location won't disappoint. Visit the award-winning Oval Beach for swimming, surfing, or just lounging on soft sand. Don't miss Saugatuck Dunes State Park, where you can climb 200-foot (61 m) dunes (or admire them from the ground—we won't judge). Or visit Mount Baldhead (via a hand-cranked ferry, the last of its kind in the U.S.), where 302 steps get you to beautiful views of Saugatuck and Lake Michigan. For more time on the water, take a cruise on the *Star of Saugatuck*, a 51-ton (46 t) stern-wheeler paddleboat that's been running since 1978.

Get your party on at the Dunes Resort. More than 40 years old, it's one of America's largest and longest-running LGBTQIA+ resorts and a rainbow oasis that comes with the motto "whatever you do, just be you!" Spend the day floating around the massive pool and the night enjoying karaoke, dance parties, cabaret, and drag shows.

Refuel with some caffeine at Uncommon Coffee Roasters, have a famous Michigan fruit pie (and some wine) at Crane's Pie Pantry Restaurant and Winery, dine alfresco at Phil's Bar & Grille, or sample locally made craft beers from Guardian Brewing Company.

Waterfront homes in the quaint town of Saugatuck sit on border channels that lead to Lake Michigan.

SAIL INTO GILDED AGE DECADENCE.

Newport, Rhode Island, U.S.A.

THE LGBTQIA+ LOWDOWN Although Newport doesn't have a big queer scene, you'll find plenty of Pride flags and welcoming smiles. Newport Pride and NewportOUT sponsor year-round events for the LGBTQIA+ community and allies.

A seaside city known as the "sailing capital of the world," Newport, Rhode Island, is also home to stately mansions (built as summer homes for the wealthy in the 1800s), a storied history (many of America's "firsts" happened here), and lovely beaches.

The must-visit mansions are clustered along Bellevue Avenue. We love the Breakers: a Vanderbilt estate with an Italian palazzo design. Built between 1893 and 1895, it sits on 13 acres (5 ha) and has astounding ocean views. Inside are 70 rooms and the Great Hall, with a 50-foot (15 m) ceiling, gold-covered walls, and intricate mosaics. Other favorites include Marble House—featuring 50 rooms, a Chinese Tea House, and Beaux Arts architecture—and the Elms, which houses a collection of Renaissance art and was modeled after an 18th-century French château.

You can reach several mansions via the 3.5-mile (5.6 km) Cliff Walk, where nice breezes and crashing waves make for a lovely stroll. For scenic views of the shoreline and mansions, head to Ocean Drive (a National Historic Landmark District). Leave plenty of time to stop at Fort Adams State Park (home to America's second largest fort), Brenton Point State Park (great for picnics, hikes, fishing, and cycling), and Gooseberry Beach for swimming in tranquil waters. Then head to Sachuest Point National Wildlife Refuge for 242 acres (98 ha) of nature trails and more than 200 species of birds.

While in town, take a "sight sailing" cruise with America's Cup Charters or Newport Sailing School & Tours. And be sure to visit Touro Synagogue (the oldest in the U.S.) and Redwood Library (the country's oldest continuously operating library). See the cool hedge sculptures at Green Animals Topiary Garden or the International Tennis Hall of Fame, which serves up history about the sport's greats.

Next, head to Thames Street, where you'll find more than a mile of stores (and pubs, restaurants, and art galleries, too). Check out Frazzleberries Country Stores for gifts and home decor and Virgin & Aged for gourmet olive oils. Then walk to nearby Bowen's Wharf, an 18th-century commercial harborside complex known as the "Anchor of Newport," with brick walkways and granite quays. Window-shop, gallery hop, and admire the boats docked in the harbor.

Nearby, try brunch at Parlor Bar & Kitchen, lobster rolls at Anthony's Seafood, or spirits at the White Horse Tavern, America's oldest restaurant (established in 1673), which is allegedly haunted.

Shop at boutiques, local cafés, and artisanal galleries at the bustling Bowen's Wharf.

NEED TO KNOW

✦ WHEN TO GO
Time your visit for a great event, like the Newport Oyster & Chowder Festival (May), Pride (June), Newport Folk Festival (July), Newport Jazz Festival (July or August), and Newport International Boat Show (September).

✦ WHERE TO STAY
The Hotel Viking has an Old World charm, luxurious beds, and a great wine list. The Francis Malbone House offers a romantic setting, beautiful rooms, and a gourmet breakfast, while the Admiral Fitzroy Inn is a historic building (built in 1854) perfectly located on the water.

✦ WHAT TO KNOW
Just 45 minutes away, Providence is worth a visit. Check out queer bars like Providence Eagle, Mirabar, and EGO Providence. See the famous "WaterFire" sculpture light up the river between May and November.

Find views of the Breakers and other opulent mansions along the Cliff Walk on Newport's eastern rocky shore.

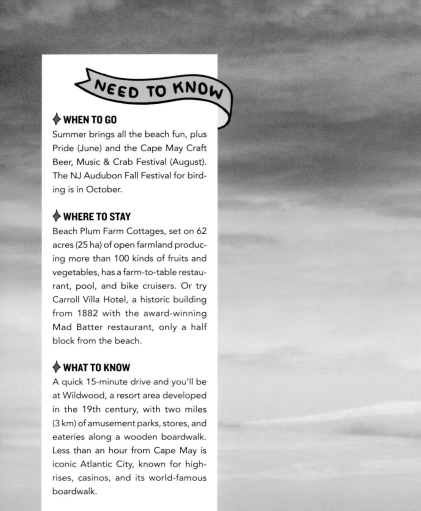

◆ WHEN TO GO

Summer brings all the beach fun, plus Pride (June) and the Cape May Craft Beer, Music & Crab Festival (August). The NJ Audubon Fall Festival for birding is in October.

◆ WHERE TO STAY

Beach Plum Farm Cottages, set on 62 acres (25 ha) of open farmland producing more than 100 kinds of fruits and vegetables, has a farm-to-table restaurant, pool, and bike cruisers. Or try Carroll Villa Hotel, a historic building from 1882 with the award-winning Mad Batter restaurant, only a half block from the beach.

◆ WHAT TO KNOW

A quick 15-minute drive and you'll be at Wildwood, a resort area developed in the 19th century, with two miles (3 km) of amusement parks, stores, and eateries along a wooden boardwalk. Less than an hour from Cape May is iconic Atlantic City, known for high-rises, casinos, and its world-famous boardwalk.

Cape May's historic lighthouse, built in 1859

ENJOY OLD-SCHOOL FUN AT THE OLDEST SEASIDE RESORT IN THE COUNTRY.

Cape May, New Jersey, U.S.A.

THE LGBTQIA+ LOWDOWN Since the '90s, the nonprofit GABLES of Cape May has helped the town be a welcoming destination to the queer community, so you'll find inclusivity and charm by the sea.

Located on New Jersey's southern tip, Cape May is named after a Dutch sea captain who explored the coast in 1621. It's America's oldest coastal resort town, designated a National Historic Landmark District, and is known for its treasured collection of more than 600 Victorian buildings and homes.

Start in the historic district to see the colorful and ornately decorated buildings such as the Painted Ladies, Stockton Row Cottages, and Emlen Physick Estate. Explore by foot or take a red trolley powered by nonprofit Cape May MAC. For another stroll, head to Washington Street Mall, a charming area of brick paths, fountains, and flowers. If you get hungry, stop at Cape May Peanut Butter Company for treats, sandwiches, and more.

Aviation and military history enthusiasts shouldn't miss the NAS Wildwood Aviation Museum, located inside a World War II hangar and listed on the National Register of Historic Places. For more history, visit the Harriet Tubman Museum, the former home to the celebrated abolitionist and other activists who worked to free enslaved people in the 1850s. Afterward, take the Center for Community Arts Underground Railroad Trolley Tour, which visits places where escaped people sought refuge from enslavement and a historic cemetery where the earliest free Black settlers are buried. Check out the renowned East Lynne Theater Company for American plays performed in a church.

Get outside at Cape May Point State Park. On the Monarch Trail, see butterflies that flock to the wildflowers every fall. Don't miss Cove Beach for stunning sunsets and great surfing and kayaking. From there, you can spot the Cape May Lighthouse and museum and climb the stairs to the top for great views. A few beach spots are known for being queer-friendly: On the west side of Cape May Point near the lighthouse, Sunset Beach is a popular hangout, while state-owned Higbee Beach is a place for long walks (beware at high tide). Higbee used to be known for nudists (it's illegal now; Higbee still tends to draw the queer community, particularly between South Voodoo Tree and the creek).

For food, head to the Lobster House for fresh seafood. The Cape May Brewing Co. has German-style brews. At Exit Zero Filling Station, Scottish owner Jack Wright serves curry dishes using recipes from his homeland, burgers, and more.

Cape May has the second highest number of Victorian homes in the country after San Francisco.

BIBA I LAGA BIBA (LIVE AND LET LIVE) IN THE COLORFUL CARIBBEAN.
Curaçao, Dutch Antilles

Cross the Queen Emma Bridge to stroll by the colorful buildings bordering the waterfront of Willemstad.

THE LGBTQIA+ LOWDOWN With a strong European influence, Curaçao is one of the most queer-welcoming locations in the Caribbean.

Though often overshadowed by neighboring Aruba, Curaçao is a beach lover's dream (with more than 38 sandy coves) and also delivers spectacular national parks, terrific museums, and vibrant neighborhoods.

We love Grote Knip for its electric blue water, dramatic cliffs, and gentle waves. It's one of Curaçao's most popular beaches, so go early or late in the day to avoid the crowds. Our other favorites include Cas Abao, which is top-to-bottom gorgeous, and Playa PortoMari, an awesome spot for snorkeling and diving and home to adorable resident pigs Willy and Woody. For more snorkeling, don't miss Playa Lagun, where boats sit on the shore and clear water makes it easy to see coral, fish, turtles, and sometimes seahorses.

Experience something truly special on a day trip to Klein Curaçao, an uninhabited island a two-hour boat ride away. Snorkel with sea turtles, see an old lighthouse and abandoned shipwreck, or relax on the white sand. Various companies run trips to Klein Curaçao, including Irie Tours, which offers a comfortable catamaran ride.

Back on the mainland, explore Curaçao's capital, Willemstad, a UNESCO World Heritage site. Stroll pedestrian-only streets, cross the floating Queen Emma Bridge (nicknamed the "Swinging Old Lady"), hang out at cafés and beach clubs, and gaze at the Handelskade, a row of brightly colored Dutch-style buildings. Don't miss the Kurá Hulanda Museum, which details the area's role in the African slave trade and its impact on enslaved people. The museum also highlights how various cultures influenced Curaçao.

Get in touch with nature at Christoffel National Park, home to more than 450 species of plants and wildlife such as the rare Curaçao white-tailed deer. Take a drive, go on gentle walks, or hike Christoffel Mountain for stupendous views (the round-trip journey takes two to three hours, but you must start before 10 a.m. due to intense afternoon heat). Then visit nearby Shete Boka National Park, where massive waves crash against volcanic cliffs and underground caves.

Curaçao has great restaurants, including Fish & Joy with tapas-style seafood; Gouverneur de Rouville, where you'll dine in an 18th-century Dutch mansion and can try Cuban banana soup and Karni stoba, a local stew; and the Wine Cellar, a family-owned French restaurant with rack of lamb and sautéed sea scallops paired with your favorite vino.

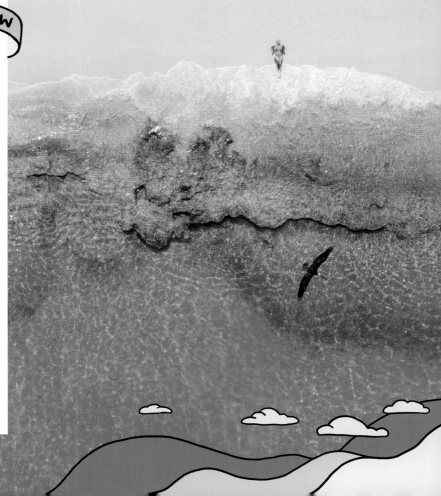

NEED TO KNOW

◆ WHEN TO GO
Anytime is lovely here, but go between January and March for Carnival, August through September for the North Sea Jazz Festival, or October for Pride.

◆ WHERE TO STAY
The Baoase Luxury Resort has top-notch digs on a private island. The Curaçao Marriott Beach Resort has a beachfront location, pool, and restaurants. Bario Hotel is a city center hotel with an artistic vibe and food hall (Bario Urban Street Food).

◆ WHAT TO KNOW
Called the "Soho of Curaçao," the Pietermaai area has trendy restaurants and nightlife, a cool art scene, and beachfront boutique hotels. It's a favorite area among travelers but also has an up-and-coming feel that some may find uncomfortable.

Curaçao's idyllic beaches are known for their turquoise waters and white sand.

⬥ NEED TO KNOW

⬧ WHEN TO GO

Swimming season is from May through October, but the shoulder seasons are less crowded. Carnival is held across the island in February. The Malta International Fireworks Festival takes place over seven nights, typically in April.

⬧ WHERE TO STAY

At Dar tal-Kaptan Boutique Maison Guesthouse, you can rent an entire home. The Xara Palace boutique hotel in a converted 17th-century palazzo is the only hotel within the walls of Mdina. Or try the Vincent hotel, a restored palazzo that's more than 400 years old with eclectic suites.

⬧ WHAT TO KNOW

An hour north of Valletta, visit the Blue Hole in Malta's sister island, Gozo, with a natural limestone rock formation that makes the perfect swimming, snorkeling, diving, scuba, and gazing spot. Then go to the Cittadella, a UNESCO site and fortified town atop a steep hill of cliffs. While in Gozo, also see Ramla Bay, a beach with reddish sand.

Soaking up the sun in lavish Malta

THIS MEDITERRANEAN MECCA HAS IT ALL.
Malta

A dazzling blue lagoon on tiny Comino, a pristine island between Malta and Gozo

THE LGBTQIA+ LOWDOWN Malta received ILGA-Europe's (International Lesbian, Gay, Bisexual, Trans, and Intersex Association) top spot on the Rainbow Index. In 2016, it became the first European country to criminalize "deceptive and harmful" conversion. It's particularly friendly for trans travelers.

Malta—with just over 120 miles (193 km) of shoreline—is a Mediterranean oasis south of Sicily with swoon-worthy beaches, renowned cuisine, and plenty of culture to explore.

Start in Paola, overlooking the Grand Harbour, at the UNESCO World Heritage site Ħal Saflieni Hypogeum, a 6,000-year-old burial site where you can go underground (note: Only 300 visitors are allowed per day). Explore its Oracle Room, famed for its acoustics, which can be heard throughout the entire structure (book your tour way in advance).

Then, in Valletta, visit St John's Co-Cathedral for the famous "Beheading of St. John the Baptist," the painting by Michelangelo Merisi da Caravaggio (1571–1610).

Across the Grand Harbour from Valletta, see three pre-served cities (Vittoriosa, Senglea, and Cospicua) to get a peek into Malta's maritime history and experience authentic life. Don't miss Fort St. Elmo, built in 1552 by knights to protect Valletta harbors, and the National War Museum that it houses.

Game of Thrones fans will want to hit up Mdina, called the "Silent City," where you can take a themed tour to see the sights of parts of King's Landing from season one. (Mdina is also the film location of other hits such as *Gladiator* and *The Count of Monte Cristo*.)

Treasures await on the western coast, including sandy Ġnejna Beach. Also worth a visit: St. Peter's Pool (a natural swimming hole) or the somewhat secluded Anchor Bay surrounded by rocky slopes. For harbor views, the fishing village of Marsaxlokk offers colorful boats, a morning market, and local seafood. It can get crowded in the afternoon, so go early.

With so many great restaurants, you'll have your pick. Go to Roger's Bakery & Pastizzeria in Żejtun for Malta's signature pastry (called *pastizzi*) that's filled with ricotta, Nutella, or peas with curry. In Valletta, visit family-owned Old Bakery's Pizza e Pasta for their signature dish, *rosette* (layers of fresh pasta with ham and a cream sauce). In Marsaxlokk, eat at Ir-Rizzu, which serves up fresh catches all day. To master the cuisine yourself, take a class at the Mediterranean Culinary Academy.

Maori is a queer bar in a building with a larger-than-life cat mural. Or head to Lollipop for a night of dancing.

WORTH SOME EXTRA LOVE

MALTA

With its idyllic islands and Mediterranean climate, Malta's stunning landscapes (like Għajn Tuffieħa beach, pictured here) are what postcards are made of. We can't get enough of the delicious cuisine, kind people, and rich history—much of it spread across three UNESCO World Heritage sites (and another seven sites are being considered for the list). And with the most official holidays in the European Union—including more than 75 religious celebrations—you're almost always guaranteed a meaningful event or a great party.

RELAX THE DAYS AWAY WITH CRYSTAL CLEAR WATER AND CORAL REEFS.
Krabi, Thailand

Colorful kayaks line the sand outside a bar at Railay (Rai Leh) Beach.

THE LGBTQIA+ LOWDOWN Thailand is a popular destination for queer travel and is known as one of the most welcoming countries for transgender people (plus a medical tourism destination for those pursuing gender-affirming surgery). Thailand is making progress to legalize same-sex civil partnerships and recently had its first trans candidate for prime minister.

The province of Krabi, on the west coast of Thailand, is known for its marine life; brilliant, clear waters; and coral reef. Krabi includes hundreds of islands off the coast and is *the* spot in Thailand for a relaxing getaway.

The Krabi Town Night Market (Friday to Sunday) is an absolute must-experience with more than 70 vendors selling crafts, Thai street food, clothing, and more. Just 10 minutes from town, visit Wat Tham Sua (Tiger Cave Temple), a complex of caves where monks live and worship. Then head up more than 1,200 steps to the "footprint of the Buddha" for a panoramic view of the Andaman Sea and its islands. For another great site, visit Khao Khanap Nam, where twin mountains sit on opposite sides of the river with caves underneath.

Hit the beach at lively Ao Nang to watch long-tail boats and scuba dive. Railay (Rai Leh) Beach, accessible only by boat, is fairly secluded and famous for rock climbing on its limestone cliffs. Or visit Khlong Thom Hot Spring with mineral pools in the rainforest and tons of greenery that act as canopies for shade. For a totally different kind of beach experience, head just outside Krabi to Susan Hoi to see the "shell cemetery," a collection of huge shale rocks formed from shellfish remains between 25 and 40 million years old.

Khao Phanom Bencha National Park is less than 19 miles (30 km) from Krabi Town and is a protected area of rainforest with two waterfalls, two circular trails, and a cave. Finally, don't miss the Phi Phi Islands, the famed film location for the movie *The Beach* (go by speedboat from Krabi in just under an hour).

Eateries in the area are plentiful. Go to Khaothong Hill for insane sunset views from a hill (take the shuttle service at the bottom). In Ao Nang, go to Red Chilli Thai Cuisine, a family-run restaurant with authentic dishes, and Tandoori Hut Restaurant & Bar for its popular chicken dopiaza.

NEED TO KNOW

◆ WHEN TO GO
Plan for the non-monsoon months of October through April.

◆ WHERE TO STAY
Go big or go home at the Sofitel Krabi Phokeethra Golf & Spa Resort with a massive swimming pool and sprawling property. The Tubkaak Krabi, near quiet Tubkaak Beach, is set away from the more commercial resort area and is perfect for a romantic stay. Or try Amari Vogue Krabi in the same area for beachfront wood houses and a spa. The eco-certified Pavilions Anana Krabi in Ao Nang offers farm-to-table dining and multiple pools.

◆ WHAT TO KNOW
Phuket, Thailand's more developed island, is a better choice if you want tons of nightlife or queer-focused activities.

The limestone cliffs of Railay Beach

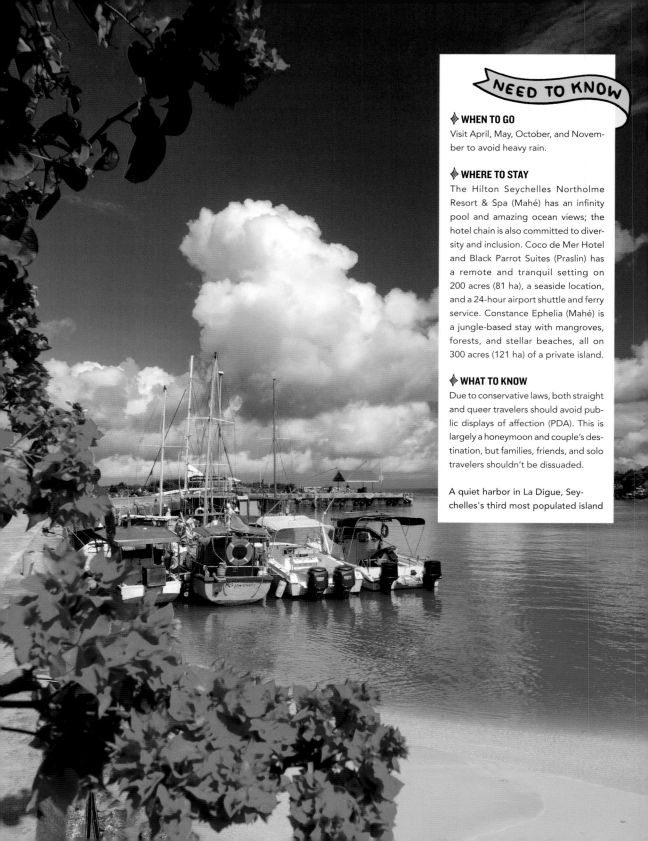

◈ WHEN TO GO

Visit April, May, October, and November to avoid heavy rain.

◈ WHERE TO STAY

The Hilton Seychelles Northolme Resort & Spa (Mahé) has an infinity pool and amazing ocean views; the hotel chain is also committed to diversity and inclusion. Coco de Mer Hotel and Black Parrot Suites (Praslin) has a remote and tranquil setting on 200 acres (81 ha), a seaside location, and a 24-hour airport shuttle and ferry service. Constance Ephelia (Mahé) is a jungle-based stay with mangroves, forests, and stellar beaches, all on 300 acres (121 ha) of a private island.

◈ WHAT TO KNOW

Due to conservative laws, both straight and queer travelers should avoid public displays of affection (PDA). This is largely a honeymoon and couple's destination, but families, friends, and solo travelers shouldn't be dissuaded.

A quiet harbor in La Digue, Seychelles's third most populated island

LIVE YOUR BEST TROPICAL LIFE.
Seychelles

A diver swims through a school of blue-striped snapper.

THE LGBTQIA+ LOWDOWN Seychelles is making progress, having decriminalized "same-sex acts" in 2016, but marriage and civil unions are still not recognized. LGBTQIA+ couples should be mindful that, although resorts and many locals are welcoming, some communities remain conservative. LGBTI Sey advocates for equality and sponsors queer-focused events.

An archipelago east of Kenya and Tanzania and north of Madagascar in the Indian Ocean, Seychelles offers amazing beaches, national parks, nature reserves, and luxurious resorts.

After arriving in Mahé, the country's largest and most populous island, explore breathtaking beaches, including Beau Vallon Beach, Anse Soleil, and Petite Anse, and visit Morne Seychellois National Park. As the country's largest national park, its land occupies more than 20 percent of Mahé. Morne Seychellois (its highest point) reaches nearly 3,000 feet (915 m). Hikers won't want to miss the moderately challenging and winding Morne Blanc Trail for a trek through a misty forest and incredible views from the summit. The park is also great for bird-watching.

Mahé's capital city, Victoria, is also worth checking out. Admire colonial buildings and Little Ben (a mini version of London's Big Ben), chat with locals in Freedom Square, visit the National Museum of History, and get fresh fish and produce at Sir Selwyn Clarke Market. Don't miss the National Botanical Garden. More than 100 years old, it has 15 acres (6 ha) of endemic and exotic plants, plus giant tortoises, flying foxes, and fruit bat colonies.

On Praslin Island, you'll find Anse Lazio, widely considered one of the world's best beaches. Getting there is a literal uphill climb, but you'll be rewarded with a dreamy stretch of beach, a coastline flanked with boulders, and striking cobalt water. Visit Anse Volbert (also known as Côte d'Or) for calm water and coral reefs. Vallée de Mai Nature Reserve is a prehistoric forest and one of the few places in the world to see a coco-de-mer (double coconut) palm, endemic to Seychelles.

From Praslin, take a boat ride to Sainte Anne Marine National Park for snorkeling, scuba diving, and nature walks, or Curieuse Island to see free-roaming giant tortoises. You can also find these gentle giants at Aldabra Atoll (it has the world's largest population), but it has a limited daily capacity and no tourist facilities or hotels. To get there, prearrange a cruise with companies such as Silhouette Cruises or Silversea.

While in Seychelles, try one of its most popular dishes, *poison ek diri* (rice with fish), best enjoyed from a beachside café or food stand. Or opt for sit-down, fresh seafood meals like grilled snapper at Les Rochers on Praslin Island or Marie Antoinette in Victoria, one of Seychelles's oldest restaurants serving local Creole dishes. Chill Out Tapas Lounge Bar (also in Praslin) offers tasty light bites and cocktails with a view of Anse Volbert.

CELEBRATE THE NIGHT AWAY WITH PARADES AND PRIDE.

Rio de Janeiro, Brazil

People flood the streets for the LGBTQIA+ Pride Parade at Copacabana Beach.

THE LGBTQIA+ LOWDOWN Rio is the queer mecca of Brazil, priding itself on initiatives like vocational training courses for trans people, anti-bullying projects to support queer students, and legislation outlawing discrimination in the city's nightclubs.

Located in eastern Brazil, Rio is world famous for its Carnival celebrations, but it's also a big and vibrant coastal city with beaches and mountains galore.

Start at Ipanema Beach, a hot spot for the queer community and one of the cleanest beaches in the city (here you'll find Rua Farme de Amoedo, a famous LGBTQIA+ street with some of the city's best queer nightlife). Also check out Copacabana, one of the world's most popular beaches, which also has a lively queer crowd, music, restaurants, and bars. Or visit Praia de Abricó beach, the city's only nudist option. It's located in the West Zone in Grumari, the only area with no residents.

Don't miss Sugarloaf Mountain, a historic landmark with a famous tramway installed in 1912. Double your fun with a cable car to the top (or hike and rock climb if you're experienced). For another iconic landmark, visit the statue of Christ the Redeemer, one of the New Seven Wonders of the World at more than 98 feet (30 m) tall (it's the fourth largest statue of Jesus Christ in the world). To get there, go to Mount Corcovado, a massive granite peak that overlooks the city, and take the challenging hike 90 minutes to the top. You can also take the Corcovado Rack Railway to the summit.

To see Rio's artistic side, check out the colorful Escadaria Selarón (Selarón Stairs), which were created by Chilean artist Jorge Selarón in 1990 with materials from construction sites. Since then, it has become a widely recognized filming location (you may have seen it in the video for "Beautiful" with Snoop Dogg, Pharrell Williams, and Uncle Charlie Wilson). For more contemporary art, visit the Niterói Contemporary Art Museum, a futuristic-looking building with 360-degree views of Guanabara Bay.

Try Churrascaria Palace for traditional Brazilian *churrasco*, different cuts of meat on skewers; Joaquina for a cozy spot offering typical Brazilian dishes by the beach; or Reino Vegetal, a family-friendly spot that has been serving vegetarian and vegan dishes for more than 25 years. If you're looking for bars, go to Barraca da Denise 63 on Ipanema Beach for daytime club vibes; Boate La Cueva, a 1960s LGBTQIA+ bar and disco designed to feel like a cave; and the popular Explorer Bar for drinks, international fare, and a jungle-like patio. You can also wind down with jazz and other soothing sounds at the Maze, overlooking downtown Rio with views across Guanabara Bay.

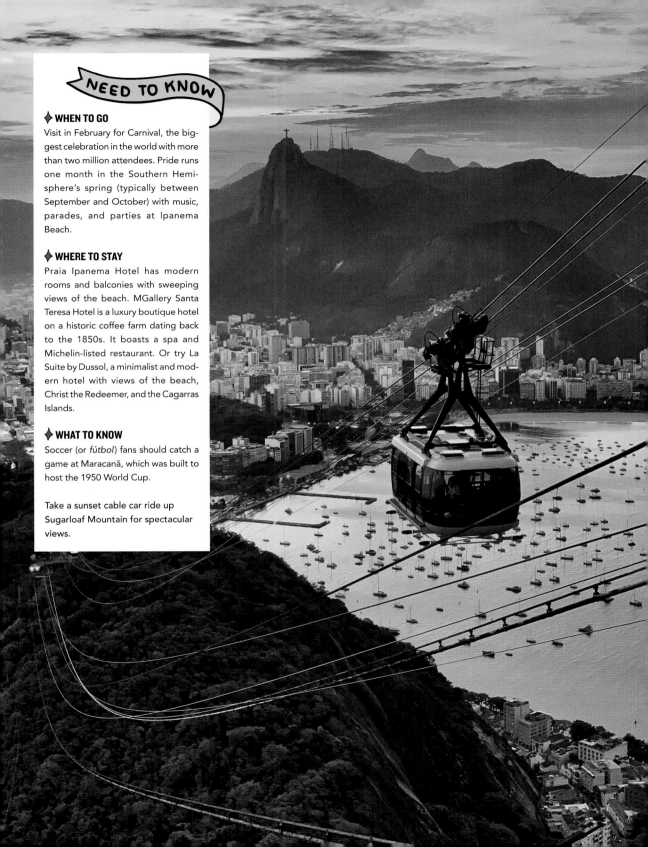

NEED TO KNOW

◆ WHEN TO GO

Visit in February for Carnival, the biggest celebration in the world with more than two million attendees. Pride runs one month in the Southern Hemisphere's spring (typically between September and October) with music, parades, and parties at Ipanema Beach.

◆ WHERE TO STAY

Praia Ipanema Hotel has modern rooms and balconies with sweeping views of the beach. MGallery Santa Teresa Hotel is a luxury boutique hotel on a historic coffee farm dating back to the 1850s. It boasts a spa and Michelin-listed restaurant. Or try La Suite by Dussol, a minimalist and modern hotel with views of the beach, Christ the Redeemer, and the Cagarras Islands.

◆ WHAT TO KNOW

Soccer (or *fútbol*) fans should catch a game at Maracanã, which was built to host the 1950 World Cup.

Take a sunset cable car ride up Sugarloaf Mountain for spectacular views.

The glassy waters of Kayangan Lake on Coron Island

LEAVE YOUR WORRIES BEHIND ON THIS LITTLE ISLAND.

Boracay, Philippines

Visitors walk along a busy strip of shops and restaurants on Boracay Island.

THE LGBTQIA+ LOWDOWN A small tropical Filipino island, often referred to as one of the queerest places in Asia, Boracay is only four miles (7 km) long and is known for its beautiful sandy beaches, resorts, and nightlife.

Boracay was once known almost singularly as a party destination. Though it's now cleaned up its act (literally, with a ban on single-use plastic and limits on how many people can be on the island at once), Boracay has gone from a wild party town to a perfect escape with clean water and plenty to do and see.

Kick things off at White Beach, known for its idyllic beauty, where you can swim, sail, and watch the sunset. Next, see Willy's Rock, a volcanic rock formation that juts out into the ocean, complete with a shrine dedicated to the Virgin Mary. To escape crowds, head north to Puka Shell Beach—formerly Yapak Beach—named for the seashells that litter the sand. For water sports (permitted May through October), go to Bulabog Beach.

To admire views of the island and surrounding beauty, head to Mount Luho—the tallest peak on Boracay at more than 300 feet (91 m) above sea level—for the panoramic observation deck. Then, put on your snorkeling gear to explore Tambisaan Beach on the island's southeast corner

for coral, clownfish, and possibly sea snakes. Ilig-Iligan Beach, a more rustic spot, has a beautiful reef that's not as crowded, especially earlier in the day. Crocodile Island (named for its crocodile-like shape) is just a few hundred feet off the coast and is known for sightings of cuttlefish, lionfish, and moray eel.

If you're up for a day trip that's only 30 minutes by boat, visit the Motag Living Museum, which takes a step back in time by highlighting Filipino culture before the islands became a modernized resort destination. Go for a totally hands-on experience at the museum: plant rice, taste traditional food, and soak up wisdom from the elders that meet with visitors for this experience.

For a hearty meal, try Nonie's Restaurant with traditional dishes, healthy vegetarian/vegan options, and locally sourced ingredients. Go to Salsa Fusion Restaurant for a Mexican/Filipino hybrid that's a local favorite. Balai Seafood Restaurant is your place for scallops, crab, oysters, and other fresh seafood.

RIDE THE WAVES AT BONDI BEACH AND PRETEND YOU'RE IN *PRISCILLA.*

Sydney, New South Wales, Australia

A dazzling nighttime view of Sydney's skyline and opera house

THE LGBTQIA+ LOWDOWN Sydney, a cosmopolitan and welcoming city, has its biggest queer scene in Darlinghurst (around Oxford Street), but the neighborhoods of Erskineville, Surry Hills, Newtown, and Redfern are also popular with the LGBTQIA+ community.

Sitting on a beautiful harbor, Australia's Emerald City is a place to find world-class museums, long stretches of beach, hopping bars, and designer shops, plus the famous Sydney Opera House. Catch a concert or behind-the-scenes tour and admire the building's shapes and angles. Grab a drink at the Opera Bar, where you'll find locals hanging out and reasonably priced wine. Stroll along the harbor and walk over the Sydney Harbour Bridge, called the "coat hanger" by locals, for incredible views. Adventure seekers, try the heart-pumping Bridge Climb.

One of the world's most famous beaches, Bondi Beach is another must. Grab a spot on its long stretch of sand (North Bondi is popular with the LGBTQIA+ community), surf the waves, and people-watch (lots of men wear Speedos, as they were invented in Sydney, after all). Or take a dip in the Bondi Icebergs Club's pool, a century-old historic landmark built on the shores of Bondi Beach (and the most photographed swimming pool on Earth).

To really stretch your legs, take the Bondi to Coogee Coastal Walk for its spectacular cliffs and water views (tip: Reverse the order for fewer crowds). You can stop at several places and see five beaches: Coogee, Clovelly, Bronte, Tamarama, and Bondi. For snorkeling or diving, Gordon's Bay (between Coogee and Clovelly) has a fantastic under-water nature trail. Alternatively, Wylie's Baths and Bronte Baths provide sheltered swimming areas.

Ferry rides are nonnegotiable. Hop on one to Manly Beach, where pine trees, striking yellow sand, and big waves make up the scenery. Don't miss Taronga Zoo to see giraffes with the Sydney Opera House behind them (they have the best view), or Cockatoo Island, a UNESCO World Heritage site that was once home to an infamous prison.

Elsewhere in the city, explore the Royal Botanic Gardens or check out artwork at White Rabbit Gallery and the Art Gallery of New South Wales. Let the hours roll by in Darlinghurst, where you can shop for new clothes created for "beach baes and pool punks" at Double Rainbouu, which puts fresh spins on Hawaiian shirts and resort wear and sells unisex attire. Save time for browsing at Bookshop Darlinghurst, a beloved space since 1982.

Reserve a meal at world-class Quay, or grab dumplings at Din Tai Fung, then spend the night dancing at ARQ and the Colombian Hotel. Or see a drag show at Universal, the Oxford, or the Stonewall Hotel, which also hosts Trans Glamoré, a celebration of trans performers and friends. In Erskineville, visit the Imperial Hotel (the setting for *The Adventures of Priscilla, Queen of the Desert*) for more dancing and drag shows.

◆ WHEN TO GO

June through August (the Southern Hemisphere's winter) are good months to spot whales. The shoulder seasons (September through November or March through May) offer fewer crowds and lower prices. February is Sydney Gay and Lesbian Mardi Gras, and Pride takes place in June.

◆ WHERE TO STAY

Brickfield Hill Inn (Surry Hills) is a boutique experience in a 19th-century house. Medusa Hotel (Darlinghurst) is lovely and near all the action. The Park Hyatt Sydney offers a resort-like experience (including a great pool) and is on the harbor.

◆ WHAT TO KNOW

Areas like Darlinghurst and Surry Hills are called suburbs but are urban neighborhoods within walking distance of the Central Business District. Groups like Heaps Gay, Trans Pride Australia, Girlthing, and Honcho Disko often sponsor LGBTQIA+ events. Quick, easy, and scenic day trips include Hunter Valley (especially great for wine lovers) and the Blue Mountains for bushwalking (both intense and gentle) in spectacular natural scenery. Don't miss the Three Sisters Lookout and Wentworth Falls.

Thousands of revelers celebrate Gay and Lesbian Mardi Gras.

◆ WHEN TO GO

Visit in June for FIRE, the first LGBTQIA+ film festival in Spain. The popular Panteresports is an LGBTQIA+ multisport tournament in September. Also in September, La Mercè festival fills the streets with parades and a Catalan tradition called Correfoc, a performance and parade where good and evil are played out on the streets with fire and fireworks.

◆ WHERE TO STAY

Kimpton Vividora in the Gothic Quarter is a pet-friendly favorite with a pool. Hotel Ohla, in the same area, is known for the 1,000 ceramic eyes on its facade and its Michelin-starred restaurant. The hetero-friendly Axel Hotel in Gaixample is also quite popular with the LGBTQIA+ community and houses Sky Bar, which features a fan of feathers representing diversity.

◆ WHAT TO KNOW

Sitges, 22 miles (35 km) southwest of Barcelona, is known for its inclusiveness and explosive Carnival celebration (at the end of Lent). But you'll find plenty more there: Garraf Massif natural area (one of the most important biological reserves in Catalonia); Sitges Film Festival's Zombie Walk, where crowds parade through the city as the undead (May); and Platja la Bassa Ronda, a popular queer-friendly beach.

Pont del Bisbe bridge in Barcelona's Gothic Quarter

HERE, YOU'RE GAUDÍ-TEED A GOOD TIME.
Barcelona, Spain

A vendor sells fresh produce, spices, and chilies at Mercat de la Boqueria, a public market in Barcelona.

THE LGBTQIA+ LOWDOWN Barcelona, the Catalan capital, is particularly welcoming to the spectrum of the queer community, with multiple LGBTQIA+ events, queer-friendly districts, and inclusive hangouts.

Northern Spain's only coastal city, Barcelona has it all: history, art, Gaudí-designed landmarks, gastronomy, and Instagrammable sites at every turn.

Start at UNESCO-listed Park Güell to see the work of architect Antoni Gaudí and Spanish entrepreneur Eusebi Güell, a sea of colored tiles with sculptures and expansive gardens.

Don't miss Palau de la Música Catalana, also a UNESCO World Heritage site. Completed in 1908, it's a tribute to Catalan music and history with floor-to-ceiling stained glass and colorful mosaics. Catch a performance of a genuine flamenco show, ballet, or concert.

Next, visit the vibrant and famous Las Ramblas street for La Boqueria Market with 400 food stalls and tile artwork by famous painter Joan Miró. Antinous, an LGBTQIA+ bookstore, hosts author talks, signings, and special events.

Head to the Gothic Quarter for winding lanes, cool shops, and popular bars. Here you'll find Cathedral Square, with the Cathedral of the Holy Cross and Santa Eulalia, constructed in the 14th and 15th centuries. Opposite the cathedral, look for Picasso's huge frieze murals (the renowned artist moved to Barcelona when he was 13).

Another trendy neighborhood, Eixample, known by the locals as Gaixample for its large LGBTQIA+ community, is great for craft beer bars, art galleries, high-end stores, modernist buildings, and the Arc de Triomf, designed as the entrance to the 1888 Barcelona World Fair. You should also visit the Gaudí houses: Casa Batlló ("House of Inspiration") and La Pedrera-Casa Milà, Gaudí's last private residence project (completed in 1912), for immersive hologram experiences.

Bogatell Beach has a family-friendly vibe and is adjacent to the Poblenou neighborhood, one of Barcelona's coolest. Go to the Design Museum, outdoor Palo Alto Market Fest, and the massive Razzmatazz Night Club and Beer Garden with multiple rooms for different types of music. Or head north of Bogatell for Mar Bella Beach (with a clothing-optional section), which is popular with the LGBTQIA+ community.

To get views from above, head to the Bunkers of Carmel at the top of Turó de la Rovira hill, 860 feet (262 m) above sea level. At the summit, you'll find ruins from the Spanish Civil War.

To eat and drink, go to Paradiso bar, named one of the world's best cocktail bars; Churrería Laietana for churros and chocolate; family-owned El Bierzo a Tope for homestyle Catalan cooking; and El Berro, a "straight-friendly" local tapas bar. Most restaurants are closed Sundays and Mondays, so plan ahead.

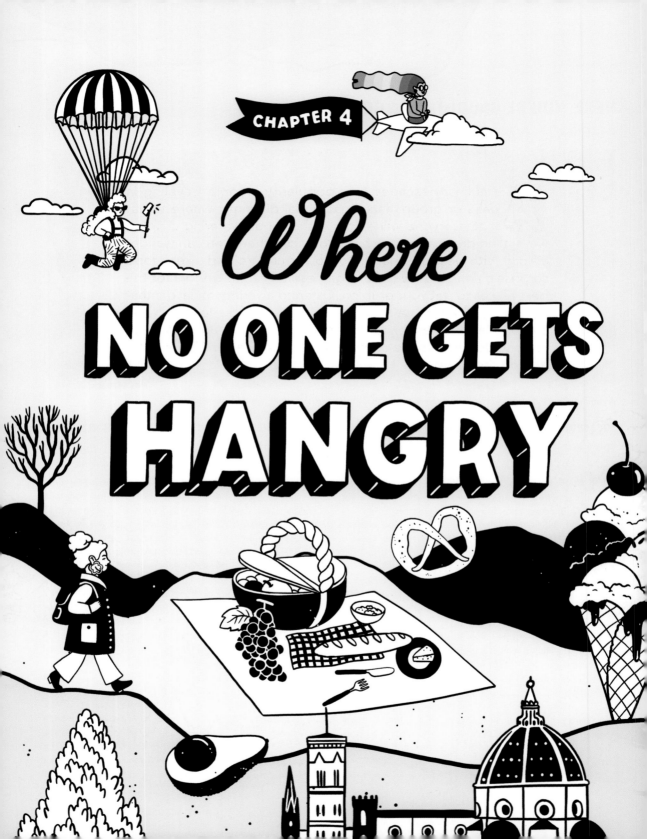

CHAPTER 4

Where NO ONE GETS HANGRY

As culinary escapes gain popularity, people traveling in pairs or groups face a potential dilemma: where to eat that everyone will enjoy. In this mouthwatering chapter, we outline destinations such as Florence, where you can wander all day with gelato in hand; Tokyo for culture and street food surprises; and Tel Aviv ("the vegan capital of the world") for the best places to get your grub on. Offering a variety of flavors that will satisfy different palates, this chapter explores food cultures and timeless culinary experiences that will satisfy—plus, what to see and do when you're between meals in these foodie hot spots around the world.

FILL UP ON GOOD FOOD AND EXPLORE THE GREAT OUTDOORS.
Boise, Idaho, U.S.A.

Vibrant colors and smells fill the Basque Market thanks to delectable Spanish dishes like paella.

THE LGBTQIA+ LOWDOWN Boise is a big city with a small-town feel—and is also Idaho's most welcoming city. It has a thriving LGBTQIA+ community and a popular Pride festival that's more than 30 years old.

Situated on the Boise River, Idaho's capital offers outdoor adventures (including fishing and floating), is a paradise for music lovers, and has some of the best food in the country.

Start at the quirky Potato Museum to explore the vegetable's history, take selfies with a massive potato statue, and eat potato cupcakes (made with potato flour) and more. Then get your rocks on at the Idaho Museum of Mining & Geology to see fluorescent minerals, meteorites, fossils, and a seismograph.

Go downtown to Freak Alley Gallery (F.A.G.), the Northwest's largest open-air, multi-artist gallery. While downtown, check out the Idaho Black History Museum, Idaho Botanical Garden, and the Anne Frank Human Rights Memorial. It's also home to the Edge, Boise's first espresso bar, which opened in the early 1980s.

Next, take a walk (or pick up some wheels at Pedego Electric Bikes) on the Boise Greenbelt, a 25-mile (40 km) path along the Boise River. For more nature, go to Camel's Back and Hulls Gulch Reserve for nature trails, birding, and native plants, or Bogus Basin for hiking, biking, and winter sports.

In Boise's historic North End, you'll find the Hyde Park district, which is listed on the National Register of Historic Places and is a hub for the LGBTQIA+ community. Wander tree-lined streets, visit shops, and grab a coffee or cocktail.

When it's mealtime, try Kibrom's Ethiopian & Eritrean Cuisine, owned by a family from the Shimelba refugee camp in Ethiopia. Family-owned and family-operated Bacon has a southern-inspired menu and bacon cinnamon rolls (their nonprofit, Bacon for Hope, supports the Hope House, a home for kids from failed adoptions). Certified Kitchen + Bakery has an all-day breakfast featuring English muffins made with a 52-year-old sourdough starter. Boise Brewing, in a converted gym, is a go-to spot for craft beer. The Lively has daily menus highlighting local ingredients, plus special events like a six-course sushi tasting menu.

In search of family fun? Base Camp Pong + Axe is a huge gastropub with ax throwing, table tennis, and a full restaurant and bar. For nightlife, visit Neurolux Lounge, an inclusive bar and music venue and favorite among locals; Somewhere Bar, an LGBTQIA+ community favorite; and the Balcony Club for dancing the night away.

NEED TO KNOW

◈ WHEN TO GO
Visit in March for Treefort Music Fest, a five-day indie rock event. The famous Idaho Shakespeare Festival runs from May through October.

◈ WHERE TO STAY
The Modern Hotel and Bar is a former Travelodge turned fun boutique hotel with a well-loved bar and restaurant. Or try Boise Guest House for its North End location and suites with plenty of privacy and space for lounging.

◈ WHAT TO KNOW
If you're overwhelmed by choices, take one of Indulge Boise's food tours, where you can eat your way through town while hearing about the cultural and historic highlights of the city.

Boise is home to numerous outdoor farmers markets.

◆ WHEN TO GO

Summer is when most events happen, with Pride in June (which includes Black Pride and Latinx Pride), the Gay Oregon Pageant at CC Slaughters (open all year), Portland's Naked Bike Ride in July, and the annual July PDX Adult Soapbox Derby, where teams race their own creations. In November, you can catch Portland's Queer Film Festival.

◆ WHERE TO STAY

McMenamins Kennedy School Hotel is a converted elementary school from 1915. You can have a pint in a classroom, enjoy an aged whiskey in detention, and see movies in the auditorium. Hotel Lucia offers a photography collection, eclectic art, and boutique accommodations in a charming building that's on the National Register of Historic Places. Or try Tiny Digs, a collection of adorable, custom-built luxury tiny houses in East Portland.

◆ WHAT TO KNOW

Portland has been nicknamed Beervana for all its noteworthy craft brews (and more than 70 breweries). Take a brew cycle group tour, or hit up places like Migration Brewing, which features a Colors of Love beer and is dedicated to Pride year-round; Old Town Brewing, which is kid friendly; Kells Brewery, a neighborhood pub with rave food and brew praise; and Ruse Brewing for small-batch craft beers (the company also works with local artists and musicians to design art paired with their beers).

Twilight over the Willamette River and Portland skyline

FIND FOOD, BOOKS, AND BREWS IN THE CITY OF ROSES.
Portland, Oregon, U.S.A.

THE LGBTQIA+ LOWDOWN At the forefront of LGBTQIA+ rights and with a history of inclusion that stretches back to the precolonial era, Portland is one of the most queer-friendly spots in the United States. In 2008, it was the first major U.S. city to elect an openly gay mayor.

With biking, hiking, and a downtown filled with possibilities, Portland is the perfect place to stay—and eat—for a few days away.

Start at Pioneer Courthouse Square, the "city's living room" in the heart of downtown. It hosts hundreds of events and is a faithful go-to for food carts (try Fried Egg I'm in Love or the Block sandwich shop). Next, visit the Portland Art Museum, the oldest art museum in the Pacific Northwest (founded in 1892). Browse artifacts and artwork from Indigenous cultures as well as contemporary art, including paintings by Monet and Picasso. For literary adventures, visit Powell's City of Books, offering almost 70,000 square feet (6,503 m²) of new and used titles, including an impressive queer selection.

Then enjoy some of Portland's parks and gardens—more than 200 of them, including Mill Ends Park (the world's smallest dedicated park) and the vast Forest Park. Don't miss the Audubon Society of Portland Nature Sanctuary, which offers 150 acres (61 ha) of bird-watching; the Portland Japanese Garden for a waterfall, teahouse, and pond garden; and the International Rose Test Garden, which has more than 10,000 rose blooms (May through October). Along the Willamette River, you can hang on the beach, swim, take a jet boat excursion, kayak, or stand-up paddleboard.

Rest your feet at Darcelle XV Showplace, which is listed on the National Register of Historic Places and will keep you thoroughly entertained with its famous drag shows.

If you can't decide what's for breakfast, lunch, or dinner, take your pick of more than 500 food courts. We like Cartlandia food cart pod, which has 30-plus food carts representing 15 different countries. Portland Mercado has Mexican, Colombian, Peruvian, Argentinian, and Venezuelan dishes. Fifth Avenue food cart pod is a casual collection of food carts in a busy downtown location. And St. Johns Food & Beer Porch has more than a dozen food carts with local brews and ciders on tap.

To dine in, go to Red Sauce Pizza for its pies, sourdough bread, and pizza-making classes. To get your fix of Asian food, try Langbaan, a 24-seat restaurant with a Thai tasting menu, or Murata, which has been serving classic Japanese dishes since 1988. Don't miss the family-owned Swiss Hibiscus (with its famous Martin's Swiss Dressing) and its sister restaurant, Bipartisan Café, which is structured around the owners' belief in community and displays artwork that represents all groups of people. And, of course, visit the famous Voodoo Doughnut—it's totally worth the line.

Sample from one (or many) of Portland's legendary food trucks and carts.

DISCOVER TRAILS, EATS, AND CHARM IN THE "PARIS OF THE SOUTH."
Asheville, North Carolina, U.S.A.

THE LGBTQIA+ LOWDOWN With progressive politics, protective laws, and a large queer community (according to the U.S. Census Bureau, Asheville has 83 percent more gay and lesbian residents than the national average), it's a place where you can travel freely and explore all the fun.

Set against the backdrop of the Blue Ridge Mountains and dubbed the Paris of the South, Asheville draws visitors and transplants from all over with its biodiversity and temperate climate.

Get to know the city on the self-guided Asheville Urban Trail. Start at Pack Place (on Pack Square) with plaque #1, "Walk Into History," and then follow the other bronze plaques and statues to discover the city's culture and history through 30 different sites.

The Asheville Museum of Science lets the whole family become geologists, discover topography, dig for fossils, and investigate a *Teratophoneus* dinosaur skeleton. The Asheville Pinball Museum features more than 75 classic machines and video games. Meanwhile, the 68,000-square-foot (6,317 m²) Asheville Art Museum showcases 20th- and 21st-century American works. For something extra fun, hit up Haywood Road for its RuPaul and Dolly Parton mural and to explore an area that's popular with the LGBTQIA+ community.

The Asheville Bee Charmer, which is queer-owned, offers a truly unique experience. They're committed to honeybee habitat protection and offer small-batch honey and a tasting bar. Nearby, Firestorm Bookstore Co-op is a queer feminist collective that's worker-owned and self-managed. For another inclusive lit spot, go to Malaprop's Bookstore & Café, which hosts popular celebrity book readings.

Have a grand experience at Biltmore, an 8,000-acre (3,237 ha) estate and the United States' largest home, built by George Vanderbilt. Admission includes access to Biltmore's gardens and Antler Hill Village & Winery, both of which focus on preservation and environmental stewardship.

For a great choice for grub, go to S&W Market & Taproom, a food hall named one of the best in the country. Or check out Highland Brewing Company; Farm Dogs with grass-fed sausages and burgers; The Hop Ice Cream, which is antibiotic free; and Bun Intended, serving award-winning Thai street food and locally sourced proteins. Or visit 12 Bones Smokehouse, where everything is smoked long and slow over hardwoods. Then chill at Bottle Riot, a listening and lounge bar with a focus on wine, small-production spirits, and European beers. O. Henry's, North Carolina's oldest queer bar, has games and a dance club in the back called the Underground. Or take a tour with queer-owned Asheville Rooftop Bar Tours, which will show you some of the best views of the Blue Ridge Mountains while you sip cocktails.

Located along the French Broad River, 12 Bones Smokehouse is a staple of the River Arts District.

WHEN TO GO

The Blue Ridge Pride Festival in September is a huge celebration of the queer community and its allies with more than 100 vendors, educational groups, and plenty of food and beverage stalls. September is also host to Goombay, a 40-year-old celebration of African Caribbean food and music. Or go in April for Asheville's Bread Festival or May for GRINDfest, a free, four-day festival that celebrates Black freedom.

WHERE TO STAY

The Lion and the Rose B&B is an 1898 residence and one of Asheville's longest-operating inns with stained glass windows, period antiques, and fireplaces. Or try the historic Princess Anne, which opened in 1924; it's on the U.S. Department of the Interior's National Register of Historic Places and follows eco-friendly practices. Cedar Crest Inn, the longest-running B&B in Asheville, is owned by a historic preservation company that's keeping its Victorian charm alive.

WHAT TO KNOW

The North Carolina Literary Map, an ongoing project that highlights the Tar Heel State's literary heritage, maintains a database of locations connected to some of our favorite reads and authors. A Thomas Wolfe and F. Scott Fitzgerald walking tour covers Asheville, or you can venture to neighboring cities and towns to visit your own interests from the map.

The must-see Winter Garden at the Biltmore Estate

NEED TO KNOW

◆ WHEN TO GO

Toscana Pride in June takes place in six cities and has celebrations, art, and parades. September brings the Florence Queer Festival inside the Cinema La Compagnia, the hub of the city's cultural activity. From April through June, you can take part in the Maggio Musicale Fiorentino (music festival), a series of internationally acclaimed classical music concerts and recitals, operas, and ballets.

◆ WHERE TO STAY

Hotel David, open since 1958, is an award-winning accommodation away from crowds but still walkable to the city center. For luxury, go to Hotel Lungarno, which is on the Arno and has Ponte Vecchio as its backdrop (some rooms have terraces).

◆ WHAT TO KNOW

To access the cathedral and other churches in the city, be prepared and dress appropriately: covered shoulders and knees, and no sandals.

The legendary All'Antico Vinaio sandwich shop

TAKE IN ALL THE ART AND VINO THIS CENTRAL ITALIAN CITY OFFERS.
Florence, Italy

THE LGBTQIA+ LOWDOWN With a history of gay artists like Michelangelo and Donatello, mostly liberal views, and the largest population of LGBTQIA+ residents in Italy, you can enjoy great food, wine, and art without worry. Bonus: Gaily Tour has LGBTQIA+ guides that will help you explore the city's gay history.

Florence, the capital of Tuscany, is known for its art history, bridges, World Heritage sites, and amazing cuisine. So how do you pack it all in?

First, hit all the musts, including the Gallerie Degli Uffizi, featuring Italian Renaissance artwork by Titian, Michelangelo, and da Vinci. See Michelangelo's "David" (and more) at the Accademia Gallery. Then visit the Duomo Complex, a UNESCO World Heritage site, which has the Cathedral of Santa Maria del Fiore and four other iconic monuments. For another highlight, cross Ponte Vecchio, one of the world's most historic bridges, famous for its three arches.

To escape the crowds and see sweeping views of the city center, go to Sacred Doors Cemetery, an outdoor collection of sculptures and monuments on a burial ground from the 1800s. Or visit the Florence Baths, which opened in 1991 and is the only gay sauna in the city.

Make sure to take in Florence's stellar cuisine. The best sandwich in Florence is at All'Antico Vinaio, in business since 1991 and known around the world (New York has an outpost, too). You'll see the line from down the street, but the food is worth it. Sant'Ambrogio indoor market features traditional fruit, vegetable, and specialty food vendors since 1873. On newer ground, Mercato Centrale's second floor is a refurbished food hall run by artisan traders offering bread and baked goods, meat and charcuterie, buffalo mozzarella and other cheeses, chocolate, gelato, fresh pasta, and wine. In Hotel Lungarno, Borgo San Jacopo overlooks the Arno River and boasts a Michelin star for its tasting menus.

Then there's the gelato. Claiming to be the birthplace of gelato, Perchè No! is a can't-miss spot and has served the creamy dessert since 1939. Or try Gelateria de' Medici, famous for its very Italian interiors and great scoops.

Though not exclusively queer, Tenax is a dance spot inspired by New York's Greenwich Village music scene where the LGBTQIA+ community gathers.

We recommend exploring the hills, villages, and history between Florence and Siena on a day trip to Chianti in Tuscany for some of the best wines in the world. Make your destination point Castello di Volpaia, a family-owned winery in a village that dates back to 1172. Then go to Siena for its charming piazza and medieval architecture, art, food, and a good bottle of Chianti.

A window display of mouthwatering sweets and candies at Florence's Caffè Gilli

A BUSTLING CITY FOR SACRED SITES AND OPEN-AIR FOOD MARKETS
Bangkok, Thailand

The Train Night Market in Bangkok

THE LGBTQIA+ LOWDOWN Bangkok is one of Asia's queerest cities, where LGBTQIA+ tourists around the world should feel safe and encouraged to visit. Same-sex activity has been legal since 1956, and the country's tourism authority has the global project "Go Thai Be Free."

A bustling city with Buddhist temples, canals, night markets, art, and more than 500,000 street vendors, Bangkok is the capital of Thailand in many ways—its diverse food scene included.

Go to Wat Phra Chetuphon, founded during the 16th century, now one of the country's oldest and most visited temples. Don't miss the reclining Golden Buddha, measuring more than 150 feet (46 m) long. Then walk to the Grand Palace, established in 1782. Here, you'll find the sacred Wat Phra Kaew, a temple holding the historic Emerald Buddha. Finally, see Phra Phuttha Maha Suwan Patimakon, which holds the world's largest gold sculpture (a Golden Buddha, of course). In Silom, a hub of queer culture, head to Lumphini Park to wander, picnic, or rent a boat. Or visit the Patpong Museum to learn the history of Silom's famed red-light district, then go to Sky Bar, located on the 63rd floor of the State Tower, for great cocktails with city and river views.

Don't miss the most popular food markets. Start with Khlong Toei, the largest market and purveyor to chefs in the city. Wang Lang Market is another local favorite packed with food stalls: authentic rice and noodle dishes, bento sets, and drinks. Talat Phlu is famous for its noodle shops, steamed rice with pork,

and desserts. And no trip to Bangkok is complete without floating markets. Bang Nam Phueng is our top pick, tucked away in a jungle-like area just outside of town. It's smaller and lesser known than others, which we think makes it a more enjoyable, authentic experience. There you'll find seafood snacks, grilled meats, tropical fruits, and mouthwatering soups.

For entertainment, Calypso Bangkok is a decadent theater that has featured transgender artists since 1988. To escape noise and crowds, go to the 200-year-old Baan Silapin (Artist's House) in the off-the-beaten-path Thonburi area. On-site is a small café, the perfect spot for a traditional Thai iced tea or coffee.

Experience authentic dining at Ruen Mallika Royal Thai Cuisine. The Michelin-starred Sra Bua by Kiin Kiin is an upscale experience with elevated dishes. For cheap eats that still impress, order pad Thai or red curry at family-owned Markintiny Restaurant. Try Double Dogs Tea Room, a traditional teahouse, where you can sip your drink with a side of delicious cake. To explore Bangkok's party scene, Lesla Party, the most famous lesbian party in Bangkok, takes place monthly. A basement speakeasy, Maggie Choo's is not well known, but those who find it fall in love with Gay Night (Sundays).

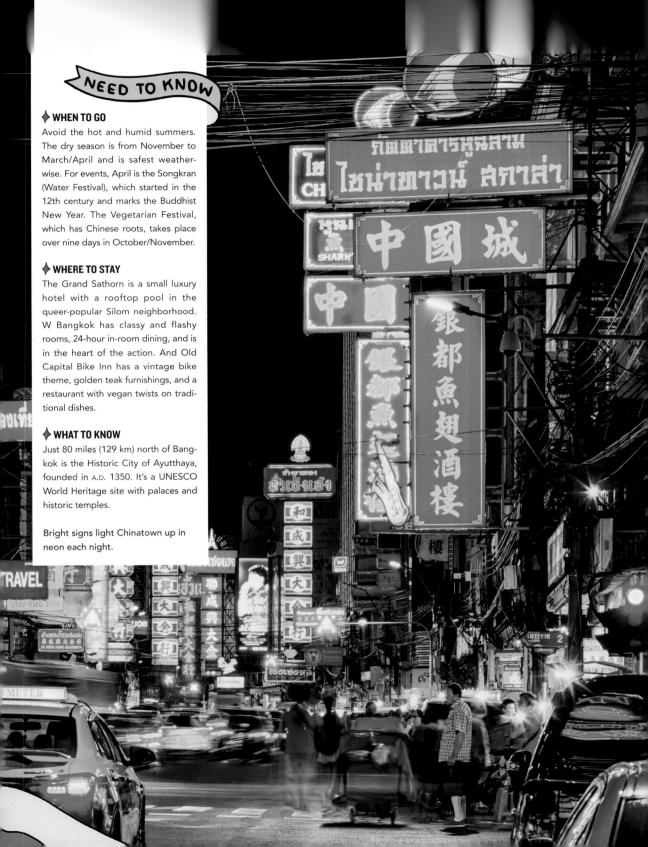

✦ NEED TO KNOW

✦ WHEN TO GO

Avoid the hot and humid summers.
The dry season is from November to
March/April and is safest weather-
wise. For events, April is the Songkran
(Water Festival), which started in the
12th century and marks the Buddhist
New Year. The Vegetarian Festival,
which has Chinese roots, takes place
over nine days in October/November.

✦ WHERE TO STAY

The Grand Sathorn is a small luxury
hotel with a rooftop pool in the
queer-popular Silom neighborhood.
W Bangkok has classy and flashy
rooms, 24-hour in-room dining, and is
in the heart of the action. And Old
Capital Bike Inn has a vintage bike
theme, golden teak furnishings, and a
restaurant with vegan twists on traditional dishes.

✦ WHAT TO KNOW

Just 80 miles (129 km) north of Bangkok is the Historic City of Ayutthaya,
founded in A.D. 1350. It's a UNESCO
World Heritage site with palaces and
historic temples.

Bright signs light Chinatown up in
neon each night.

BANGKOK

With more than 40,000 temples still standing in Bangkok, you can lose yourself in the beauty and architecture of the city's religious history. And even though the country is primarily Buddhist, you can still find plenty of Hindu influences in Thailand. One of the most popular Hindu temples, Wat Benchamabophit Dusitwanaram (aka the Marble Temple, pictured here) is a sight to behold. Its name actually translates to "the monastery of the fifth king near Dusit Palace" and refers to King Chulalongkorn the Great (Rama V).

TAKE A TAPAS TOUR AND SIT BY THE SEA.
San Sebastián, Spain

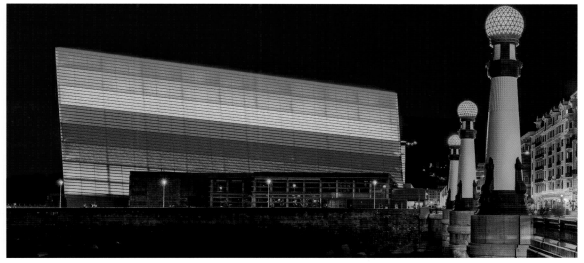

In celebration of Pride, rainbow lights cover the Kursaal Congress Centre and Auditorium, a conference center in San Sebastián.

THE LGBTQIA+ LOWDOWN This city was named after Saint Sebastian, often referred to as a gay icon and the patron saint of homosexuality. The saint has been referenced by gay writer Oscar Wilde; Yukio Mishima in *Confessions of a Mask* (1949), which has a gay protagonist; and others.

In the mountainous Basque region of Spain, this resort town is known for its picturesque bay, green spaces (more than 20 percent of its urban area), and an abundance of *pintxos* (tapas) and wine, plus world-renowned restaurants—the most Michelin stars per capita in the world.

Experience a cultural and foodie phenomenon at Petritegi Sagardotegia, a typical cider house in the country. Fill up on cured sausage, Basque steak, and other traditional dishes all while drinking cider from the barrel in a *sidrería* (cider room). When you pour, say, "Txotx!" (pronounced choch), and you'll be doing it right.

On Thursday nights, hit the town for traditional pintxos (usually served with toothpicks or skewers). For an upscale vibe, try Beti Jai Berria or Borda Berri. Atari is a cool spot with a heated terrace, cocktails, and music. And Baztan is a great pick for traditional pintxos.

Continue eating your heart out by visiting La Cuchara de San Telmo for beef cheeks, crispy pork ears, and more. Michelin-starred Arzak was an Anthony Bourdain favorite. Pub Dionis is a popular queer bar that excels at drinks.

Between bites and sips, have some fun at Monte Igueldo Amusement Park. Ride the wooden cars of the funicular to the top for the best views. We recommend visiting the San Telmo Museum (Plaza Zuloaga) in Old Town to learn about Basque history and culture, then taking the path that goes up Monte Urgull to the statue of Jesus Christ.

Don't miss the beloved Parte Vieja (Old Town). Wander narrow streets to Plaza de la Constitución (formerly a bull-ring), the Church of San Vicente, and the 18th-century Basilica of Santa María.

For a festive beach day, go to Zurriola, a surfer's paradise. Puerto is an alternative for sunsets and a peaceful vibe (venture upstairs to La Mejillonera, where you can get take-out food to eat at the port).

In October, visitors will be treated to the Gastronomic Congress of San Sebastián, a four-day culinary event when chefs from all over the world come for competitions. Attendees can take part in wine tastings, eat street snacks, and participate in master cooking classes with Michelin-starred and renowned chefs.

YOU CAN EAT YOUR HEART OUT IN THIS ENCHANTED SEASIDE CITY.

Tel Aviv, Israel

Israel's largest indoor food mall, Sarona Market in Tel Aviv, offers street food, produce, cheeses, wines, and more.

THE LGBTQIA+ LOWDOWN Israel is often praised as the most accepting Middle Eastern country, and Tel Aviv is undoubtedly at its heart. With approximately 25 percent of its population identifying as LGBTQIA+, it's been known internationally as a welcoming place for decades.

The second largest city in Israel, Tel Aviv offers clean beaches, culture, and great food (especially for vegans, as it's the "vegan capital of the world").

Start at the Tel Aviv Port, a revitalized area in the north, for blue seas, boutique shops, restaurants, and two landmarks: the Reading Power Station (dating back to the eighth century) and lighthouse. Next, visit Shuk HaNamal at Hangar 12 on the boardwalk, Israel's first covered market. It's a shopper's dream for produce, cheeses, olives, spreads, fresh pasta, handmade sausages, spices, and pastries. Afterward, go to Shuk HaCarmel, Tel Aviv's most famous market, bustling since 1920 and brimming with clothing, electronics, spices, and traditional Israeli food.

Explore the city's famous Bauhaus architecture in the "White City" on a tour with the Bauhaus Center. You'll learn about a collection of more than 4,000 Bauhaus-style buildings (the largest collection in the world) that Jewish-German architects first constructed in the 1930s. For more walking, hit up the southern neighborhood of Florentin and see its bright and bold graffiti.

Then use the Tayelet, an almost nine-mile (14 km) paved path that runs along the beach to Jaffa, the oldest and most culturally rich part of the city. See the Jaffa Clock Tower (in the center of the town square), which was built from limestone in 1901 and incorporates two towers. The Jaffa Flea Market offers Judaica, antiques, jewelry, eco-artist wares, restaurants, and bars. Finally, head to the Wishing Bridge, adorned with the signs of the zodiac. Legend has it that if you touch your sign and make a wish, it will come true.

Taste the best at one of the oldest hummus restaurants in Israel: Abu Hassan. Also make sure to try other traditional foods: *shakshuka* (an egg and tomato dish originally from Tunisia) from Shukshuka in Carmel Market; falafel at Frishman Falafel & Frishman Sabich or the Falafel Banin stand, open since 1958 (with a gluten-free option that gets huge raves); and *sabich* (a typical street food sandwich with eggplant, chopped eggs, and tahini) from Aricha Sabich, which locals love.

Some additional restaurant highlights include Port Said, a gastropub and record bar; Shpagat, an institutional gay bar; Dalida, a blend of Arab, Italian, and French cultures and flavors; Herzl 16 café for all-day fare and a DJ night spot in a 1920s building; and POC Café for pastries and coffee.

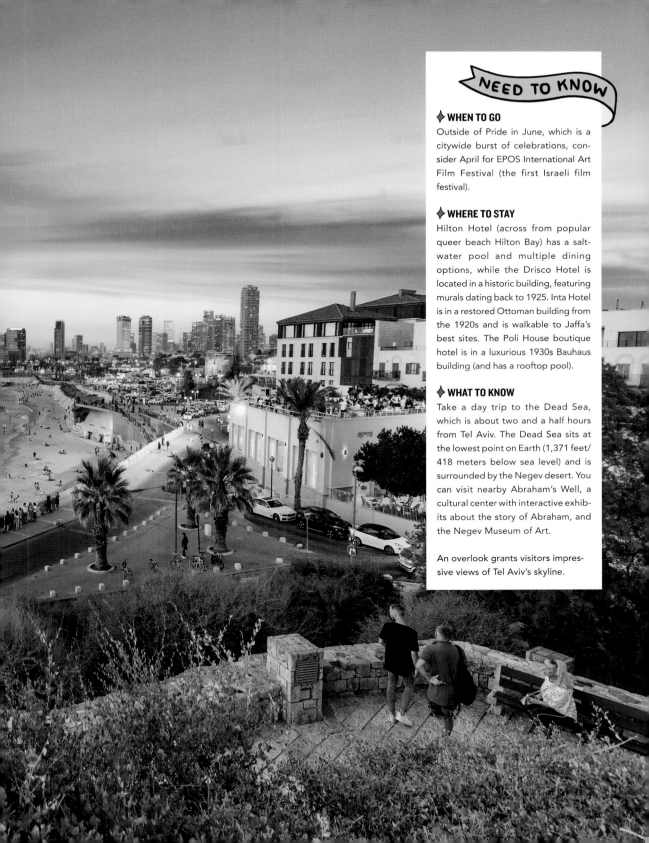

NEED TO KNOW

◆ WHEN TO GO
Outside of Pride in June, which is a citywide burst of celebrations, consider April for EPOS International Art Film Festival (the first Israeli film festival).

◆ WHERE TO STAY
Hilton Hotel (across from popular queer beach Hilton Bay) has a saltwater pool and multiple dining options, while the Drisco Hotel is located in a historic building, featuring murals dating back to 1925. Inta Hotel is in a restored Ottoman building from the 1920s and is walkable to Jaffa's best sites. The Poli House boutique hotel is in a luxurious 1930s Bauhaus building (and has a rooftop pool).

◆ WHAT TO KNOW
Take a day trip to the Dead Sea, which is about two and a half hours from Tel Aviv. The Dead Sea sits at the lowest point on Earth (1,371 feet/ 418 meters below sea level) and is surrounded by the Negev desert. You can visit nearby Abraham's Well, a cultural center with interactive exhibits about the story of Abraham, and the Negev Museum of Art.

An overlook grants visitors impressive views of Tel Aviv's skyline.

FALL IN LOVE WITH BATHHOUSES, QUEER BARS, AND VIBRANT MARKETS.
Tokyo, Japan

Varieties of dried squid for sale at the Tsukiji Outer Market

THE LGBTQIA+ LOWDOWN Tokyo has some of the most progressive LGBTQIA+ rights in Asia, with antidiscrimination laws around gender identity and sexual orientation, plus hundreds of queer bars in the Shinjuku district.

Japan's capital city is full of glitz, skyscrapers, bathhouses, and great food. With more than 150,000 restaurants (including 200-plus with at least one Michelin star), this is the place to play and dine.

Visit Shinjuku Gyoen National Garden for its bright cherry blossoms. The Tokyo National Museum is the place to see hundreds of sculptures, paintings, and more.

Shinjuku (called Ni-Chome, or Nicho) is the LGBTQIA+ heart of the city. It's full of queer bars (but not all welcome foreigners, so consider a tour with Out Asia Travel to find the best ones). Don't miss Piss Alley (also known as Nonbei Yokocho or Drunkard's Alley), an illegal drinking area in the 1940s now famous for its bars and yakitori restaurants.

Trying a bathhouse is a must. For beginners, an *onsen* uses volcanic spring water and a *sento* uses tapwater. These communal baths, a centuries-old tradition, are plentiful and separated by gender (required by law). Also, you either need to be nude or in a towel. The 24 Kaikan is for gay men and can be more of a scene than a traditional experience. Niwa no Yu is a popular coed bathhouse with separate pools and central mixed-gender areas in which to hang out.

To experience Tokyo's famous markets, go to Tsukiji, the world's biggest fish market, or Nakamise Dori for one of the oldest shopping streets in the city. Try Tsukiji Cooking or ABC Cooking Studio to learn how to make *onigiri* (rice ball sets), sushi, and more.

To taste your way through Tokyo, Tamawarai has dishes made from scratch with locally grown buckwheat. Ao is a tiny neighborhood restaurant with an omakase menu in a 70-year-old Japanese traditional-style house. Sushi Tou is a hidden gem popular with locals. (Note that eel, or *unagi*, is endangered, so consider carefully before ordering.) Go to Shiro-hige's Cream Puff Factory for anime character–shaped sweets. Dorobune restaurant caters to queer women. Go for their specialty, *okonomiyaki*, a savory pancake topped with different condiments. Rainbow Burritos is a fun Mexican restaurant run by members of Tokyo's LGBTQIA+ community. Donyoku is a café with onsens (to soak your feet only) that's proud of its Pride.

When drinks are on the agenda, go to Ozawa Sake Brewery or the Kosoan teahouse overlooking gorgeous gardens. Campy! Bar has drag queens and great drinks. Or try Tac's Knot, owned by a local gay artist, for a fun time out plus art.

THIS IS THE PLACE TO INDULGE IN ALL THE DANISH DELIGHTS.
Copenhagen, Denmark

Copenhagen food markets offer traditional delicacies, such as Danish open-faced sandwiches (*smørrebrød*).

THE LGBTQIA+ LOWDOWN Denmark is an open and welcoming country where same-sex relations have been legal since 1933. In 1989, it became the world's first country to legalize same-sex unions. Copenhagen, the capital, is said to be the most queer-friendly Scandinavian city, a label it proudly bears.

Beloved for its hygge (coziness), food scene, great architecture, and reputation as one of the happiest places in the world to live, Copenhagen checks all the boxes for a great time.

Begin at Frederiksberg Gardens with its castle, canals, lakes, and stretches of green space. Its underground art space, the Cisterns, features locally made, modern glass art. Then hit one of our favorite streets, Studiestræde, an LGBTQIA+ hub. Check out its boutique shops, restaurants, art galleries, and colorful buildings (stop at Next Door Café or Kiss Kiss Bar & Café). Don't miss Nyhavn, Copenhagen's famous row of boldly colored town houses along the canal.

Head to Den Blå Planet National Aquarium Denmark to see thousands of animals in more than 1.8 million gallons (7 million L) of water. Then check out the National Museum (Denmark's largest), which houses objects from Viking raids, Egyptian mummies, and a children's museum. Also consider the Round Tower, the oldest observatory in Europe (dating back to 1642), where you can climb the spiral stairs to stargaze from a platform. To bike on an old railroad, go to

Amagerbanen, a scenic 0.9-mile (1.5 km) path of greenery.

Tivoli Gardens is the world's second oldest amusement park and boasts the Tivoli Food Hall. Browse 15 food stalls with baked goods, Michelin-starred outposts, and modern twists on traditional favorites such as *smørrebrød* (Danish open-faced sandwiches), North African food, authentic Indian fare, craftsman pizza, and Japanese street food. Also worth a visit in the park is Nimb's organic vegetable restaurant. To wander street markets, visit Aarhus Street Food, Lighthouse Street Food, and Storms Pakhus.

Try a traditional dining experience at Restaurant 1733, founded by Danish friends and known for marinated herring and fried pork belly; Radio, a Michelin-starred restaurant with an award-winning wine list; Lagkagehuset (one of the city's best bakeries); and Aamanns for drool-inducing, Instagram-worthy open-faced sandwiches.

Have drinks at Oscar Bar & Café (a popular nonsmoking LGBTQIA+ spot), Men's Bar, and Vela, a lesbian bar that opened in 2004. For drag and jazz, Centralhjørnet is the oldest LGBTQIA+ drinking hole in Copenhagen.

◆ WHEN TO GO

Distortion is a festival of parties that unfolds across the city during June's Pride month. MIX COPENHAGEN LGBTQ+ Film Festival is one of the oldest in the world and typically happens in October.

◆ WHERE TO STAY

Hotel d'Angleterre is a luxurious historic landmark and home to Michelin-starred restaurant Marchal. Axel Guldsmeden is an eco-conscious boutique hotel with an organic breakfast and a jungle-like courtyard. Or try Urban House Copenhagen, a fun hotel with a game zone, cinema room, and accessible areas/rooms.

◆ WHAT TO KNOW

Swimming in Copenhagen is allowed only in permitted areas, but if you go during the summer months, visit Islands Brygge Harbour Bath, which has five basins and skyline views, and is just across the bridge from the city center. Helgoland is a complex with three ocean pools: male, female, and mixed.

Copenhagen's Tivoli Gardens, built in 1843, is the world's second oldest amusement park.

Twilight in Lima's central main square, the Plaza de Armas

SOUTH AMERICA'S FOOD CAPITAL IS WORTH SAVORING.
Lima, Peru

After touring Parque del Amor's central sculpture and mosaic-covered walls, dine alfresco at a café in the Miraflores district.

THE LGBTQIA+ LOWDOWN Although Peru has a growing queer community, it's still a conservative country where the LGBTQIA+ rights movement has a long way to go. In 2019, Lima held its first Pride, and awareness and acceptance continue to steadily grow. But Lima is still largely conservative, so keep that in mind.

Make your first stop at the Larco Museum to learn about Peruvian history dating back 5,000 years. You'll find an extensive gold and silver collection and archaeological exhibits from ancient Peru housed in an eighth-century colonial building. At the nonprofit MATE museum, see the work of Mario Testino, one of Peru's beloved LGBTQIA+ artists, who rose to fame with his *Vanity Fair* portraits of Princess Diana in 1997.

Don't miss Lima's historic center, or Ciudad de los Reyes (City of Kings), founded in 1535. This UNESCO site is a largely preserved colonial town that's survived despite major earthquakes between 1940 and 1974. One of our favorite parts is Circuito Mágico del Agua, a park featuring 13 fountains that put on a high-tech show complete with music and lasers.

We also love El Malecón, a cliffside walk in Miraflores, a popular and buzzing district. Running six miles (10 km) and set above the Pacific Ocean, it's perfect for biking, strolling, and shopping. You can even spot the Faro la Marina, a famous lighthouse built in 1900, in the Parque Antonio Raimondi area.

Try Peru's renowned cuisine, such as ceviche (its national dish), *causa limeña* (with potato, tuna, avocado, and tomato),

lomo saltado (a meat dish), *tacu tacu* (Peruvian dumplings with rice and beans), and more, at its popular markets: Festival Gastronomia in the Plaza Municipal comes alive on Sunday evenings, the Surquillo Market has fewer tourists, and Bio Feria offers organic fare.

Exquisito Perú has earned a huge fan following for their street food tours, which combine Peruvian history with rich food culture. On the Ultimate Peruvian Food Tour, wind through historic Peru as you taste Peruvian coffee, empanadas, ceviche, and artisanal gelato with Peruvian flavors, and learn how to make your own pisco sour. Plus, the Exquisito promise is hard to beat: They can adapt the menu for almost any diet or restrictions.

Lima is home to many of the world's top restaurants, including Astrid & Gastón, known for Peruvian home cooking, and Maido, with a Japanese twist on contemporary food. Other worthy dining options are family-owned Sonia's and El Muelle, both local ceviche spots; El Pez Amigo, a neighborhood seafood restaurant; and El Chinito, a traditional *sanguchería* (sandwich spot) opened by Chinese immigrant Félix Yong in 1960. For great cocktails, try Open Deck Bar and Café, an LGBTQIA+ hangout in Miraflores.

CHAPTER 5

Romantic RENDEZ-VOUS

One of the joys of travel is sharing new experiences with your significant other, especially with the full freedom to be yourselves along the way. Here, we've curated destinations where you don't have to justify who you are, who you love, or why you want "just one bed, please." Our top spots are perfect for couples planning a first trip, newlyweds heading off on their honeymoon, or those looking to rekindle a flame or just get some R & R. Favorites include strolling the canals in Venice, sleeping in your very own overwater bungalow in the Maldives, and exploring colorful buildings in the UNESCO-listed Old Town Cartagena. And though all these destinations have romantic vibes, many are also great for family getaways, time away with your besties, and solo adventures, too.

GET CHARMED BY SOUTHERN DECADENCE.
Charleston, South Carolina, U.S.A.

Swoon over the gorgeous waterside views at the Battery.

THE LGBTQIA+ LOWDOWN Charleston is very queer friendly, with two Pride festivals—Charleston Pride (November) and Park Circle Pride (June)—plus year-round LGBTQIA+ events. Its numerous community groups include the Alliance for Full Acceptance (AFFA) and We Are Family, focusing on LGBTQIA+ youth.

Set along South Carolina's coastline, Charleston's cobblestone streets, harborfront park, and colorful and historic buildings make this destination a real charmer.

Wander scenic King Street for antique and local shops, take selfies with famously pastel-colored homes on Rainbow Row, and find shade under an oak tree at White Point Gardens. Browse more than 300 stalls for handmade baskets and other souvenirs at the Charleston City Market. Grab lunch to go and find a bench next to the iconic Pineapple Fountain in Waterfront Park. For sweeping views, walk or bike over the Arthur Ravenel Jr. Bridge.

Discover queer history with the Real Rainbow Row Tour with Walk and Talk Charleston. Guides take you to sites and share stories connected to Oscar Wilde, Armistead Maupin, Gertrude Stein, Alice B. Toklas, and Dawn Langley Simmons (who made headlines in the late 1960s for her gender-affirming surgery and interracial marriage). Tour proceeds benefit the South Carolina LGBTQ Oral Histories, Archives, and Outreach at the College of Charleston.

Visit the historic sites at the Aiken-Rhett House, Nathaniel Russell House, and Fort Sumter, the site of the first battle of the U.S. Civil War. Museum lovers, don't miss the International African American Museum, Gibbes Museum of Art, the Old Slave Mart Museum, and the Charleston Museum.

Just 20 minutes from the city, Folly Beach is both lively and lovely, offering swimming, surfing, and water sports, plus plenty of beach bars. (Get your fill of tacos and margaritas at colorful Taco Boy.) Also, not far from Charleston, Sullivan's Island exudes small-town charm with its lovely cottages and scenic shores. Poe's, a restaurant housed in the former home of Edgar Allan Poe, has terrific burgers. Kiawah Island, about an hour from Charleston, has the amazing Beachwalker Park and is a wonderful place for bike rides, kayaking, and nature trails.

Enjoy a date night at some of Charleston's best restaurants including 82 Queen, FIG, Husk, and Halls Chophouse. Zero George Restaurant & Caviar Bar has its own cooking school so you can learn to make meals together. Then enjoy cocktails and city views at Stars Rooftop and Grill, Citrus Club, or the Rooftop Bar at Vendue.

Don't miss Dudley's on Ann, a popular LGBTQIA+ bar, or drag bingo and other events hosted by renowned drag queen Patti O'Furniture.

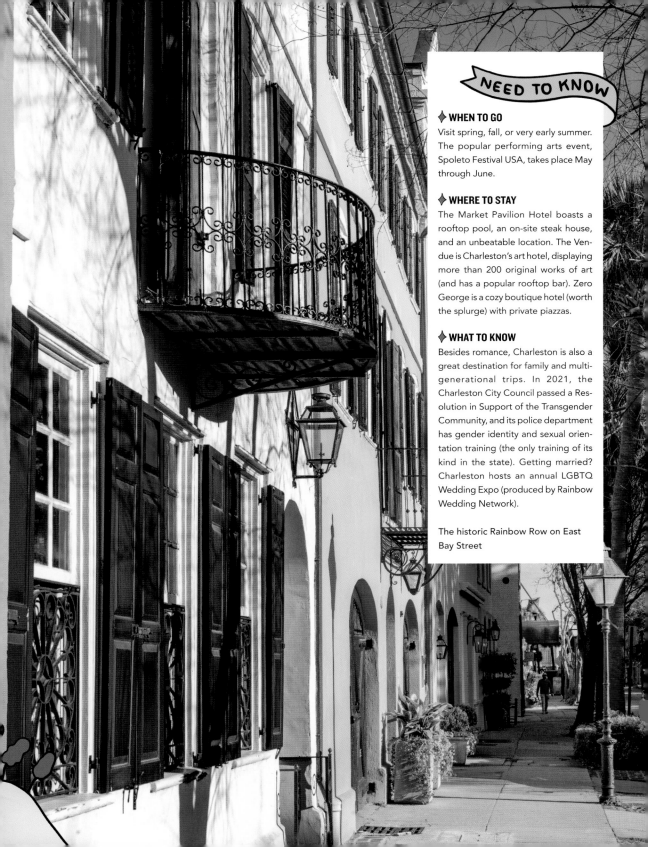

✦ WHEN TO GO

Visit spring, fall, or very early summer. The popular performing arts event, Spoleto Festival USA, takes place May through June.

✦ WHERE TO STAY

The Market Pavilion Hotel boasts a rooftop pool, an on-site steak house, and an unbeatable location. The Vendue is Charleston's art hotel, displaying more than 200 original works of art (and has a popular rooftop bar). Zero George is a cozy boutique hotel (worth the splurge) with private piazzas.

✦ WHAT TO KNOW

Besides romance, Charleston is also a great destination for family and multi-generational trips. In 2021, the Charleston City Council passed a Resolution in Support of the Transgender Community, and its police department has gender identity and sexual orientation training (the only training of its kind in the state). Getting married? Charleston hosts an annual LGBTQ Wedding Expo (produced by Rainbow Wedding Network).

The historic Rainbow Row on East Bay Street

GET COZY AMID ROLLING HILLS AND ADORABLE TOWNS.
The Berkshires, Massachusetts, U.S.A.

THE LGBTQIA+ LOWDOWN An artist enclave, the Berkshires has long been super welcoming. In 2004, Massachusetts was the first U.S. state to legalize gay marriage, and the Berkshires has celebrated Pride since 2017. Local LGBTQIA+ community organizations include Berkshire Trans Group, Rainbow Seniors of Berkshire County, and Berkshire Stonewall Community Coalition.

In this gem of western Massachusetts, you'll feel the romance in the air while strolling through quaint villages or setting up a picnic amid rolling hills and mountains.

With its spectacular greenery and a fantastic lineup of performers, Tanglewood, a world-renowned music venue (it's hosted James Taylor, Bonnie Raitt, and Janis Joplin) is the perfect date night. Its 524 rolling acres (212 ha) provide room to spread out under the sun or stars—just remember to BYOBB (bring your own blankets and beverages, of course).

Since 1955, the Williamstown Theatre Festival has assembled some of the most talented performers in the United States to stage world-premiere plays and musicals as well as rich revivals. Or head to Jacob's Pillow, a historic landmark and one of the country's premier dance venues. In addition to amazing shows, you can participate in talks and dance classes.

Love museums? At MASS MoCA in North Adams, you can spend a day or more taking in the galleries and performing arts spaces. Just six miles (10 km) west in Williamstown, you'll find the renowned Clark Art Institute, a local favorite since 1950 featuring a vast art collection, including works by Monet and Renoir. Even if you don't consider yourselves an artsy couple, the grounds alone are worth the trip. It's hard to beat the sprawling lawns, meadows, hills, and stunning reflecting pool.

The Mount in Lenox, former summer cottage of Pulitzer Prize–winning author Edith Wharton, is also a spectacular spot. Wharton loved a good party, and you'll totally feel like high society in her extravagant gardens.

Get in touch with nature on a couple's hike at Mount Greylock or Monument Mountain, wander the Berkshire Botanical Garden, or hit the slopes at Jiminy Peak.

Don't miss Stockbridge, home to the Norman Rockwell Museum, quaint antiques shops, and the historic Red Lion Inn on Main Street. Dating back to 1773, the inn is the best spot for relaxing on a rocking chair, enjoying dinner and drinks next to a roaring fire, and tucking in for the night.

The Berkshires has an excellent dining scene, including many farm-to-table, vegan, and vegetarian restaurants. Some of our favorite places include Mezze Bistro + Bar (Williamstown), Dottie's Coffee Lounge (Pittsfield), Frankie's Ristorante (Lenox), and the Old Inn on the Green (New Marlborough), which has a beautiful candlelit dining room.

Picturesque horse barns and green pastures dot the countryside of Berkshire County.

SWEEPING COASTAL VIEWS INSPIRE ROMANCE AND RENEWAL.
Monterey Bay, California, U.S.A.

THE LGBTQIA+ LOWDOWN Located just two hours south of San Francisco, Monterey Bay has been frequented for decades by the queer community seeking respite from the city. Monterey Bay has plenty of Pride with an annual celebration and activism throughout the year.

Put on the map by John Steinbeck's *Cannery Row,* Monterey Bay draws visitors for its rugged cliffs and stretches of beach dotted with cypress trees, and it includes the adorable towns of Carmel-by-the-Sea and Pacific Grove. The bay is one of the largest national marine sanctuaries in the U.S. With its progressive culture and dramatic landscapes, this is a popular destination for LGBTQIA+ elopements and weddings.

In Monterey, start at Cannery Row, site of the booming 1900s sardine industry. There, visit the Monterey Bay Aquarium and be mesmerized by a massive jellyfish exhibit. From nearby Fisherman's Wharf, catch a tour with Discovery Whale Watch to see migrating whales in season. Then take the walking/biking path (or drive) north to Pacific Grove.

In this seaside enclave, you'll find Victorian-era homes and Lovers Point Beach, with deep blue ocean views from rocky cliffs. Don't miss the monarch butterfly migration (October through March), where thousands nestle in the treetops at Monarch Butterfly Sanctuary. Back in Monterey, visit the Monterey County Youth Museum (MYM), an inclusive nonprofit where families of all kinds can go for a safe and colorful place to play.

Finally, drive south to Carmel-by-the-Sea, a fairy-tale town with cobbled paths, art galleries, quaint shops, and historic Carmel Mission downtown. Experience one of the country's best sunsets at Carmel Beach. Hop back in the car for the famously scenic 17-mile (27 km) drive along the coast. Cruise along the Pacific Coast Highway (also called State Highway 1), or zip through Carmel Valley for a romantic day out. Or drive to Point Lobos State Natural Reserve for the Cypress Grove Trail or a more challenging 7.5-mile (12 km) hike along the Loop Trail.

To taste your way through the towns, try the strudel and cinnamon roll at Alta Bakery (Monterey). Hula's Island Grill is a tiki-inspired restaurant with amazing coconut ceviche (Monterey). In Carmel-by-the-Sea, memorable Mexican food can be had at Cultura Comida y Bebida: Order the plantain burrito to go, or try their mole (with smoked pork cheeks), enchiladas, or tacos. Trendy restaurant Stationæry will give you all the laid-back California feels over brunch.

For a fun date night in nearby Seaside, go to Lynn's Arcade, a pinball parlor with almost 40 machines; it's family friendly until 9 p.m. Folktale Winery (in Carmel Valley) has 15 acres (6 ha) and is a romantic spot for wine tasting with views.

Watch schools of fish swim past at the Monterey Bay Aquarium's "Open Sea" exhibit.

◆ WHEN TO GO

With its damp northern coast climate, summers are often fogged in, but late summer and early fall bring nicer weather. Visit for September's Monterey Jazz Festival or the AT&T Pebble Beach Pro-Am (usually in February). Monterey Car Week is a massive event that car enthusiasts delight in every August.

◆ WHERE TO STAY

The pet-friendly Cypress Inn, in walkable downtown Carmel, is a boutique hotel and oasis with a Mediterranean feel (once co-owned by queer icon, legendary singer, actress, and animal activist Doris Day). Bernardus Lodge is set among the area's wine country with a pool, a spa, and great restaurants. The Hyatt Regency Monterey Hotel and Spa overlooks Del Monte Golf Course, the oldest operating course west of the Mississippi. It also has a great weekend brunch.

◆ WHAT TO KNOW

Take a ride to Big Sur to see the giant arch of Bixby Bridge, completed in 1932, with magnificent ocean views. Then continue to Nepenthe on famous Highway 1, which towers above sea level, with a restaurant that dates back to the pioneer days of Big Sur. If you come for romance, plan to return and tie the knot with the officiant-and-photographer team of Ellen Scher and Tatiana Scher (the author's mother and sister-in-law!), known for intimate LGBTQIA+ weddings—including on stunning cliffside locations that are challenging to access on your own.

Bixby Creek Bridge on scenic Highway 1 offers some of the best views of the Pacific Ocean.

NEED TO KNOW

◆ WHEN TO GO

May through October have the best weather.

◆ WHERE TO STAY

Navutu Stars Resort, in the Yasawa Islands, offers an adults-only escape you may never want to leave. Six Senses Fiji, in the Mamanuca Islands, has splurge-worthy pool villas to accompany stunning beaches. The InterContinental Fiji Golf Resort & Spa on the Coral Coast offers grand-scale facilities and services and has adults-only areas.

◆ WHAT TO KNOW

The Mamanuca Islands can also be visited as a day trip from Nadi, with many beach clubs offering day passes. Most excursions leave from Port Denarau. Embrace the warm Fijian spirit by using local words like *bula* (the official Fijian greeting) and *vinaka* (thank you).

Paradise found at the Warwick Fiji resort on the main island of Viti Levu's Coral Coast

EMBRACE THE FRIENDLY SPIRIT IN THIS SOUTH PACIFIC PARADISE.

Fiji

THE LGBTQIA+ LOWDOWN Fiji has become more progressive with LGBTQIA+ rights over the past few decades. Generally, the people here are super friendly, as it is illegal to discriminate against a person based on sexual orientation or gender identity, and same-sex relations were made legal in 2010. Queer travelers are largely welcome, but it's best to use caution and avoid PDA.

A country in the South Pacific Ocean, Fiji is considered the "soft coral capital of the world" and comprises 333 islands surrounded by swoon-worthy blue water. Whether you want to spend the day lounging on a pristine beach, playing in the ocean, or going on spectacular nature hikes, Fiji is any couple's dream.

Because you'll most likely be flying into Nadi on the island of Viti Levu, it's worth spending at least a few days there. Close to the airport, Denarau Island is a well-maintained area with lots of resorts. The beaches aren't the best, so this is more of a place to relax in a fancy pool at your hotel. In Nadi, visit the impressive Sri Siva Subramaniya Swami Temple, the largest Hindu temple in the Southern Hemisphere. The Garden of the Sleeping Giant is perfect for lovely strolls among 2,000 varieties of orchids. Don't miss Navala, a traditional Fijian village where thatched bures and mountain views set the scene as residents share their ceremonies and customs.

Head to the Coral Coast for Viti Levu's best beaches. In addition to powder-soft sands and blue waters, you'll find a host of adventurous activities such as surfing and diving with tiger sharks at Beqa Lagoon. Beyond the beach, visit Sigatoka Sand Dunes National Park, a 650-acre (263 ha) protected area with dunes up to 200 feet (61 m). Hiking here goes from the beach to forests to meadows before reaching the grand finale at the dunes.

To experience the Fiji you've seen on postcards, ferry out to the Mamanuca Islands, where you'll find *very* blue water, white beaches, terrific snorkeling (look for rays, turtles, reef sharks, and colorful fish), and overwater bungalows. Visit the uninhabited Monuriki Island, where the movie *Cast Away* was filmed (just please leave your volleyball at home), or have wood-fired pizza and cocktails on the floating Cloud 9.

A little farther out, the Yasawa Islands are equally breathtaking. Visit the limestone Sawa-i-Lau caves, famous for their saltwater pools, or swim with manta rays near Drawaqa Island.

Love hiking and waterfalls? Beeline to Taveuni (known as the Garden Island) for a trek to Tavoro (Bouma) Falls in Bouma National Park and cool off in a swimming hole. Or try the Lavena Coastal Walk for a scenic stroll along the beach, through the forest, and past more waterfalls. On the island of Kadavu, you'll find eco-resorts and the Great Astrolabe Reef, one of the world's largest barrier reefs, where you may spot whales, dolphins, wrasse, and more.

A hawksbill turtle and school of fish swim over coral in Fiji's Namena Marine Reserve.

SIT ALONG THE CANALS AND CHAT THE DAYS AWAY.
Venice, Italy

White porcelain masks are a deeply rooted Venetian tradition.

THE LGBTQIA+ LOWDOWN Though Venice's record on inclusiveness hasn't always been one to write home about, it has made progress. Thanks to the Venice Film Festival, which awards the Queer Lion trophy, and queer artist representation at the famous international Biennale art exhibition, Venice continues to expand its inclusiveness.

The capital of Northern Italy's Veneto region, Venice has a collection of islands and canals that many couples dream of. With its charming waterways, winding paths lined with restaurants and historical buildings, Venice is one of our favorite places in the world to wander.

Start at the Rialto Bridge, constructed in A.D. 1173 as a pontoon bridge. It's the oldest bridge of four on the Grand Canal, and the surrounding area is a bustling place to shop or just people-watch the day away. Then grab Northern Italy's favorite cocktail, an Aperol spritz, and take a gondola ride down the canal. After that, join the crowds and peruse Mercato di Rialto, a canal-side market with fresh seafood, fruits, and vegetables (typically open until noon).

Don't miss St. Mark's Square, which dates back to the 12th century and is the most famous square in Venice—packed with galleries, people, and great views of St. Mark's Basilica and the brick bell tower (which you can climb for panoramic city views). Tip: Spring for a drink at one of the cafés on St. Mark's Square around 7 p.m., when three orchestras

compete for applause under the moonlight—it's pure magic.

After you take in your fill of the art and beautiful canal views outside, venture inside the Peggy Guggenheim Collection museum, which offers accessibility for visitors who are blind or visually impaired and features a sculpture garden plus masterpieces of 20th-century European and American art. It's located in a stunning waterside palace called Palazzo Venier dei Leoni, which itself is made of Istrian stone.

Stop for *cicchetti* (small bites or snacks) at Ai Garzoti, a cozy, exposed-brick spot with outdoor tables and canal views, or at the bar of Osteria al Portego, also for cicchetti plus regional wines. La Zucca has great pasta and vegetarian-focused meals in a quiet location on a tucked-away canal. For gelato, Gelatoteca Suso is a must—its vegan options earn bonus points.

To learn how to make Italian fare for yourself, check out Mama Isa's Cooking School, a beloved and popular LGBTQIA+-welcoming institution with classes on breads, pizza, tiramisu, and more.

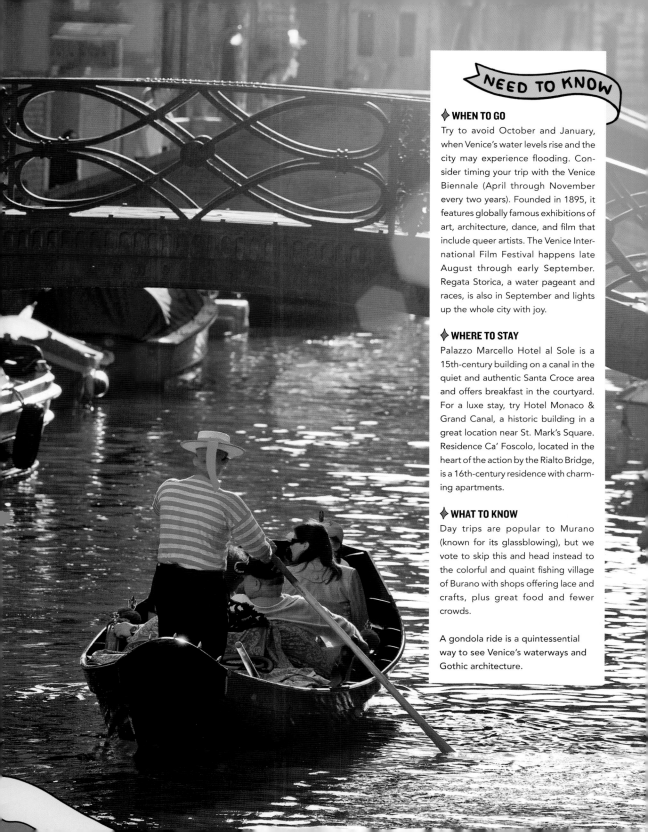

◈ WHEN TO GO

Try to avoid October and January, when Venice's water levels rise and the city may experience flooding. Consider timing your trip with the Venice Biennale (April through November every two years). Founded in 1895, it features globally famous exhibitions of art, architecture, dance, and film that include queer artists. The Venice International Film Festival happens late August through early September. Regata Storica, a water pageant and races, is also in September and lights up the whole city with joy.

◈ WHERE TO STAY

Palazzo Marcello Hotel al Sole is a 15th-century building on a canal in the quiet and authentic Santa Croce area and offers breakfast in the courtyard. For a luxe stay, try Hotel Monaco & Grand Canal, a historic building in a great location near St. Mark's Square. Residence Ca' Foscolo, located in the heart of the action by the Rialto Bridge, is a 16th-century residence with charming apartments.

◈ WHAT TO KNOW

Day trips are popular to Murano (known for its glassblowing), but we vote to skip this and head instead to the colorful and quaint fishing village of Burano with shops offering lace and crafts, plus great food and fewer crowds.

A gondola ride is a quintessential way to see Venice's waterways and Gothic architecture.

WORTH SOME EXTRA LOVE

VENICE

One of our favorite places on the globe, Venice never gets old. From sitting along the Grand Canal (pictured here) sipping a delicious glass of wine to visiting the shops and galleries, Venice offers one of the most romantic places in the world. For the best days, don't make a plan. Instead, wander your way through the city's winding streets and waterfront sidewalks to discover restaurants, bars, and artists' treasures that will create the kind of memories that call you back year after year.

HERE, CHERRY BLOSSOMS AND LOVE BLOOM BOLDLY.
Kyoto, Japan

A riverboat passes the shore in the district of Arashiyama, famous for its beautiful scenery and bamboo grove.

THE LGBTQIA+ LOWDOWN Kyoto is a friendly place, and LGBTQIA+ travelers should enjoy the generally tolerant culture, though they won't spot much open queer life. The Kansai Queer Film Festival (September) has become a significant part of local queer culture.

Japan's cultural center, Kyoto is home to multiple UNESCO World Heritage sites, temples, sprawling gardens, ancient shrines, diverse restaurants, and tons of charm—and is the birthplace of Kabuki theater.

Start in Hanamikoji, the geisha district in Gion and the most famous, historical part of the city, once the entertainment district in the Sengoku period (1467 to the late 1500s). Experience traditional Japan by strolling its wooden buildings and shops and spotting geisha (women trained in music, dance, and other arts). Book tickets for the Minamiza Theatre, housed in a 1920s building and renowned for its Kabuki shows and classical Japanese performances. You can also see Kiyomizu-dera Temple, a UNESCO World Heritage site founded in A.D. 780. On its grounds are Jishu Shrine, which is dedicated to the deity of love and matchmaking, a waterfall that visitors can safely drink from, and stunning views of cherry blossoms or fall foliage, depending on the season.

Near Inari Station, pay a visit to the popular Fushimi Inari-Taisha shrine, dedicated to the Shinto god of rice. The shrine's thousands of distinctly orange gates (torii) extend through a forest leading to sacred Mount Inari. Avoid the crowds early in the morning or after sunset.

In northern Kyoto, explore magical Arashiyama Bamboo Grove, which is more than 1,640 feet (500 m) long.

Couples who love manga should visit the Kyoto International Manga Museum to see more than 50,000 books or watch professional manga artists sketch in the studio.

For kaiseki dining (set meals served in a particular order), try Guilo Guilo Hitoshina for a rare affordable take. For authentic Kyoto sushi, go to Izuju, a 100-plus-year-old institution in front of the historic Yasaka Shrine (formerly Gion Shrine). Another traditional meal can be had at Katsukura: Get the *tonkatsu*, a breaded, deep-fried pork cutlet dish. For a classic sake bar, try Takahashi. Tsuen Tea (established in A.D. 1160) is the oldest teahouse in the world, located near the Uji Bridge, the oldest in Japan.

Azure is a bar for gay men, and Kitsune is a queer-friendly dance club. Bar Look Me is the city's beloved lesbian bar.

ENJOY A SPLASH OF ROMANCE WITH AMAZING SNORKELING AND YOUR OWN OVERWATER BUNGALOW.

Maldives

Stroll the immaculate beaches of Malahini Kuda Bandos.

THE LGBTQIA+ LOWDOWN The Maldives is a conservative Muslim country where being queer can put you at serious risk, yet many resorts are welcoming bubbles for the LGBTQIA+ community. In these spaces, you shouldn't encounter issues and should be treated respectfully.

With almost 1,200 coral islands (but only 200 inhabited ones) spread across 26 atolls, the Maldives is a big diving and snorkeling draw. Whether you want to play in the water, watch dramatic sunsets over the Indian Ocean, lie on picture-perfect beaches, or have private pool time in your overwater bungalow, the Maldives is a place to unplug and enjoy your time together.

Though you may be eager to arrive at your resort, getting there can be a lengthy journey. Most visitors fly into Velana International Airport, located near the capital island of Male, then take a plane or speedboat (sometimes both) to their resort. The process is typically arranged by hotels, but be cognizant of layovers or arriving too late in the day to transfer to your resort and having to spend a night in or around Male.

One of the world's densest cities, it's not quite the tropical island vibe you might've envisioned (and, again, we urge queer travelers to use caution here), but if you'd like to explore local culture, check out Artificial Beach, a famous human-made seashore; the Male Fish Market; Old Friday Mosque, the oldest in the Maldives (dating to 1656); and the National Museum for historical artifacts and antiques. Try Sala Thai for glass noodle soup or Symphony Restaurant for Maldivian fish curry.

When it's time to depart, grab a taxi and head to the airport or adjacent speedboat jetty.

Around the islands, one of the best places to swim with whale sharks is at Alifu Dhaalu Atoll. Or snorkel at Banana Reef (Kuda Kalihi), which has a variety of soft coral and fish. To see giant manta rays, go diving at Manta Point off Lankanfinolhu Island. Maaya Thila (North Ari Atoll) is best for diving with gray reef sharks and exploring caves. Hanifaru Bay, a UNESCO Biosphere Reserve, is known for manta rays and sea turtles.

In addition to diving and snorkeling, the Maldives has water sports galore: kayaking, paddleboarding, Jet Skiing, parasailing, kitesurfing, windsurfing, and more! After all this activity, soothe your sore muscles with a couple's spa day, and enjoy romantic dinners on the beach, booked through your resort. At dinner, sample Maldivian dishes such as *roshi* (flatbread) and spicy fish cakes. Experiencing the Sea of Stars on Vaadhoo Island, where microscopic plankton glow under the moonlight thanks to bioluminescence, is truly magical.

NEED TO KNOW

◆ WHEN TO GO

November through April have the best weather. From May through October, the wet season will shower you with better resort prices if you're willing to roll the dice with the sun.

◆ WHERE TO STAY

Many resorts offer coveted overwater bungalows, beachfront locations, and all-inclusive packages, so it really comes down to your budget. Some of our favorites, based on value and commitment to inclusiveness, include the Pullman Maldives Maamutaa, a huge all-inclusive resort in a prime snorkeling location with pools and lots of dining options, including a vegetarian restaurant. The W Maldives is a five-star private island resort with one of the best reefs in the Maldives, plus four restaurants and two bars. And the Conrad Maldives Rangali Island Resort has seven restaurants, including one that's underwater, and both family-friendly and adults-only pools.

◆ WHAT TO KNOW

At the resorts, food and drinks are very expensive (think U.S. $60 for a pizza) so we recommend going with an all-inclusive option. Transport from Male to your resort often comes with an added cost, which some resorts charge hundreds of dollars for, so be sure to get that info up front. Outside of hotels, it's best to avoid PDA (generally frowned upon for both queer and straight couples).

The Maldives is home to the seventh largest coral reef system in the world.

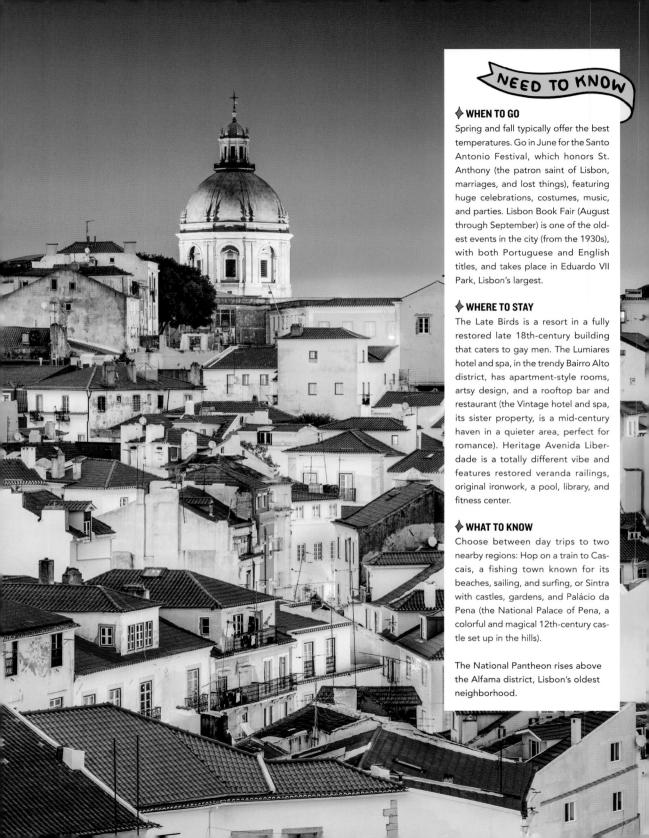

NEED TO KNOW

◆ WHEN TO GO

Spring and fall typically offer the best temperatures. Go in June for the Santo Antonio Festival, which honors St. Anthony (the patron saint of Lisbon, marriages, and lost things), featuring huge celebrations, costumes, music, and parties. Lisbon Book Fair (August through September) is one of the oldest events in the city (from the 1930s), with both Portuguese and English titles, and takes place in Eduardo VII Park, Lisbon's largest.

◆ WHERE TO STAY

The Late Birds is a resort in a fully restored late 18th-century building that caters to gay men. The Lumiares hotel and spa, in the trendy Bairro Alto district, has apartment-style rooms, artsy design, and a rooftop bar and restaurant (the Vintage hotel and spa, its sister property, is a mid-century haven in a quieter area, perfect for romance). Heritage Avenida Liberdade is a totally different vibe and features restored veranda railings, original ironwork, a pool, library, and fitness center.

◆ WHAT TO KNOW

Choose between day trips to two nearby regions: Hop on a train to Cascais, a fishing town known for its beaches, sailing, and surfing, or Sintra with castles, gardens, and Palácio da Pena (the National Palace of Pena, a colorful and magical 12th-century castle set up in the hills).

The National Pantheon rises above the Alfama district, Lisbon's oldest neighborhood.

THIS CITY HAS STREET ART, CASTLES BY THE SEA, AND HISTORY.
Lisbon, Portugal

A tram transports residents and visitors up and down the cobbled streets of Lisbon's historic neighborhoods.

THE LGBTQIA+ LOWDOWN Portugal is widely hailed as one of the world's most queer-friendly destinations. It's a rare country whose constitution includes a ban on discrimination based on sexual orientation. And with Lisbon at the heart of Portugal's queer community and culture, expect to feel all the welcoming vibes here.

The coastal town and capital of Portugal, Lisbon is known for its pastel buildings, beautiful beaches, and hilltop views.

Experience the highlights with Tram 28, which runs yellow trams from the 1930s that are a quintessential way to travel through the city. Its hour-long route passes through narrow streets and historic districts, climbing the hills for mesmerizing views. Highlights include Basílica da Estrela with a domed roof and baroque architecture; Se Cathedral and St. Anthony Church (St. Anthony is the patron saint of Lisbon, along with lovers); and the area near St. George Castle, where you can disembark to walk up a hill to reach the castle—worth it for the incredible vistas.

In the charming, buzzy area of Barrio Alto, you'll be inspired to walk hand in hand. With its cobbled streets, culinary delights, and famous street art, you'll have plenty to talk about. To cover all the amazing murals, take a guided stroll with Lisbon Street Art Tour, where part of the price goes to funding the creation of more art. Or make masterpieces as a couple with Drink and Draw, an eco-friendly and LGBTQIA+-welcoming event series that takes place in artsy spots around the city. It's popular with locals for its casual atmosphere, social scene, and motto of "fun art, not fine art."

Then head to the intersection of the Atlantic Ocean and Tejo River and take the very short walk over the small bridge to Belém Tower, built in 1514 and the point of arrival and departure for Portuguese explorers. An example of Manuelino-style (Portuguese late Gothic) architecture, the tower was named a UNESCO World Heritage site in 1983. You'll also see Jerónimos Monastery, another UNESCO site and a national monument honoring Portuguese explorer Vasco da Gama.

A trip to Lisbon isn't complete without visiting Time Out Market, a curated food hall with more than 53,819 square feet (5,000 m²) of culinary hot spots from top chefs, plus cooking classes and other events. To try traditional tapas, try Há Tapas no Mercado!!! ("There are tapas in the market"), a little restaurant with small bites like the typical Serra da Estrela cheese and cured meats. Popular local spot A Cevicheria was founded by award-winning chef Francisco Martins, better known as Chef Kiko, who puts his Portuguese touch on Peruvian ceviche. If you feel like a true experience in fine dining, go to Alma, a Michelin-starred restaurant that has earned "best meal of my life" comments by diners from around the world thanks to its tasting menus. For after-dinner entertainment, head to Boys Just Want to Have Fun, an inclusive LGBTQIA+ sports club.

WHERE THE OCEAN MEETS THE SEA AND YOUR WORRIES MELT AWAY
Los Cabos, Mexico

Watch for humpback whales breaching off the coast of Cabo San Lucas.

THE LGBTQIA+ LOWDOWN Cabo San Lucas is particularly welcoming, hosting an annual LGBTQIA+ Pride march. It's also home to many inclusive resorts and businesses.

On the southern tip of the Baja California peninsula, the Los Cabos region includes the popular towns of Cabo San Lucas and San José del Cabo, connected by the Corridor: 20 miles (32 km) of walkable beaches, golf courses, resorts, and great spots for snorkeling and fishing.

Visit Cabo San Lucas's popular Medano Beach, crammed with oceanfront hotels and plenty of places to sip margaritas all day. Just across from the beach, you'll see the landmark El Arco, a three-story limestone arch where the Pacific Ocean meets the Sea of Cortez. Take a water taxi to Lovers Beach, a beautiful swimmable beach on the Sea of Cortez side of the arch.

Cabo San Lucas has a lively party scene, shopping, and dining choices galore—especially downtown. As Los Cabos is considered the "marlin capital of the world," fans of sport fishing should head to the marina and take a charter out to sea to catch marlin, yellowfin tuna, dorado, and more. San José del Cabo has a historic center featuring the San José missionary church and Plaza Mijares, the town square. From

there, explore the surrounding art galleries, trendy dining, and boutiques.

Get the local beach experience without all the crowds and hang out at Chileno Bay, located in the Corridor. The water is calmest in the mornings, and it's one of the best swimming and snorkeling areas in Los Cabos.

Take in a different view of the region when you hike the Sierra de la Laguna Mountains, a UNESCO Biosphere Reserve, peaking at 6,000 feet (1,828 m) with views of both the Pacific Ocean and Sea of Cortez. The reserve is also home to pine and oak forests and more than 75 species of birds.

Cabo is well loved for its cuisine, and there's plenty to explore. Los Tres Gallos in downtown Cabo San Lucas is a magical, twinkle-lit patio restaurant with great classic Mexican dishes and a fun vibe. On Medano Beach, eat while listening to live music at the Office with your feet in the sand. Flora's Field Kitchen is a chic farm-to-table restaurant on a 25-acre (10 ha) organic farm in San José del Cabo. At Carbón Cabrón, dine surrounded by the sights and scents of a mesquite grill with a romantic, dimly lit, and trendy vibe.

◆ WHEN TO GO

May and June are the best months, before it gets too hot or crowded and hurricane season hits.

◆ WHERE TO STAY

ME Cabo (by Melía) on Medano Beach puts you near all the action; walk to town or sit by the pool with views of the sea and El Arco, then join the parties along the busy beach strip at night. It also holds the Queer Destinations Committed distinction, an internationally recognized standard of inclusivity for the LGBTQIA+ community. To truly unwind, stay at Hilton Los Cabos (located in the Corridor) with a stunning infinity pool overlooking the Sea of Cortez, one of the best breakfasts we've ever had, and the only swimmable beach in the area. All rooms have ocean views, many with balconies or extended terraces. For a super romantic getaway, splurge for a room with a private plunge pool.

◆ WHAT TO KNOW

Consider a side trip to Los Barriles (90 minutes away), Baja's most famous spot for windsurfing and kitesurfing. For a different kind of experience, Yoga with Sarah offers LGBTQIA+-welcoming beachfront classes (all levels) facing the glistening Sea of Cortez. Todos Santos (60 minutes away from Cabo) is a picturesque village founded in 1724, designated a Pueblo Mágico (a national program highlighting a rural area's unique heritage and offerings) and full of galleries, laid-back vibes, and colonial charm.

The Arch of Cabo San Lucas rock formation, at the tip of the Baja California peninsula

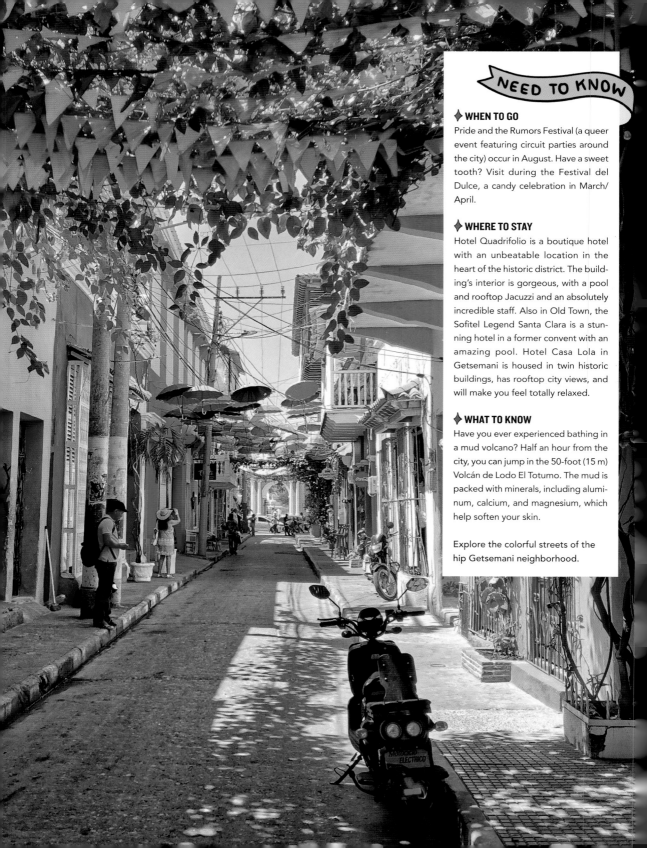

◆ WHEN TO GO

Pride and the Rumors Festival (a queer event featuring circuit parties around the city) occur in August. Have a sweet tooth? Visit during the Festival del Dulce, a candy celebration in March/April.

◆ WHERE TO STAY

Hotel Quadrifolio is a boutique hotel with an unbeatable location in the heart of the historic district. The building's interior is gorgeous, with a pool and rooftop Jacuzzi and an absolutely incredible staff. Also in Old Town, the Sofitel Legend Santa Clara is a stunning hotel in a former convent with an amazing pool. Hotel Casa Lola in Getsemani is housed in twin historic buildings, has rooftop city views, and will make you feel totally relaxed.

◆ WHAT TO KNOW

Have you ever experienced bathing in a mud volcano? Half an hour from the city, you can jump in the 50-foot (15 m) Volcán de Lodo El Totumo. The mud is packed with minerals, including aluminum, calcium, and magnesium, which help soften your skin.

Explore the colorful streets of the hip Getsemani neighborhood.

PLAY ON THE SAND, THEN GET LOST IN THE OLD CITY.

Cartagena, Colombia

Vendors greet shoppers with vibrant produce—and smiles—on the streets of Cartagena.

THE LGBTQIA+ LOWDOWN Colombia is a South American trailblazer that decriminalized homosexuality in 1981 and legalized same-sex marriage in 2016.

Going to Cartagena feels like traveling back in time, only with modern conveniences. One of the most popular destinations in Colombia, this gem enchants visitors with its walled city (the neighborhoods of El Centro and San Diego). Filled with winding, cobblestoned streets, historic sites, restored buildings, bustling plazas, and many great places to eat, shop, and stay, the area is best explored on foot.

On Calle de Don Sancho, arguably the city's most scenic street, you'll find brightly colored buildings with ornate hanging flowers set against the backdrop of the yellow Cartagena Cathedral—one of the oldest episcopal sees in the Americas. Linger here as long as you like; we won't judge.

Also yellow and totally unmissable is the Torre del Reloj, Cartagena's most recognizable landmark: a clock tower built in 1601 that was the original gate to the old city. The surrounding plaza is filled with street vendors and performers. Other notable sights include San Pedro Claver church, home to Indigenous and African art galleries, and the lovely Plaza Bolívar, with the Palacio de la Inquisición. Though brightly colored, the building has a dark history: It's where prisoners were tried and tortured during the Spanish Inquisition. Today, it's a museum but not for the faint of heart.

When you need a break from the outdoors, head to La Serrezuela, an enormous complex of boutiques, eateries, and performance spaces that was transformed from a former bullring, or browse the books at Ábaco Libros y Café.

Just outside the walls is the booming neighborhood of Getsemaní, filled with colorful murals, restaurants and nightlife, and the fabulous Plaza de la Trinidad (when you want to dance in the street, this is the place). At the Castillo San Felipe de Barajas fortress, you'll get impressive city views and have a chance to explore underground passages.

Escape the city on a 45-minute boat ride to the Rosario Islands. Spend the day swimming, kayaking, snorkeling, or diving. Playa Blanca is especially stunning.

After catching a beautiful sunset, hit up Cartagena's restaurant scene. Carmen is great for seafood, Alquímico is fun for a jazz-era vibe and great cocktail bar, and Mar y Zielo has amazing ceviche in a lovely historic house. Le Petit is a restaurant and LGBTQIA+ bar.

CHAPTER 6

HOLIDAY SEASON ESCAPES

and Where to Escape the Holidays

Love or hate the holidays, we've got you covered. Let's start with visits to the best holiday markets and festive locations—from strolls through an LGBTQIA+ Christmas market in Cologne (mulled wine in hand, of course) and a Bavarian village in Washington State to celebrating Kwanzaa and Hanukkah in Atlanta. For those of us who prefer to escape the holidays, consider booking beach time in Tahiti or dancing at queer bars in San Juan, where you'll find more palm trees than Christmas trees. Though we're all for traditions, a vacation for (or away from) the holidays gives you the gift of celebrating on your own terms.

DECK THE HALLS IN A BAVARIAN VILLAGE.
Leavenworth, Washington, U.S.A.

Leavenworth becomes a dreamy winter wonderland around the holidays.

THE LGBTQIA+ LOWDOWN Leavenworth doesn't have an obvious queer scene, but, like much of Washington, LGBTQIA+ residents and visitors are welcomed. Thirty minutes away, Wenatchee Pride sponsors events for the LGBTQIA+ community and allies in the north-central Washington area.

Two and a half hours from Seattle, Leavenworth offers a taste of the Alps in the Pacific Northwest. In this Bavarian-inspired town, you'll find lots of holiday cheer and festivities surrounded by the Cascade Mountains.

Leavenworth didn't always look like somewhere out of Europe. The town was built to serve the timber industry in the late 1800s; when business dried up in the 1950s, the area fell into a depression. Enter two men from Seattle, who just happened to be a gay couple, as well as friends and business partners. They resurrected Leavenworth with a German-style makeover.

Their plan worked. Today Leavenworth is one of Washington's most popular destinations. During the holidays, you'll find several jolly sights and activities, including lighting celebrations and a Christkindlmarkt, where you can buy handmade arts and crafts and eat sausages, spaetzle, and giant pretzels.

Don't miss the Gingerbread Factory, serving fresh-baked gingerbread houses, and the Nutcracker Museum, home of 7,000 decorated figures from all over the world. The Village of Lights: Christmastown features more than half a million lights, plus caroling, appearances by Santa, and, of course,

glühwein (mulled wine). In January, weekends come alive with Leavenworth's Winter Karneval (celebrating the German tradition of *Fasching*), which includes ice carving, fireworks, ice-skating, and live performances.

In addition to holiday attractions, you can ski or sled just minutes away from downtown at the Leavenworth Ski Hill, or head 45 minutes outside of town to Stevens Pass for more than 50 runs for skiers and snowboarders of all levels.

If you're into snowshoeing, visit the Icicle Gorge Nature Loop, a four-mile (6 km), mostly gentle trek along scenic Icicle Creek. To see nature without the legwork, go on an adventure with Leavenworth Sleigh Rides (yes, there's a Santa-themed version). Don't miss Lake Wenatchee State Park, which transforms into Sno-Park from the late fall to the end of winter. Go cross-country skiing, snow tubing, or build a snowperson.

Back in town, browse indie stores such as A Book for All Seasons, Black Swan, and the Cheesemonger's Shop. Grab a bite to eat at Mana for organic dishes and wine, the Watershed Cafe for farm-to-table Pacific Northwest cuisine, or Mozart's Steakhouse for European fine dining. Or try some of the best German dishes at Sausage Garten or München Haus.

NEED TO KNOW

◆ WHEN TO GO
Visit after Thanksgiving to mid-January for the holiday festivities.

◆ WHERE TO STAY
The Posthotel has luxe rooms with cozy fireplaces, private patios or balconies, and hand-carved soaking tubs. The Bavarian Lodge is just steps away from beer gardens, shops, and restaurants. The dog-friendly Obertal Inn has breathtaking views of the Cascade Mountains, plus a complimentary breakfast, including fresh-baked strudel.

◆ WHAT TO KNOW
Leavenworth is a great choice for a family vacation. Though winter totally charms, the warmer months offer opportunities for camping, white-water rafting, and incredible hiking in the Okanogan-Wenatchee National Forest and the Enchantments hiking area, with its gorgeous alpine lakes.

Ski or hike the backcountry near the summit of Ansgar Pass in the Cascade Mountains.

Earth Goddess during Atlanta Botanical Garden's Garden Lights, Holiday Nights

A FESTIVE CITY, NO MATTER WHAT YOU'RE CELEBRATING
Atlanta, Georgia, U.S.A.

THE LGBTQIA+ LOWDOWN Well known as an extremely diverse city, Atlanta has perfect scores on the Human Rights Campaign's Municipal Equality Index and has ordinances prohibiting discrimination based on sexual orientation or gender identity in both public and private employment.

The capital (and most populous city) of the Peach State, Atlanta is known for its culture, civil rights movement history, music, and vibrant arts industry.

No matter the time of year you're visiting, start at Centennial Olympic Park, run by the Georgia World Congress Center Authority, for a sprawling 22-acre (9 ha) green space. Originally built for the 1996 Olympics, the park is home to the National Center for Civil and Human Rights, which details the civil rights movement and houses the LGBTQ Institute. In the Centennial Park District, you'll also find the Georgia Aquarium with its seven major galleries (awarded for being sensory inclusive) and the World of Coca-Cola, exploring the history of the brand in a 20-acre (8 ha) complex (its holiday illumination from November through January only adds to the fun).

Don't miss Martin Luther King, Jr. National Historical Park, a tribute to the reverend's work and life (the civil rights leader was born here). You can take a guided tour of the home where MLK was born; view the D.R.E.A.M. gallery exhibitions, with images that depict the close bond between Jimmy Carter's and MLK's families through the years; and wander through the "I Have a Dream" World Peace Rose Garden.

For holiday festivities, head to the Atlanta Botanical Garden for Garden Lights, Holiday Nights. Enjoy sculptures, fountains, and endless light shows. Also check out Atlanta Christkindl Market, brimming with craft and gift vendors as well as food and drinks. At the Children's Museum of Atlanta, you'll find multicultural celebrations and performances for Christmas, Hanukkah, Las Posadas, and Kwanzaa throughout the month. If you can, catch the annual Atlanta Gay Men's Chorus—the first LGBTQIA+ chorus in the South and one of the few in the world—for an uplifting holiday concert.

Take in a show at the Out Front Theatre Company, focusing on the voices and experiences of the queer community. Shop at Charis Books & More for feminist and cultural studies titles, plus kid lit. Antiques lovers should head to Chamblee's Antique Row District to shop more than 350 dealers selling antiques and collectibles across 300,000-plus square feet (27,870 m²).

Try family-owned La Hacienda Midtown for authentic Mexican fare, traditional music, and a queer crowd. Home Grown is a retro diner and a favorite breakfast spot. South City Kitchen is great for sophisticated southern classics (get their signature fried green tomatoes), and Bones Restaurant has earned the coveted "best steak house" title many times over since it opened in 1979. Or try drag dining at its best at Lips and drinks at My Sister's Room, a beloved lesbian bar for more than 24 years.

Downtown Atlanta's World of Coca-Cola highlights the history of the company.

THIS PLACE HAS POSTCARD-WORTHY CHARM AND CHEER.

Woodstock, Vermont, U.S.A.

THE LGBTQIA+ LOWDOWN Vermont is a liberal and welcoming state (one of the most queer friendly in the U.S.). In 2000, Vermont was the first state to legalize civil unions for same-sex couples and extended full marriage rights to gays and lesbians nine years later. Woodstock follows suit with its inclusive attitudes.

One of America's prettiest places, Woodstock is a picturesque New England village, home to historic buildings, rolling hills, colonial architecture, and lots of boutique shops and restaurants to explore. For the holidays, Woodstock transforms itself with twinkling lights, decorates its historic homes, and hosts a parade that unfolds throughout town.

Start in the Green, the heart of town, and visit the Norman Williams Public Library, a gorgeous pink sandstone building from 1883 with impressive collections (including racial justice resources), a kids' space, and a children's garden. For history, check out exhibits at the Historical Society of Woodstock, founded in 1929 by a group of artists, writers, academics, and local citizens; they host a Holiday Market Fair that is open in the first half of December. Then go to F. H. Gillingham & Sons, Woodstock's oldest store, operating since 1886, for maple syrup, local cheeses, granola, gourmet goods, and holiday decor.

Wassail Weekend, two days full of festive events (and inspired by an English tradition) will really put you in the holiday spirit. Visit Billings Farm & Museum, a working dairy farm with a historic farmhouse where you can experience 19th-century life. During Christmas at the Farm, you can sip hot chocolate under a towering Christmas tree, go snowshoeing, and dip your own candles. Also check out the Woodstock Town Hall Theatre, a concert hall that hosts celebrations all year. The Holiday Showcase at the Grange (which includes performances by local talent) and the Vermont Holiday Festival (in nearby Killington, with contests, food, and gifts) are both fun events that take place over a weekend in December (check the schedule ahead of time).

When it's time for brekkie, grab a locally sourced meal and coffee at Mon Vert Cafe, famous for its espresso. Red Rooster at Woodstock Inn serves American fare with New England charm. Worthy Kitchen is a rustic and cozy farm-to-table stop with comfort food and local brews (and is committed to protecting the environment and supporting the community). Ransom Tavern is a gem that serves authentic Italian, and South Woodstock Country Store is perfect for breakfast, lunch, and baked goods; both are located in the Kedron Valley Inn.

The center of Woodstock, known as the "village green"

◆ WHEN TO GO

Though December has holiday events, consider coming back another time for stunning fall foliage.

◆ WHERE TO STAY

The beloved Woodstock Inn has traditional Vermont charm, and its Tubbs Snowshoes & Nordic Adventure Center offers expert-led winter excursions. Try the Farmhouse Inn for an eco-friendly stay where breakfast is sourced locally, including honey from their bees. The lesbian-owned Lincoln Inn & Restaurant at the Covered Bridge has all the farmhouse vibes. At the edge of the property is the oldest covered bridge of its kind in the U.S. (built in 1877). Make a reservation at the inn's restaurant for its seven-course tasting menu under the stars.

◆ WHAT TO KNOW

For a little road trip, tour New England's famed covered bridges, such as Middle Covered Bridge near the Green, Route 4's Taftsville Covered Bridge, and Lincoln Covered Bridge (next to the historic Lincoln Inn & Restaurant, famous for both its accommodations and food).

The 139-foot (42.4 m) Middle Covered Bridge spans the Ottauquechee River.

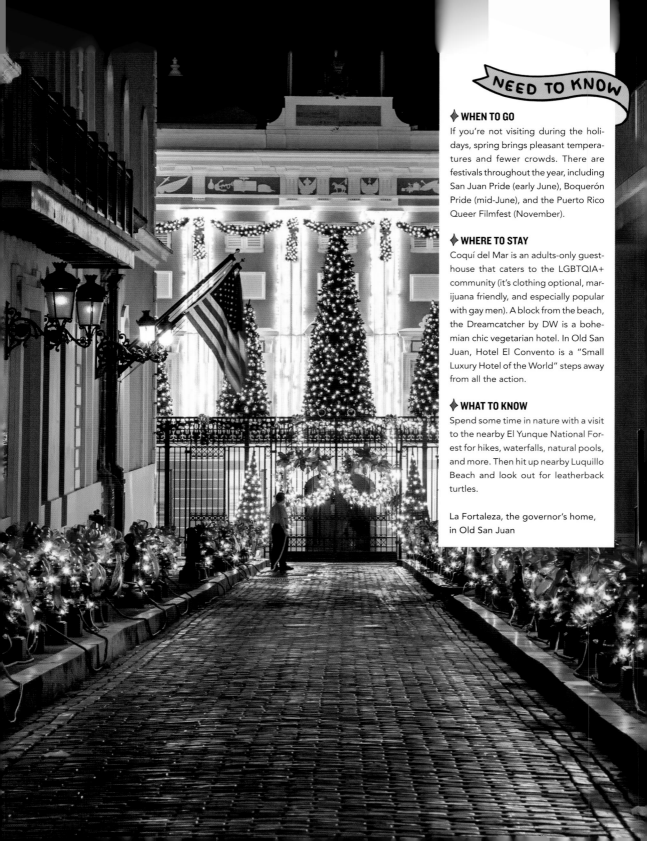

◆ WHEN TO GO

If you're not visiting during the holidays, spring brings pleasant temperatures and fewer crowds. There are festivals throughout the year, including San Juan Pride (early June), Boquerón Pride (mid-June), and the Puerto Rico Queer Filmfest (November).

◆ WHERE TO STAY

Coquí del Mar is an adults-only guesthouse that caters to the LGBTQIA+ community (it's clothing optional, marijuana friendly, and especially popular with gay men). A block from the beach, the Dreamcatcher by DW is a bohemian chic vegetarian hotel. In Old San Juan, Hotel El Convento is a "Small Luxury Hotel of the World" steps away from all the action.

◆ WHAT TO KNOW

Spend some time in nature with a visit to the nearby El Yunque National Forest for hikes, waterfalls, natural pools, and more. Then hit up nearby Luquillo Beach and look out for leatherback turtles.

La Fortaleza, the governor's home, in Old San Juan

SUN-KISS THE HOLIDAYS AWAY WITH SANDY BEACHES AND CARIBBEAN BEATS.

San Juan, Puerto Rico, U.S.A.

THE LGBTQIA+ LOWDOWN In the Caribbean's most queer-welcoming destination, LGBTQIA+ couples can freely hold hands and singles won't have a hard time finding a dance partner.

Located on the Atlantic coast, San Juan is Puerto Rico's largest city and more than just a tropical getaway. Puerto Rico's capital has colorful historic buildings, expansive forts, great gastropubs, and lively, welcoming dance parties.

We can't think of a better way to melt holiday stress than by relaxing on a blissful beach. Head to the Condado area, where the section of sand and surf between Calle Vendig and Condado Avenue is popular with the LGBTQIA+ community.

Next, go to Old San Juan and stroll the Paseo de la Princesa, a waterfront promenade that dates back to 1853. Don't miss the Fuente Raíces, a fountain commemorating the 500th anniversary of the "discovery" of America and depicting Puerto Rico's multiethnic heritage.

While in Old San Juan, wander cobblestone streets and admire Spanish-inspired architecture at the Casa Rosa (a former barracks that's now a day care center), Casa Blanca (where Juan Ponce de León once lived), and La Fortaleza (the governor's residence). Save plenty of energy to explore the city's famous forts: Castillo San Felipe del Morro (begun in 1539 with ramps, tunnels, and dungeons) and Castillo San Cristóbal (with five freestanding structures connected by a moat and tunnels). After sightseeing, try a piña colada, Puerto Rico's national drink, at its alleged birthplace Barrachina, a restaurant in Old San Juan. (Two different bartenders at the Caribe Hilton also claimed they were the first to make the tropical treat.)

Among San Juan's great gastronomy options, some of our favorites include Princesa Cocina Cultura, Old San Juan's first gastro bar; 1919, known for its "ocean-to-table experience"; Lote 23, an outdoor gastronomic food court with a cocktail garden and event space; and Cayo Caribe, serving home-cooked Puerto Rican cuisine with dishes such as mofongo with lobster and *chuletas* (pork chops).

Post-dinner, the Santurce neighborhood is the place to be. Before hitting the bars, walk down Calle Loíza and check out the cool galleries and colorful murals, then hit up the city's most popular drag shows at Tía María Liquor Store, SX (more for men), and Kweens Klub. Be sure to stop at La Placita, a fruit market by day and a spirited area packed with restaurants, bars, and salsa dancers at night. El Hangar is a collective-run community space that hosts queer events.

Escape the holidays in Old San Juan overlooking the Atlantic Ocean.

SOAK UP THE CULTURE IN CENTRO HISTÓRICO AND MARVEL AT THE MAYA RUINS.

Mérida, Mexico

Holiday cheer in festive Mérida

THE LGBTQIA+ LOWDOWN Mérida is one of North America's safest cities, including for the queer community. It has an artistic soul and welcoming vibe that attracts LGBTQIA+ visitors from around the world.

Yucatán's capital, Mérida, is a cosmopolitan city blending Maya and Mexican cultures with European influences. Its colorful historical center, hip arts scene, and nearby heritage sites draw expats, digital nomads, and the queer community alike. And with winter temps in the 80s, you can do the holidays in shorts and flip-flops.

In December, the Paseo de Montejo sparkles with bright lights and Christmas trees. Even without the decorations, it's a lovely street filled with restaurants, stores, museums, and striking historical buildings. Don't miss Casas Gemelas (Twin Houses), a set of beaux arts mansions finished in 1911; Palacio Cantón, the city's anthropology and history museum; and the massive Monumento a la Patria (Monument to the Fatherland). Hand-carved by Colombian sculptor Rómulo Rozo Peña, it's spectacular when lit up at night.

In Plaza Grande, Mérida's largest square, you'll find a life-size nativity and vendors selling gifts. See the Catedral de San Ildefonso, one of the Americas' oldest cathedrals. Also, check out Casa de Montejo, a 16th-century home turned museum. Palacio de Gobierno is the seat of the executive government branch and houses must-see murals. Outside of Mérida's historic center, visit El Gran Museo del Mundo Maya de Mérida (the Great Museum of the Maya World), which details Maya history and showcases a large collection of artifacts in an airy space.

Save time to soak in a cenote: natural limestone swimming holes considered sacred by ancient Maya. We loved Cenotes Hacienda Mucuyché.

In the evening, take your pick of eateries in Mérida's booming food scene. Some of our favorite spots include Apoala, La Chaya Maya, the Museum of Yucatecan Gastronomy, La Bottega, Mercado 60 (a bustling food hall), and El Apapacho (it's also a bookstore with an emphasis on feminist works). Wherever you go, try excellent local pork dishes like *cochinita pibil* (slow-roasted pork) and *poc chuc* (marinated cutlets) or *sopa de lima* (lime soup). For drinks, meet friendly locals at Papis, a popular queer bar with a mixed crowd, or see drag shows at Dix Bar or Banana's Club. Woman- and queer-owned Cadadía has craft cocktails and events with LGBTQIA+ and feminist focuses, and it bills itself as hetero friendly.

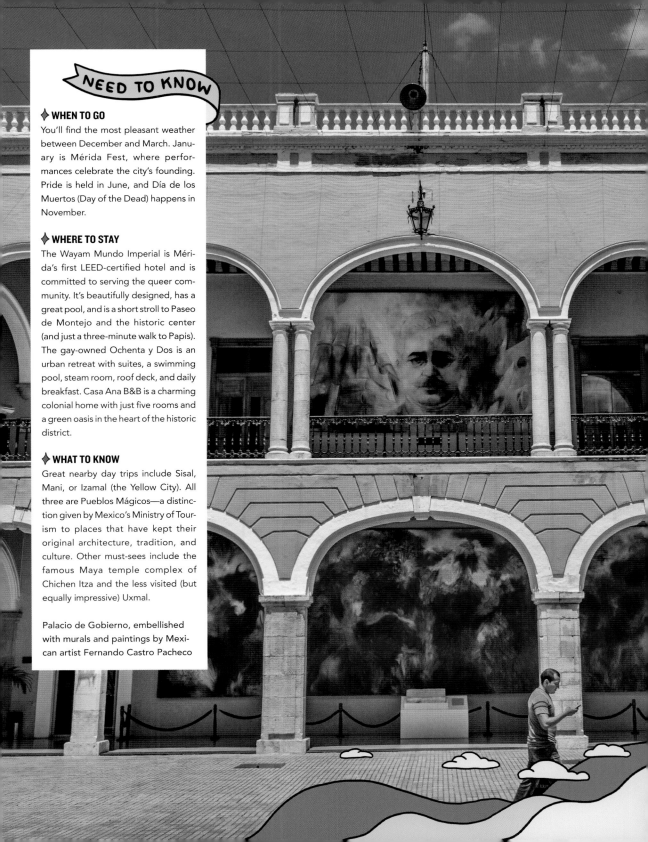

NEED TO KNOW

◆ WHEN TO GO

You'll find the most pleasant weather between December and March. January is Mérida Fest, where performances celebrate the city's founding. Pride is held in June, and Día de los Muertos (Day of the Dead) happens in November.

◆ WHERE TO STAY

The Wayam Mundo Imperial is Mérida's first LEED-certified hotel and is committed to serving the queer community. It's beautifully designed, has a great pool, and is a short stroll to Paseo de Montejo and the historic center (and just a three-minute walk to Papis). The gay-owned Ochenta y Dos is an urban retreat with suites, a swimming pool, steam room, roof deck, and daily breakfast. Casa Ana B&B is a charming colonial home with just five rooms and a green oasis in the heart of the historic district.

◆ WHAT TO KNOW

Great nearby day trips include Sisal, Mani, or Izamal (the Yellow City). All three are Pueblos Mágicos—a distinction given by Mexico's Ministry of Tourism to places that have kept their original architecture, tradition, and culture. Other must-sees include the famous Maya temple complex of Chichen Itza and the less visited (but equally impressive) Uxmal.

Palacio de Gobierno, embellished with murals and paintings by Mexican artist Fernando Castro Pacheco

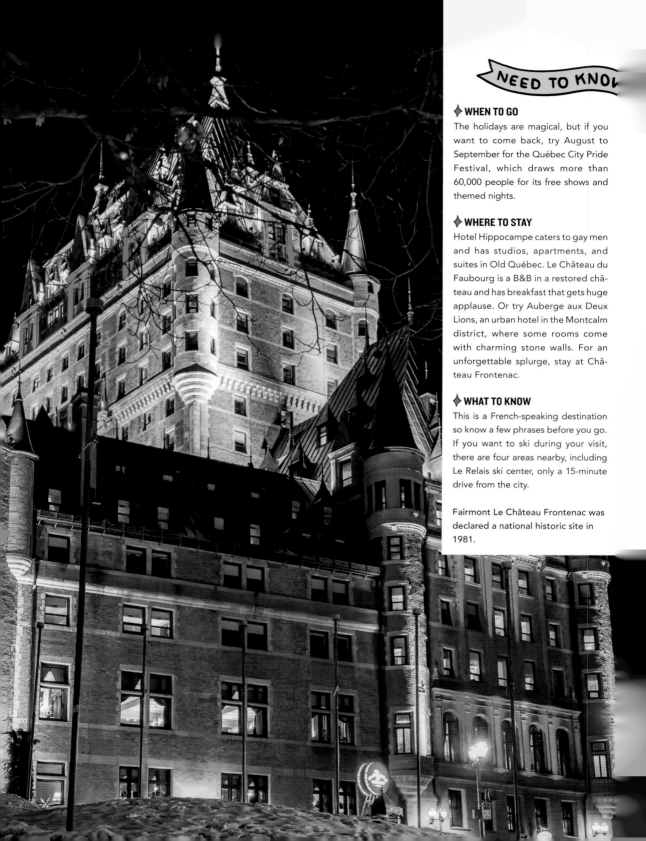

◆ WHEN TO GO

The holidays are magical, but if you want to come back, try August to September for the Québec City Pride Festival, which draws more than 60,000 people for its free shows and themed nights.

◆ WHERE TO STAY

Hotel Hippocampe caters to gay men and has studios, apartments, and suites in Old Québec. Le Château du Faubourg is a B&B in a restored château and has breakfast that gets huge applause. Or try Auberge aux Deux Lions, an urban hotel in the Montcalm district, where some rooms come with charming stone walls. For an unforgettable splurge, stay at Château Frontenac.

◆ WHAT TO KNOW

This is a French-speaking destination so know a few phrases before you go. If you want to ski during your visit, there are four areas nearby, including Le Relais ski center, only a 15-minute drive from the city.

Fairmont Le Château Frontenac was declared a national historic site in 1981.

VISIT A QUAINT VILLAGE WITH CLIFF-TOP VIEWS.
Québec City, Québec, Canada

Elf puppets in Christmas-themed shop La Boutique de Noël

THE LGBTQIA+ LOWDOWN Canada was one of the first countries in the world to legalize same-sex marriages (in 2005). Rue Saint-Jean, a historic street and shopping area (near Old Québec), is home to many rainbow flags and LGBTQIA+-owned businesses, cafés, and shops.

With 18th-century French-infused charm and a historic downtown village, Québec City is Canada's only walled city. Its historic downtown is a walkable village and a UNESCO World Heritage site.

Start your city tour at Dufferin Terrace, a cliff-top boardwalk with views of the St. Lawrence River. It's a great place to toboggan (especially during the Toboggan Festival from December 28 to 31) and surrounds the famous Château Frontenac, a grand hotel from the 1800s that was designated a national historic site in 1981. It's especially beautiful decked out for the holidays.

From here, take the historic funicular (running since 1879) to Petit-Champlain (Old Québec) and explore its quaint shops, traditional restaurants, and fairy-tale atmosphere. Don't miss the Notre-Dame-des-Victoires, the oldest stone church in North America. Old Québec is also the site of the Québec German Christmas Market, which hosts more than 90 local artisans.

Be sure to visit the Plains of Abraham (aka Battlefields Park), one of the most historic parks in Canada, with trails, a museum, and cultural events all year. It's the main site for the Québec Winter Carnival, a tradition since 1894, featuring parades and shows typically held in the first week in February.

To warm up, visit Aquarium du Québec, which is wheelchair accessible and has 10,000 animals, including more than 300 species of jellyfish, seahorses, walruses, and polar bears. Or try for an outdoor thermal experience at Strøm Nordic Spa (in Old Québec), where you can soak in outdoor tubs, float in a pool full of Epsom salt, sweat in a marble steam bath, and relax the day or night away.

To dine in style, go to BEClub Bistro Bar for everything made from scratch (even their ketchup) plus more than 200 wines. For poutine (Canada's signature dish of french fries with cheese curds and gravy), dine at Le Chic Shack (in a historic house) or Poutineville, a chain with build-your-own options.

For after-dinner fun, Le Drague Cabaret Club is Québec City's most well-known LGBTQIA+ bar, where you can sip through a fun show. Taverne Jos Dion is one of the oldest taverns in North America, serving since 1933.

QUÉBEC CITY

If fairy tales really do come true, they spring to life in Québec City. From its Gothic architecture (see Fairmont Le Château Frontenac, a nice waterfront stay built in the 20th century) and cozy cafés and bars to breathtaking river views, it's a four-season destination worthy of fanciful imaginations. The Old World charm in this wonderful place will inspire you to roam—and not rush—savoring every minute of your time here.

WALK THROUGH CHRISTMAS MARKETS, A WORLD-FAMOUS CATHEDRAL, AND HISTORY GALORE.
Cologne, Germany

Costumed revelers line the street for Cologne Carnival, which has been celebrated for two centuries.

THE LGBTQIA+ LOWDOWN Cologne competes with Berlin for the most queer-friendly city in Germany. You'll find one of Europe's biggest Pride festivals, two distinct LGBTQIA+ neighborhoods (Rudolfplatz-Schaafenstrasse in the west and Heumarkt-Mathiasstrasse in the east), and lots of queer spaces.

Few places do the Christkindlmarkt better than Germany, and the progressive university town of Cologne is no exception. Each market offers a chance to sip warm glühwein, browse handmade arts and crafts, take in ornate decorations, and sample Wiener schnitzel.

The biggest and most famous Christkindlmarkt can be found in front of the city's most iconic landmark, Kölner Dom (Cologne Cathedral), where a giant Christmas tree and pretty overhead string lights set a jolly atmosphere.

After browsing a maze of stalls, take in the views of the cathedral and its 515-foot (157 m) twin spires soaring into the sky. Begun in 1248, it's the largest Gothic church in northern Europe and a UNESCO World Heritage site that somehow withstood WWII bombing. Head inside to see significant religious relics like the Shrine of the Three Kings (a gold tomb for which the cathedral was built, believed to hold the remains of the Three Wise Men).

Other Christmas markets include Heumarkt with an ice-skating rink and ice-dancing performances; the Angels' Market with twinkling stars and a romantic vibe; and the Fairytale Christmas Market with mini–ski lifts, ornate gates decorated with puppets, and themed alleyways. In the (holiday) spirit of inclusiveness, don't miss Heavenue, a queer Christmas market featuring sexy St. Nick, live shows, and stalls bursting with color.

Save some energy for Cologne's other fantastic sites. Wander the twisting streets of Old Town and cross the Rhine River via a walk over Hohenzollern Bridge, then take in views of the Cologne Cathedral and Groß St. Martin, a 12th-century Romanesque church with a famous crossing tower.

To satisfy your hunger, visit Diner's, where you'll find cuisine and flags from around the world—the Pride flag included. For microbrews (be sure to try a local beer, Kölsch) and classics like pork chops with dumplings, head to Peters Kölsch. Or try Bei Oma Kleinmann, a lively family-owned restaurant that's been serving schnitzels and other German favorites since 1949. Among the many options for nightlife, Ex Corner is popular with men, while Die Mumu draws a mixed crowd. Amadeus and Exile are great for drag shows, and Iron Cocktail Lounge is a bit more upscale.

NEED TO KNOW

◆ WHEN TO GO
Beyond the holidays, visit for Carnival (February/March), the Come Together Cup (a May soccer festival that celebrates diversity), and Christopher Street Day/Cologne Pride (July).

◆ WHERE TO STAY
The Mercure Hotel Koeln City Friesenstrasse offers friendly service close to Old Town and the nightlife. The Excelsior Hotel Ernst am Dom is a five-star luxury option steps from the Cologne Cathedral. Maison Marsil is a family-owned boutique hotel with lots of character in the heart of the city.

◆ WHAT TO KNOW
Cologne also has some terrific museums, including the Museum Ludwig, with works by Picasso, Lichtenstein, and Warhol. The Wallraf-Richartz Museum is great for Gothic art and works by Degas, Monet, and more. For something yummy, try the Cologne Chocolate Museum. Another great choice is the Fragrance Museum, where eau de Cologne was invented in the 18th century.

Ice-skating at Cologne's Heumarkt Christmas market

NEED TO KNOW

◆ WHEN TO GO

The holidays here can feel magical but winters in general are very cold and filled with darkness. We like autumn (which begins in August) for the colors, and it's also a good time for viewing the aurora borealis.

◆ WHERE TO STAY

The Arctic TreeHouse Hotel offers nest-like sleeping quarters in a pine forest, panoramic windows to look for the auroras, and an on-site restaurant. If you've dreamed of sleeping in an igloo, head to Santa's Igloos Arctic Circle with 360-degree glass roofs, a sauna, and an outdoor whirlpool. The Arctic Light Hotel is an award-winning boutique accommodation in the heart of Rovaniemi.

◆ WHAT TO KNOW

During the holiday season, you can take the Santa Claus Express overnight train from Helsinki to Rovaniemi. Flights are also available, so consider adding on a few days to explore Helsinki's cool museums and design scene.

The forests of Lapland, Finland's northernmost region

CROSS THE ARCTIC CIRCLE TO SEE SNOWMAN WORLD IN SANTA'S "OFFICIAL" HOMETOWN.
Rovaniemi, Finland

Meet Santa Claus and his elves at his "real" office in Lapland.

THE LGBTQIA+ LOWDOWN In this open-minded country, queer travelers are welcome everywhere. Finland legalized same-sex marriage in 2017, and the capital of Finnish Lapland, Rovaniemi, has held a weeklong Arctic Pride since 2013.

Some people think Santa's home is the North Pole. Others say to look about 1,700 miles (2,735 km) south to Rovaniemi. Located in Finland's far north, Rovaniemi is a storybook holiday escape complete with reindeer, evergreen trees frosted with snow, and St. Nick himself.

At Santa Claus Village, visit with Santa, meet reindeer, listen to Mrs. Claus tell stories, and snap selfies as you cross the Arctic Circle. The village also has restaurants, shops, and Snowman World with an ice-skating rink, snow slides, a snow labyrinth, and an ice bar. For more Christmas-themed activities, head to SantaPark, an indoor amusement park, to ride a magic train, make cookies with Mrs. Gingerbread, cross the Arctic Circle again (this is the only place in the world you can do so underground), and attend Elf School for a diploma and a hat.

While in Rovaniemi, look for the northern lights (depending on the season), take a reindeer- or husky-pulled ride through snowy forests, snowshoe along the Kemijoki river, hit the slopes, cross-country ski, or snowboard at the Oun-asvaara Ski Resort. Warm up with a traditional Finnish sauna.

Around town, browse textiles, artwork, clothes, and other locally made goods (including adult pleasure products) at the Arctic Design Shop. Visit the Arktikum Science Centre and Museum for exhibits about the history and culture of Lapland. Don't miss the Korundi House of Culture, which combines the Rovaniemi Art Museum and the Lapland Chamber Orchestra's 340-seat concert hall. It is housed in a former mail-truck depot, one of Rovaniemi's few buildings not destroyed in WWII.

The area also offers some great day trips. Drive an hour south to Ranua Wildlife Park, an animal sanctuary dedicated to protecting endangered species such as polar bears (it's home to the only two in Finland) and wolverines. It also cares for and rehabilitates arctic foxes, reindeer, and moose.

Grab tasty waffles at Cafe & Bar 21. At Gustav Kitchen & Bar, find local and international cuisine such as panfried arctic char and penny bun risotto. Arctic Boulevard has traditional dishes such as reindeer and salmon.

WHEN IN BATH, DO AS THE ENGLISH DO.
Bath, England, U.K.

Explore the grounds of Bath's Prior Park Landscape Garden, including the 18th-century Palladian Bridge.

THE LGBTQIA+ LOWDOWN With an LGBTQIA+ history dating back to the 18th century and Gay West, the longest-running queer group in the southwest of England, this destination is rich in community as well as history.

Just over 100 miles (160 km) from London, at the edge of the Cotswolds Area of Outstanding Natural Beauty, you'll find Bath. Considered one of the most beautiful towns in England, and named for its Roman-built baths, Bath is the place to enjoy museums, Georgian architecture, memorable restaurants, and relaxing walks.

Be sure to visit the Roman Baths, where you'll walk through the Sacred Spring, Roman Bath House, Roman Temple, and a museum with treasures including the gilt bronze head of the goddess Sulis Minerva. To have your own bathing experience, go to Thermae Bath Spa, Britain's original natural thermal spa, where you can soak in spectacular indoor and outdoor baths in naturally warm, mineral-rich water.

Around town, see Pulteney Bridge (built in 1774), which was inspired by Ponte Vecchio in Florence and has small shops all along it; Royal Crescent, an architectural marvel that's a collection of beautiful Georgian town houses made from stone; and Alexandra Park, set above the city on a wooded hill where you'll get incredible views. For bibliophiles, the Jane Austen Centre is a must-visit to learn more about her life and work.

Then head to the Regency Tea Room, which has earned the Tea Guild's Award of Excellence (book in advance).

Ring in the holidays at the American Museum & Gardens, where you'll be treated to trails full of spectacular lights, food, and drinks. Sudeley Castle's Spectacle of Light is a magical after-dark experience with an illuminated trail around the castle grounds. Wookey Hole's Winter Wonderland offers a family-friendly evening where you can see more than 100,000 lights in a cave and meet Santa and his elves at Santa's North Pole Grotto.

For restaurants, try Sotto Sotto for Italian fare in candlelit cellars with beautiful stone walls. Pintxo de Bath is the place to sample Basque-style tapas and sherry. Go to Chaiwalla for street food–inspired Indian dishes. The Ivy Bath Brasserie is a sophisticated and cheery spot for almost any meal (including vegetarian). Mandalyns is the city's popular and long-standing LGBTQIA+ bar. Komedia is Bath's first community-owned venue, housed in a restored cinema with hundreds of events a year (including comedy, cabaret, kids' shows, and drag bingo).

NEED TO KNOW

◆ WHEN TO GO
Winter is stunning; LGBT+ History Month in February has events across the city hosted by local businesses and universities.

◆ WHERE TO STAY
Marlborough House, a B&B awarded four stars by the English Tourism Council, features rooms with Edwardian, Georgian, and other themes. The Roseate Villa, a five-minute walk from the town center, is a boutique luxury hotel in two converted Victorian houses. The Cedars, a family-run B&B in a village a few minutes from Bath (the bus runs regularly in between), has warm hosts and a locally sourced full English breakfast.

◆ WHAT TO KNOW
If the weather is good, walk along the Cotswold Way, a 102-mile (164 km) path inaugurated as a National Trail. It winds through the Cotswold Hills from Bath to Chipping Campden, a picturesque village in Gloucestershire. Stop in Bibury, a village that British poet, novelist, and artist William Morris called the "most beautiful in England." In Snowshill, another quaint countryside village, stop for lunch at the Lygon Arms, originally a coaching inn with a history dating back to the 1300s.

More than 3,000 rainbow ribbons color the walkway of St. Lawrence Street.

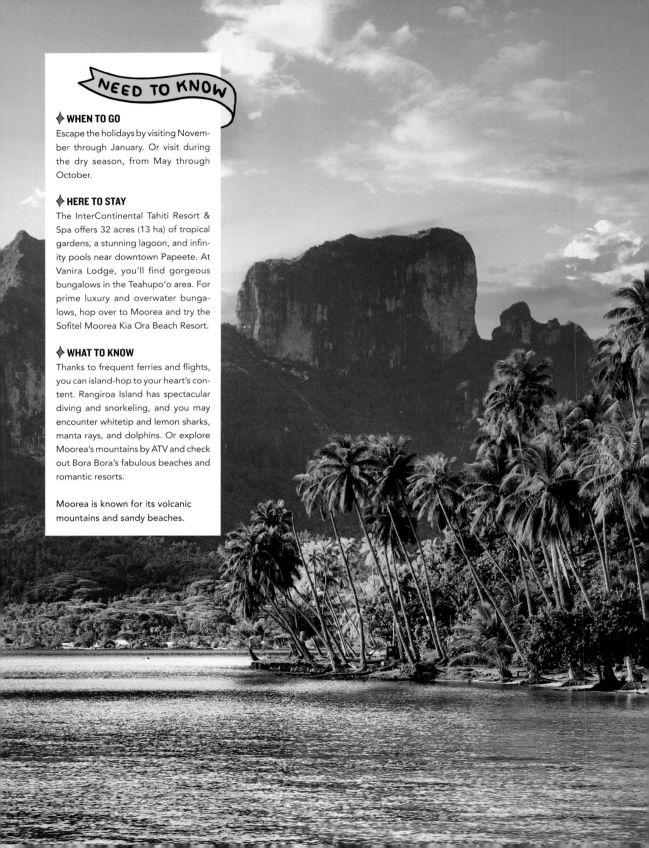

NEED TO KNOW

♦ WHEN TO GO

Escape the holidays by visiting November through January. Or visit during the dry season, from May through October.

♦ HERE TO STAY

The InterContinental Tahiti Resort & Spa offers 32 acres (13 ha) of tropical gardens, a stunning lagoon, and infinity pools near downtown Papeete. At Vanira Lodge, you'll find gorgeous bungalows in the Teahupo'o area. For prime luxury and overwater bungalows, hop over to Moorea and try the Sofitel Moorea Kia Ora Beach Resort.

♦ WHAT TO KNOW

Thanks to frequent ferries and flights, you can island-hop to your heart's content. Rangiroa Island has spectacular diving and snorkeling, and you may encounter whitetip and lemon sharks, manta rays, and dolphins. Or explore Moorea's mountains by ATV and check out Bora Bora's fabulous beaches and romantic resorts.

Moorea is known for its volcanic mountains and sandy beaches.

TRADE YOUR SNOW HATS FOR SNORKEL GEAR AND HIKING BOOTS.
Tahiti, French Polynesia

Celebrate the holidays the Tahitian way with tropical flameflower wreaths and leis.

THE LGBTQIA+ LOWDOWN French Polynesians are known for their warm welcome, including for queer travelers. Because French law governs the islands, the LGBTQIA+ community is protected against discrimination and has rights for marriage, adoption, and gender-affirming surgery. Tahitian culture recognizes different gender identities, including the Māhū, people who exhibit both (traditionally) masculine and feminine traits and don't conform to a specific gender.

On French Polynesia's largest island (there are about 130 of them), you'll get the gift of gleaming white sand and super-clear water; nature sites that include rainforests and volcanic landscapes; an infusion of Tahitian, French, and Chinese cultures; romantic overwater bungalows; and some of the freshest seafood around.

This is your chance to hide away from the holidays. Start by exploring the capital area of Papeete, especially the Marché de Papeete market with overwhelming sights and sounds—but also one of the best places in town to absorb Polynesian culture and shop for fresh fruit, flowers, fish, and souvenirs. Then stroll along the waterfront, and find a shady spot at Pā'ōfa'i Gardens, with walking trails, exotic trees, and ornamental fish ponds. Don't miss cool street art at the Gare Maritime Ferry Terminal, featuring 3D-designed robots created by Leon Keer and an eye-popping mural by Soflès and Soten on Rue Edouard Ahnne.

Only 15 minutes from Papeete is Fautaua Waterfall, Tahi-ti's tallest waterfall. To see the 443-foot (135 m) wonder, you'll need to take a semi-challenging hike, but you'll be in a shady rainforest and rewarded with amazing views. Cool off in the natural pools.

More waterfalls, rainforests, and swimming can be found in Tahiti's northwest at Les Trois Cascades (Faarumai Waterfalls). Into surfing? Teahupo'o is one of the world's best (and most dangerous) surfing areas thanks to its fast, heavy, and huge waves. You'll find gentler waters at La Plage de Maui, and the Huahine Natural Aquarium has a shallow lagoon off Mahuti Bay that's great for snorkeling.

After working up an appetite, join the locals by the roulettes (food trucks) at Place Vai'ete, where you'll get authentic food and humongous portions at a fraction of resort prices. Try tuna, mahi-mahi, and Tahitian specials like *poisson cru* (raw fish served with coconut milk) and poi (a creamy pudding made of taro flavored with banana and other fruit).

FEEL THE LION CITY'S CHEER AND (HOLIDAY) ROAR.
Singapore

New Year's Eve fireworks burst above Marina Bay and the Singapore Flyer Ferris wheel.

THE LGBTQIA+ LOWDOWN Singapore has been slow to fully embrace the LGBTQIA+ community, but it's making progress. In 2022, the country decriminalized sex between men. Generally, we find locals to be queer welcoming (especially younger generations) but recommend using discretion due to lingering conservative attitudes.

A sovereign country in Southeast Asia, Singapore is culturally diverse (speaking four official languages: English, Tamil, Malay, and Mandarin) with endless entertainment options and a great food scene.

The festivities start when you arrive at Changi Airport, often called one of the world's best. The seasonal Changi Festive Village (November through January) includes a 50-foot-tall (15 m) Christmas tree and a retro-style amusement park. The airport also has a butterfly garden, movie theater, swimming pool, and one of the world's tallest indoor waterfalls: the 130-foot (40 m) HSBC Rain Vortex.

Starting in mid-November, Orchard Road (famous for its enormous selection of stores and high-tech malls) transforms into the "Great Street." At this 40-plus-year tradition, find a display of illuminations, tons of decorations, and Christmas carols blasting through the street. With hundreds of stores, you're bound to find gifts for everyone on your nice list (or treat yourself to some retail therapy).

Gardens by the Bay is one of Singapore's most popular attractions and hosts a Christmas Wonderland with extravagant light sculptures, Santa sightings, and carnival games. Visit the Flower Dome, the world's largest greenhouse, to see plants from all over the world and the Cloud Forest, which includes a 114-foot (35 m) mountain, a waterfall, and aerial walkways. Don't miss the Supertree Grove, where 18 futuristic vertical gardens standing at more than 160 feet (49 m) tall put on an electrifying light and sound show set to holiday tunes; seven of the Supertrees are designed to harvest solar energy. More than just a spectacle, the Supertrees also house 162,900 plants of more than 200 species.

Take a break from holiday happenings and get something to eat at one of Singapore's famous hawker centers. We love Maxwell Food Centre in Chinatown, where more than a dozen vendors sell the best street food, from fish soup and oyster cakes to handmade Chinese fritters. Join the line at Tian Tian Hainanese Chicken Rice, where they serve arguably the best chicken rice in town. For sit-down experiences, Zen, Burnt Ends, and Meta have been named among the world's top 100 restaurants. Wash down your meals with drinks at queer-popular Tantric Bar, May Wong's Cafe, Backstage Bar, Dorothy's, and Taboo.

◆ NEED TO KNOW

◆ WHEN TO GO

Situated at the equator, Singapore is hot and sticky year-round, so December is great for those who desire warmth as their holiday gift. August is IndigNation, a month-long Pride celebration.

◆ WHERE TO STAY

The Quincy Hotel is a boutique spot just a quick stroll from Orchard Road and has a fantastic rooftop pool and other amenities such as outdoor lounges, a sauna, and steam rooms. With a famous rooftop infinity pool, Marina Bay Sands is a splashy splurge. The W Sentosa Cove has gorgeous rooms and views. If you're traveling as a couple, most hotels won't question that you've reserved one bed, but it's best to avoid PDA.

◆ WHAT TO KNOW

Universal Studios Singapore, about 30 minutes away on Sentosa Island, also packs in Christmas parades and live performances. Experience thrill rides such as Battlestar Galactica: Human vs. Cylon, and watch Santa and a band of merry performers take the stage. While on the island, visit Palawan Beach, continental Asia's southernmost point. Pink Dot SG is a nonprofit that sponsors rallies and events supporting the "freedom to love," and there are numerous queer-owned and queer-supported online businesses such as Heckin' Unicorn, Purposeful Skincare by ALLIES (PSA), Tomscout, and Little Sarong for your shopping pleasure.

Special lights decorate Supertrees for Gardens by the Bay's Christmas Wonderland.

CHAPTER 7

Walk on THE WILD SIDE

There's nothing like seeing wildlife in the actual wild. Here we highlight some of the world's most incredible friendly animal encounters, including seeing lions and elephants on a South African safari; snorkeling with sea turtles and spotting giant land tortoises in the Galápagos Islands; looking for moose and bears in Alaska; and getting an up close view of penguins, seals, and whales in Antarctica. Though you can choose from many experiences, we've highlighted organizations and destinations that prioritize conservation and rescue, and where laws and practices are welcoming to LGBTQIA+ travelers.

SPOT ORCAS AND TAKE IN THE FRESH PINE-SCENTED AIR.
San Juan Islands, Washington, U.S.A.

Kayak from Friday Harbor to explore the scenic coast of San Juan Island.

THE LGBTQIA+ LOWDOWN The San Juan Island Pride Foundation provides information, health resources, and safe spaces. It also organizes social events, including the San Juan Island Pride Festival.

If you need to de-stress, look no further than the mellow vibes and wild spirit of northwestern Washington's San Juan Islands, an archipelago of more than 170 islands and reefs in the Salish Sea.

What can be more relaxing than walking among Douglas firs, cycling through green pastures, or kayaking in a secluded cove? The San Juan Islands are truly something special, with each of the three most visited islands—San Juan, Orcas, and Lopez—offering its own unique activities and vibe.

San Juan Island is home to charming Friday Harbor with restaurants, shops, and lovely inns. It's a prime location for orca spotting (they're year-round residents). See them from the water with companies such as San Juan Safaris and Maya's Legacy Whale Watching charters, or on land at Lime Kiln Point State Park (also known as Whale Watch Park), where orcas, minke whales, porpoises, seals, sea lions, otters, and bald eagles can often be spotted along the shoreline. San Juan Island National Historical Park offers more amazing spots to see whales, including the Haro Strait and Grandma's Cove, which is also a nice place to swim.

For nature lovers, Orcas Island (the largest of the San Juans) offers lots of opportunities for hiking, biking, nonmotorized boating, and swimming. Don't miss Moran State Park, which covers more than 5,000 acres (2,023 ha) of ruggedly beautiful forest and lakes. It's a great place to camp and is home to Mount Constitution. Standing at 2,399 feet (731 m), the peak is the highest point in the San Juan Islands. A hike to its summit offers views of the North Cascades, San Juan archipelago, and Mount Baker (you can also drive to scenic lookouts).

Lopez Island is the place for scenic cycling through rolling pastures (biking is the best way to get around in general). Visit family-run Lopez Island Vineyards for locally made wine and check out the shops and restaurants in Lopez Village. Or enjoy the outdoors at Shark Reef Sanctuary, where a gentle 10-minute walk through woodlands leads you to a picturesque rocky shoreline (look out for seals). Stop at Iceberg Point for fabulous views of the Olympic Peninsula (another good spot for orca viewing), as well as Spencer Spit State Park, a 138-acre (56 ha) space for camping, complete with fishing, crabbing, picnicking, hiking, or kayaking.

NEED TO KNOW

◆ WHEN TO GO

May through September offer the best weather and prime wildlife-viewing opportunities. Go in June for Pride celebrations and the Orcas Island Lit Fest, which brings together renowned authors and avid readers for three days of readings and events celebrating the literary culture of the Pacific Northwest. Orcas Island Pride (June) features speakers and performers who identify as trans, nonbinary, and BIPOC.

◆ WHERE TO STAY

The Earthbox Inn & Spa on San Juan Island is well located with a vintage chic vibe. On Orcas Island, the Rosario Resort & Spa offers kayaking, cruises, and outdoor pools. Lopez Farm Cottages, on Lopez Island, has Scandinavian-inspired cottages and glamping on 29 pastoral acres (12 ha).

◆ WHAT TO KNOW

The Washington State Ferry leaves from Anacortes (90 minutes from Seattle), while Kenmore Air and the San Juan Clipper offer Seattle departures. Ferries also run between the islands. We strongly recommend booking in advance for summer months.

Shark Reef Sanctuary on Lopez Island

NEED TO KNOW

◆ WHEN TO GO

To avoid the crowds and have the best chances of seeing wildlife at Yellowstone and Grand Teton, try for April through May or September through October. For the National Elk Refuge, the best time to visit is December through April.

◆ WHERE TO STAY

In Yellowstone, the Old Faithful Inn is a classic rustic gem overlooking the eponymous geyser. In Grand Teton, Jackson Lake Lodge is so pretty you may not want to leave. Outside of the parks, hundreds of accommodations offer rustic vibes and nature feels, including A Stone's Throw Bed & Breakfast in Livingston (Montana), Chamberlin Inn in Cody (Wyoming), or the Lodge at Jackson Hole (Wyoming).

◆ WHAT TO KNOW

Yellowstone is huge, and it takes a while to drive between the sights. Consider spending at least four days here and staying in different areas of the park. Lodges within the parks fill up fast, so book in advance. When you need a break from the parks, have a relaxing soak at Chico Hot Springs (near Pray, Montana) or Bozeman Hot Springs (in Bozeman, Montana).

Thermophiles (heat-loving bacteria) create vibrant colors in the Grand Prismatic Spring at Yellowstone National Park.

SEE BEARS, BISON, AND GEYSERS IN TRUE WESTERN SPLENDOR.

Grand Teton National Park, Wyoming, and Yellowstone National Park, Wyoming and Montana, U.S.A.

THE LGBTQIA+ LOWDOWN Montana and Wyoming are historically conservative states, but the National Park Service proudly supports diversity and inclusion. Areas around Grand Teton and Yellowstone are queer welcoming with LGBTQIA+-owned businesses.

Welcome to Yellowstone and Grand Teton, two of America's most spectacular national parks, where on any given day, you might spot bison, bears, moose, elk, bighorn sheep, and wolves.

Start in Yellowstone (the oldest national park in the U.S.), famous for its geysers, geothermal activity, and hot springs. Yellowstone is home to more than 5,000 bison, and it's the only place in the U.S. where the massive mammals have continuously roamed since the prehistoric era. Hayden Valley and Lamar Valley are often reliable spots to see bison chilling in the grass or brazenly crossing the street. You might also spot bears.

With more than 2.2 million acres (890,310 ha), Yellowstone has so much to offer that you can spend a week here and barely scratch the surface, especially if you want time to hike, picnic, or swim. In addition to spotting wildlife, visit Grand Prismatic Spring, Mammoth Hot Springs, the Grand Canyon of the Yellowstone (especially Artist Point, for terrific waterfall views), Yellowstone Lake, West Thumb Geyser Basin, and Upper Geyser Basin. The latter is where you'll find Old Faithful. After watching Old Faithful's eruption, take your time exploring. Who knows, you might just witness a less frequently erupting geyser do its thing (we saw Daisy Geyser go off, and it was quite spectacular).

Nearby Grand Teton boasts equal opportunity to see wildlife and enjoy the outdoors. Don't make the mistake of doing a rushed drive-through. Instead, take your time and spend at least a whole day or two (more if you can) to get the most out of its hiking trails, gorgeous alpine lakes, and abundant wildlife. Drive the park's scenic 42-mile (68 km) loop and look for wildlife at Schwabacher Landing (a popular site for moose) and Oxbow Bend (for elk, moose, bears, and beavers). Other great areas for wildlife spotting include Antelope Flats (especially for bison) and a drive along Moose-Wilson Road for—you guessed it—moose, as well as deer, elk, and grizzly bears.

While exploring the park, stop at Snake River Overlook (made famous by Ansel Adams in 1942), Mormon Row Historic District, and Jenny Lake for hiking (try Inspiration Point and Hidden Falls or combine that with the longer Jenny Lake Loop trail). Just outside of Grand Teton is Jackson, Wyoming, a picturesque mountain town loaded with places to eat, shop, and gather. Don't miss the National Elk Refuge. With almost 25,000 acres (10,120 ha) of protected lands, this is one of the greatest places in the world to observe elk. The area is also a haven for trumpeter swans, bald eagles, wolves, and mountain lions.

The Grand Tetons at Schwabacher Landing, along the eastern edge of the Snake River

GO WILD IN THE LAST FRONTIER.
Alaska, U.S.A.

THE LGBTQIA+ LOWDOWN Alaska has a conservative reputation but is becoming more queer and welcoming. Identity Alaska in Anchorage and the Southeast Alaska LGBTQ+ Alliance in Juneau provide community support, resources, and advocacy, as well as sponsoring Pride and other events.

The largest state in the U.S. is for adventurous hearts and curious minds. Base yourself in Anchorage for a few days to explore the 11-mile (18 km) Tony Knowles Coastal Trail and the Alaska Native Heritage Center. In Chugach State Park (one of America's largest) and Kincaid Park, look for bears, moose, bald eagles, and wolves. For birding, Potter Marsh is popular.

Visit other great wildlife-spotting areas such as Seward, a scenic two-and-a-half-hour drive from Anchorage. Along the way, stop at the Alaska Wildlife Conservation Center, which cares for injured caribou, lynx, bears, and eagles, returning them to nature whenever possible. Also en route, admire the amazing views at Turnagain Arm and look for whales and seals at Beluga Point. For another cool detour, stop and walk up to Exit Glacier, located just off the Seward Highway, about four miles (6 km) north of Seward. In the area, more seasoned hikers can try the strenuous (but scenic) eight-mile (13 km) loop along the Harding Icefield Trail.

In the lovely town of Seward, hop on a boat tour to Kenai Fjords National Park. The spectacular scenery includes fjords and tons of glaciers flowing from the Harding Icefield. You'll have a chance to see orcas, whales, puffins, sea otters, seals, and sea lions. We even saw some jellyfish! For a truly memorable experience, try kayaking in Resurrection Bay.

For brown bears, it's hard to beat Katmai National Park, home to more than 2,000 of the hulking omnivores. You'll need to arrange a flight from Anchorage, but the hassle is worth it. Popular places to see bears include the Brooks Falls Trail and from viewing platforms overlooking the falls. In June and July, hordes of bears take advantage of the salmon rush in Brooks Fall, and it's quite the sight to behold. Don't miss the Valley of Ten Thousand Smokes, an ash-covered landscape formed by the eruption of Novarupta in 1912 (the largest volcanic eruption of the 20th century).

An epic five-hour drive from Anchorage, Denali National Park is one of Alaska's most visited sites. At more than 20,000 feet (6,096 m), the snowcapped Denali (formerly Mount McKinley) is North America's highest mountain and an awe-inspiring sight—if you're lucky enough to see it. Denali makes its own weather, and clouds may obstruct the view.

You've likely also come to spot some incredible wildlife. Go on an off-trail hike (encouraged here), or hop on a park tour bus and look out for bears, moose, wolves, and caribou behind the safety of your window.

The annual Running of the Reindeer at the Fur Rendezvous festival

NEED TO KNOW

✦ WHEN TO GO

May through September bring the best weather and long summer days.

✦ WHERE TO STAY

The gay-owned A Wildflower Inn (Anchorage) offers a true feel-at-home experience with very friendly innkeepers and is just minutes from all the sights. Resurrection Lodge on the Bay (Seward) has an amazing location right on the water where you can look for whales, sea otters, and sea lions from your private deck. In Denali, stay in a cabin just outside of the park at McKinley Creekside Cabins. Brooks Lodge (Katmai) is the closest accommodation to Brooks Falls you can get. The property gives you views of Brooks River and the aquamarine Naknek Lake.

✦ WHAT TO KNOW

In Denali, private vehicles can only drive to mile 15 on Denali Park Road, so you'll need to take a transit or sightseeing bus to the rest of the park (all of our wildlife sightings were past mile 15).

Watch the aurora borealis above Denali National Park from August through April.

NEED TO KNOW

◆ WHEN TO GO

December through May bring the best weather.

◆ WHERE TO STAY

You'll be sleeping on your ship of choice. As an alternative, you can get a hotel on the inhabited islands—San Cristóbal, Isabela, Floreana, or Santa Cruz—and visit other islands during the day. The Finch Bay Eco Hotel is a popular choice on the beach and is an easy walk from attractions. Golden Bay Galápagos is another eco-hotel facing the sea and is close to the airport for access to other islands. At Galápagos Safari Camp, you'll spend the night in luxury tents and have a chance to explore the stunning surroundings.

◆ WHAT TO KNOW

Before or after you visit the islands, it's worth spending a few days in Quito, especially its historic center. Don't miss Plaza Grande, Compañia de Jesús for its striking gold interior, and the lively La Ronda, with cobblestoned streets, stores, galleries, restaurants, and bars. You can also walk between the Northern and Southern Hemispheres at the Mitad del Mundo (or the more geographically accurate Intiñan Site Museum). You'll want to ride the cable car up Volcán Pichincha for mesmerizing views.

Giant tortoise numbers are on the rise on Santa Cruz Island.

SEE GIANT TORTOISES, MARINE IGUANAS, AND OTHER ENDEMIC SPECIES BY LAND AND SEA.

Galápagos Islands, Ecuador

THE LGBTQIA+ LOWDOWN Ecuador has its conservative side, but the country legalized same-sex marriage in 2019, and cities like Guayaquil and Quito (common gateways to the Galápagos) have visible LGBTQIA+ communities, queer film festivals, Pride events (including Trans Pride), and queer nightlife. The Galápagos Islands have a long history of welcoming LGBTQIA+ travelers, too.

In the Galápagos Islands, you'll encounter wildlife at seemingly every turn. But these remote islands, hundreds of miles from mainland Ecuador, offer more than just animals. Think amazing snorkeling, volcanic landscapes, and (literally) breathtaking hikes.

Famously visited by Charles Darwin in 1835, the archipelago is the only place in the world to see marine iguanas. You'll also have opportunities to spot blue-footed boobies and giant Galápagos tortoises, sea turtles, rays, seals, sea lions, sharks, dolphins, whales, and Galápagos penguins. And with a limited number of visitors each day, you won't have to fight crowds to get a good look.

To cover the most land (and sea), we recommend sailing between the islands on small ships, which are less harmful to the ecosystem and can offer diverse routes and shore landings (your itinerary is predetermined and typically limited to a few islands, so don't expect to see all the Galápagos in one trip).

Popular stops, and some of our favorites, include Rábida Island for a striking red sand beach and lots of sea lions; Fernandina, the youngest of the Galápagos Islands (a mere million years old), home to the largest colony of marine iguanas, flightless cormorants, and the most volcanic activity (the last eruption was in 1995); and Isabela, the largest island with several highlights, including Darwin Lake, giant Galápagos land tortoises, and the amazing hiking on the Sierra Negra volcano.

We also love Pinnacle Rock on the island of Bartolomé, where you can climb to the top of an extinct volcano and take in postcard-worthy views. The good news is there are stairs, but the bad news is there are 372 of them. Pinnacle Rock is also excellent for snorkeling alongside Galápagos penguins and playful sea lions.

For more wonderful snorkeling sites, don't miss Punta Vicente Roca (on Isabela Island), known for its sea turtles. It's also where you may get lucky and see a 2,000-pound (907 kg) ocean sunfish (mola). Tagus Cove (also on Isabela) is a nutrient-rich playground teeming with marine life. Head to Kicker Rock (on San Cristóbal) for turtles and giant manta rays, and Gardner Bay (on Española), where you can snorkel off a beautiful beach or just sunbathe on the sand.

Back on land, Santa Cruz has enough to keep you busy, too. Explore the Charles Darwin Research Station, located in the bustling town of Puerto Ayora. Or visit Tortuga Bay Galápagos (a great stretch of beach for swimming and snorkeling), the super-green Santa Cruz Highlands featuring Los Gemelos (impressive twin sinkholes), and the El Chato Reserve, which is a private ranch for giant tortoises.

Galápagos sea lions bask in the sunshine on Española Island's Gardner Bay.

GET READY TO GO BEYOND THE BELOVED BIG FIVE.
Cape Town, South Africa

Clifton's four Atlantic coast beaches are a haven for sun lovers in the De Waterkant area.

THE LGBTQIA+ LOWDOWN Cape Town is widely considered the most queer-friendly city in Africa. Many queer bars, clubs, and welcoming restaurants are located in the De Waterkant area.

Travelers flock to South Africa with the hope of seeing the big five: lions, leopards, rhinos, elephants, and African buffalo. Beyond the big five, there's cheetahs, giraffes, hippos, and so much more to draw you to this African port city.

Base yourself in Cape Town, on the southwest coast. In the city, stroll the Victoria & Alfred Waterfront, a working harbor that's full of great shopping and fantastic restaurants with delicious and affordable South African wine, and features the Zeitz Museum of Contemporary Art Africa. Then hike or take a cable car to the top of Table Mountain—at more than 3,500 feet (1,065 m), the ocean views are incredible. Breathe in the flowers at Kirstenbosch National Botanical Garden, and catch a ferry to Robben Island, where Nelson Mandela served 18 years of his 27-year prison sentence, to learn about the country's chilling history of apartheid.

For popular day trips from Cape Town, visit Hermanus, a seaside town that's one of the world's best places to see southern right whales, humpbacks, and Bryde's whales. Also, consider Gansbaai for an adrenaline-pumping experience in "Shark Alley," where you can cage dive with great whites or see them from a boat.

Enjoy some beach time at Clifton Third or Sandy Bay (both popular with gay men). Or head to Boulders Beach and Foxy Beach (connected by a wheelchair-accessible boardwalk), where African penguins are sure to make you smile.

When it's time for a safari, consider Africa's largest wildlife reserve, Kruger National Park, an amazing place to live out your wildest dreams. You'll find lots of accommodations for different interests and budgets.

The Sabi Sands Game Reserve, which borders Kruger National Park, is one of the world's best places to look for leopards (an elusive big fiver). Because there aren't barriers between the two parks, animals can move freely.

Love elephants? It doesn't get much better than Addo Elephant National Park, which has a lovely conservation story. When it was first declared a national park in 1931, it had just 11 elephants. Today, about 600 roam the grounds.

Other amazing options include Hluhluwe Imfolozi Park, widely regarded as one of the country's most beautiful parks. iSimangaliso Wetland Park was South Africa's first park to become a UNESCO World Heritage site and is known for its hippos and Nile crocodiles, plus elephants, dolphins, turtles, and whales.

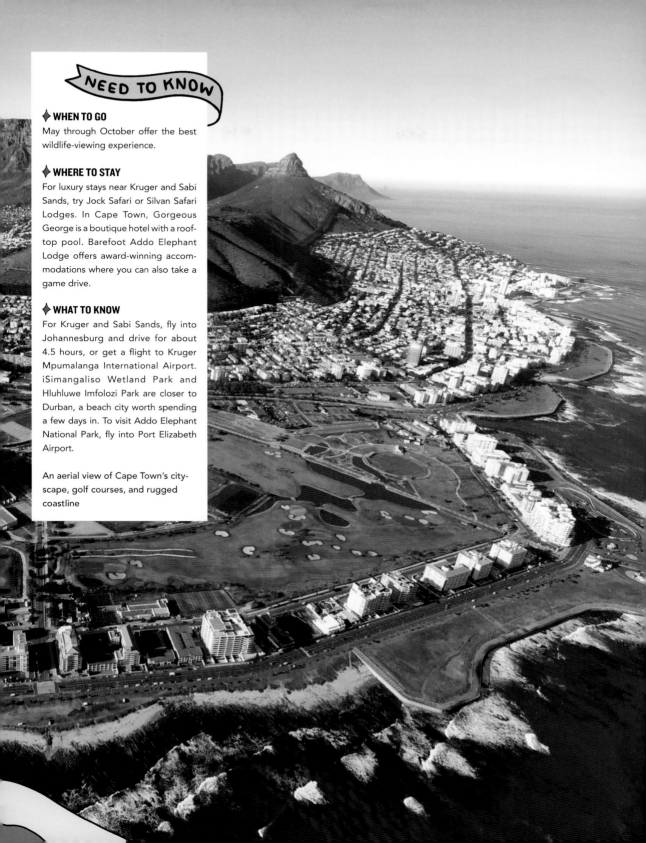

◆ WHEN TO GO

May through October offer the best wildlife-viewing experience.

◆ WHERE TO STAY

For luxury stays near Kruger and Sabi Sands, try Jock Safari or Silvan Safari Lodges. In Cape Town, Gorgeous George is a boutique hotel with a roof-top pool. Barefoot Addo Elephant Lodge offers award-winning accommodations where you can also take a game drive.

◆ WHAT TO KNOW

For Kruger and Sabi Sands, fly into Johannesburg and drive for about 4.5 hours, or get a flight to Kruger Mpumalanga International Airport. iSimangaliso Wetland Park and Hluhluwe Imfolozi Park are closer to Durban, a beach city worth spending a few days in. To visit Addo Elephant National Park, fly into Port Elizabeth Airport.

An aerial view of Cape Town's cityscape, golf courses, and rugged coastline

KRUGER NATIONAL PARK

South Africa has so many safari options, but few can match the "People's Park," which includes a range of accommodations and DIY wildlife-spotting opportunities. Kruger National Park stretches 7,580 square miles (19,633 km^2), has several ecosystems, and safeguards more than 140 species of mammals. You may go in search of giraffes, zebras, and the big five, but you also have the chance to spot Kruger's big six: a collection of birds (more than 500 live here) that includes lappet-faced vultures, martial eagles, saddle-billed storks, Kori bustards, Pel's fishing owls, and ground hornbills.

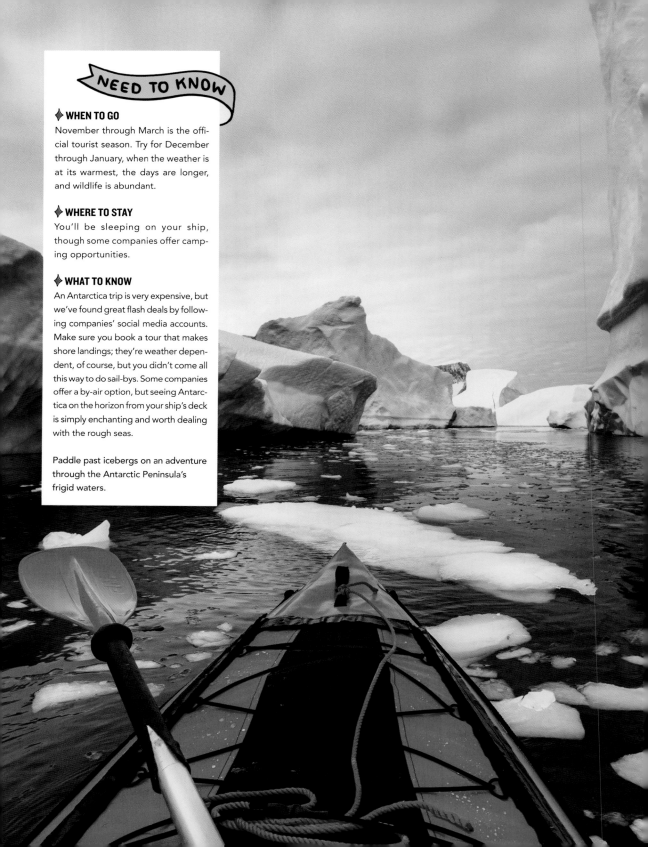

NEED TO KNOW

◆ WHEN TO GO

November through March is the official tourist season. Try for December
through January, when the weather is
at its warmest, the days are longer,
and wildlife is abundant.

◆ WHERE TO STAY

You'll be sleeping on your ship,
though some companies offer camping opportunities.

◆ WHAT TO KNOW

An Antarctica trip is very expensive, but
we've found great flash deals by following companies' social media accounts.
Make sure you book a tour that makes
shore landings; they're weather depen-
dent, of course, but you didn't come all
this way to do sail-bys. Some companies
offer a by-air option, but seeing Antarctica on the horizon from your ship's deck
is simply enchanting and worth dealing
with the rough seas.

Paddle past icebergs on an adventure
through the Antarctic Peninsula's
frigid waters.

MARCH WITH THE PENGUINS AT THE END OF THE WORLD.
Antarctica

A penguin colony in Port Lockroy overlooks snow-covered rocks and the pristine bay.

THE LGBTQIA+ LOWDOWN Antarctica has been called the least hospitable place on Earth, but queer travelers are very welcome. The nonprofit Planting Peace, which focuses on humanitarian initiatives, has named it the "world's first LGBTQ-friendly continent."

It might sound cliché, but going to Antarctica is an experience like no other. A land of extremes, the world's southernmost continent is 99 percent ice covered and holds most of the world's fresh water in its ice sheet (that's nearly 5.5 million miles/8.9 million kilometers long). From the incredible scenery—including massive icebergs and other-worldly volcanic islands—to extraordinary wildlife encounters, going to the end of the earth will be an everlasting memory.

Though it's never guaranteed, you'll have excellent chances to see seals, orcas, penguins (such as chinstrap, gentoo, and Adélie), and humpback and minke whales.

The most common way to journey to Antarctica is a cruise or expedition ship from Ushuaia, Argentina (which stakes the claim as the world's southernmost city), with companies such as National Geographic Expeditions, Lindblad Expeditions, or Quark Expeditions. Before boarding, visit the Martial Glacier and Tierra del Fuego National Park.

Once on board, settle in with a good book—it takes about two days to reach Antarctica. First, you'll sail through the Beagle Channel, a relatively smooth ride past mountains and tidewater glaciers. Then you'll cross into the Drake Passage, known as the world's roughest waters. Have some seasickness medicine on hand—you just might experience the infamous "Drake Shake." Along the way, look for dolphins, penguins, and the elusive albatross. Itineraries vary with each cruise ship, but here's an idea of what your journey may include:

At Half Moon Island, gray skies are brightened by a visit with adorable chinstrap penguins (more than 3,000 breeding pairs). Watching them hop between rocks and waddle down their "penguin highways" is incredible (just be sure to stay at least 15 feet/4.6 meters away, per official visitor guidelines). The island is also known for storm petrels, blue-eyed shags, and fur seals.

Brown Station, on Antarctica's mainland, has more glaciers calving and penguins, or take in sweeping views of Paradise Harbor.

On Deception Island, in the caldera of an active volcano—Antarctica has the world's largest number of them with almost 140—it's like walking among the craters of the moon thanks to volcanic ash, mountains, and glaciers streaked with ash. Loads of penguins and seals hang out on the beach.

Cuverville Island is home to the largest colony of gentoos in the Antarctic Peninsula—more than 12,000 of them! Look out for the gentoos swimming in the water, where they can reach speeds of 22 miles an hour (35 km/h).

Plus, there's Zodiac boat rides for closer looks at icebergs and unbelievable encounters with whales and seals. When you can get close enough to hear a minke whale breathe or see a humpback breach, it makes the whole journey worth it!

SEE SACRED TEMPLES AND MEET ELEPHANTS AT ETHICAL SANCTUARIES.
Chiang Mai, Thailand

A family of elephants dry off after a mud bath at Elephant Nature Park.

THE LGBTQIA+ LOWDOWN Thailand is one of Asia's most queer-friendly countries. Find an open LGBTQIA+ scene and queer-friendly establishments in Chiang Mai. Pride has returned (it was canceled for several years due to clashes with protesters) and is supported by locals and tourists.

Affectionately called the "Rose of the North," Chiang Mai is the largest city in northern Thailand, and it blooms with ancient temples, historical sites, terrific night markets, great food, and nearby mountains and national parks. It's also one of the best places in Thailand to ethically visit with elephants—if you do your research.

If you love these gentle giants, head straight to Elephant Nature Park. Founded in 1995 by award-winning conservationist Lek Chailert, this is one of Thailand's most respected elephant sanctuaries and home to more than 100 free-roaming elephants. You won't find elephants giving rides or doing tricks. Instead, you'll see them frolicking and bathing around the grounds or in the river, pool, or mud pits. Come for the day, spend the night, or stay a week as a volunteer to gain more time with these incredible animals.

The Chiang Mai area is home to several other ethical sanctuaries, including the Lanna Kingdom Elephant Sanctuary and Burm and Emily's Elephant Sanctuary. Another wonderful choice is Elephant Freedom Village, which works with the Karen hill tribe, so in addition to spending time with elephants, you'll learn about the community's history and culture. Note: For many of these sanctuaries, you need to book far in advance.

Never choose a "sanctuary" that allows guests to ride the elephants, keeps them in chains, rents elephants for show (as opposed to caring for them full time), or practices whipping or other abuse. Please also resist having a "tiger experience," as the big cats are treated inhumanely, including being heavily sedated, forced to live in cages, and malnourished.

Save some time to explore the impressive Wat Phra That Doi Suthep, a mountaintop temple that dates back to the 14th century and is considered among Thailand's most sacred places. After climbing more than 300 steps (or taking the lift), you'll see sweeping city views, a nearly 80-foot (24 m) golden *chedi* (a Buddhist stupa), and ornate statues of Buddha.

For more natural beauty, visit Doi Inthanon National Park, a great spot for nature hikes and bird-watching on Thailand's highest peak.

Back within Chiang Mai's old city walls, stroll around town and visit more remarkable temples, including Wat Phra Singh, Wat Chedi Luang, and Wat Phan Tao. Or shop at the Night Bazaar and Sunday Walking Street Market. For queer nightlife, check out the popular cabaret show at Ram Bar or more risqué shows at Adam's Apple. Have drinks alfresco at Orion, and dance and sing karaoke at Route181 HostBar.

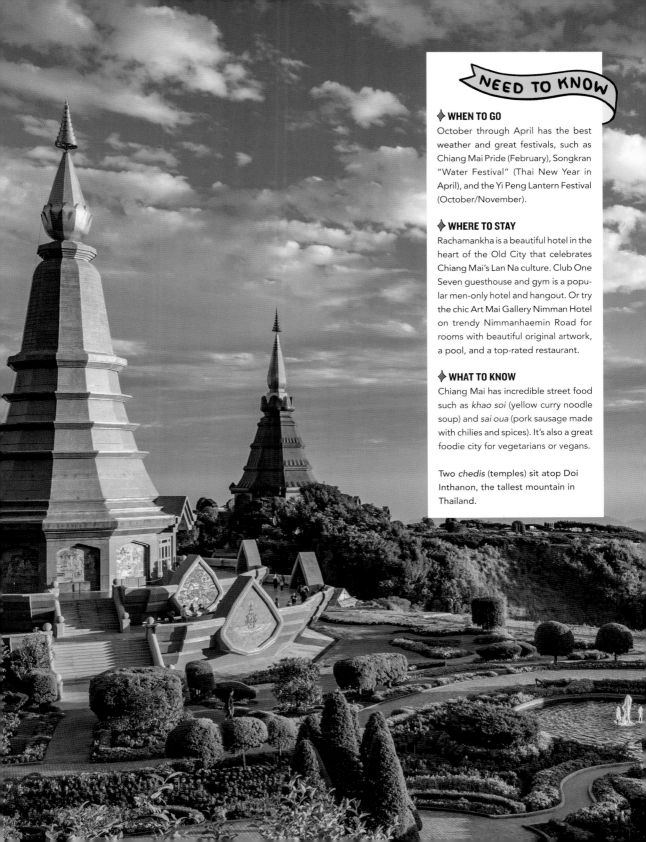

✦ WHEN TO GO
October through April has the best weather and great festivals, such as Chiang Mai Pride (February), Songkran "Water Festival" (Thai New Year in April), and the Yi Peng Lantern Festival (October/November).

✦ WHERE TO STAY
Rachamankha is a beautiful hotel in the heart of the Old City that celebrates Chiang Mai's Lan Na culture. Club One Seven guesthouse and gym is a popular men-only hotel and hangout. Or try the chic Art Mai Gallery Nimman Hotel on trendy Nimmanhaemin Road for rooms with beautiful original artwork, a pool, and a top-rated restaurant.

✦ WHAT TO KNOW
Chiang Mai has incredible street food such as *khao soi* (yellow curry noodle soup) and *sai oua* (pork sausage made with chilies and spices). It's also a great foodie city for vegetarians or vegans.

Two *chedis* (temples) sit atop Doi Inthanon, the tallest mountain in Thailand.

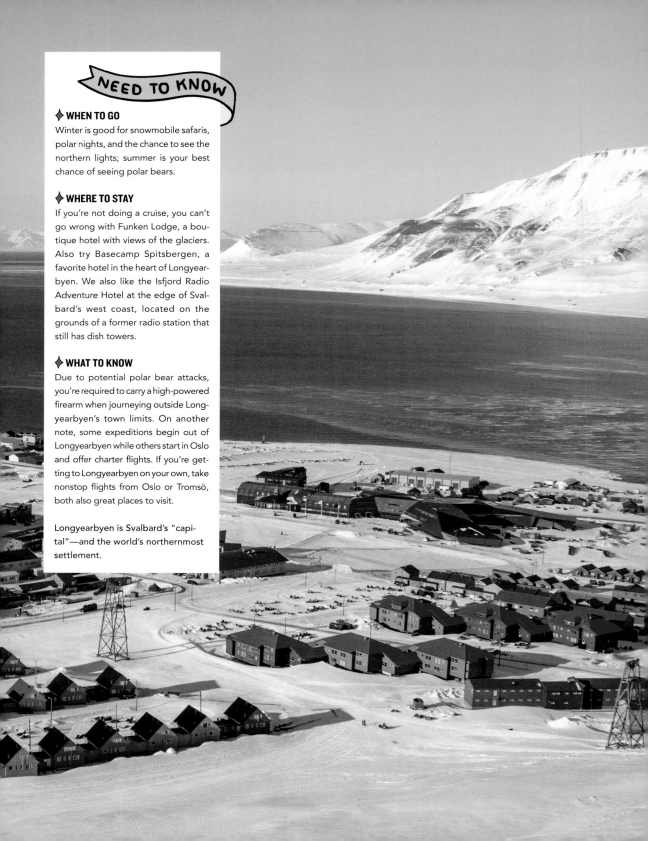

NEED TO KNOW

◆ WHEN TO GO

Winter is good for snowmobile safaris, polar nights, and the chance to see the northern lights; summer is your best chance of seeing polar bears.

◆ WHERE TO STAY

If you're not doing a cruise, you can't go wrong with Funken Lodge, a boutique hotel with views of the glaciers. Also try Basecamp Spitsbergen, a favorite hotel in the heart of Longyearbyen. We also like the Isfjord Radio Adventure Hotel at the edge of Svalbard's west coast, located on the grounds of a former radio station that still has dish towers.

◆ WHAT TO KNOW

Due to potential polar bear attacks, you're required to carry a high-powered firearm when journeying outside Longyearbyen's town limits. On another note, some expeditions begin out of Longyearbyen while others start in Oslo and offer charter flights. If you're getting to Longyearbyen on your own, take nonstop flights from Oslo or Tromsö, both also great places to visit.

Longyearbyen is Svalbard's "capital"—and the world's northernmost settlement.

GO POLAR BEAR PEEPING NEAR THE NORTH POLE.
Spitsbergen, Norway

Roughly 300 polar bears consider the area (and ice) around Spitsbergen home.

THE LGBTQIA+ LOWDOWN Norway's progressive spirit celebrates the queer community this far north. Svalbard even has its own Pride celebration in Longyearbyen, a town of 2,700 people.

Halfway between Norway and the North Pole, the island of Spitsbergen (in the Svalbard archipelago) offers a dramatically rugged landscape and Longyearbyen, the world's northernmost settlement, complete with hotels, museums, and a craft brewery.

More than 3,000 polar bears live throughout Svalbard (outnumbering humans). Though encountering one walking around Longyearbyen is rare (and potentially dangerous), guided snowmobile excursions and cruise expeditions offer chances to see polar bears from a safe distance.

A popular winter activity, snowmobile safaris typically venture to the east coast, which is colder and has more ice. You'll see breathtaking scenery like glaciers and frozen rivers, and you may spot reindeer, arctic foxes, and, what you likely came here for, polar bears. As a bonus, visiting Spitsbergen in the winter gives you the chance to go dogsledding and possibly see the magical northern lights.

If you have the time and resources, a summer cruise expedition considerably ups the odds of seeing polar bears. Ships, including those offered by National Geographic Expeditions, will spend more time looking for the bears and can get you closer to pack ice and coastal areas where they might be. Plus, you'll have the unforgettable experience of sailing the Svalbard archipelago under the midnight sun, taking smaller boat rides alongside incredible glaciers and icebergs, and visiting places like Hornsund (one of the most beautiful fjords in Svalbard) and Northwest Spitsbergen National Park (a great spot for hiking and kayaking).

If a cruise isn't an option, you can still do plenty from Longyearbyen. Take day trips to spot whales, seals, and the mighty walrus; go on a kayak tour; or join guided hikes to Plateau Mountain, Hiorthfjellet, Trollsteinen (also known as Troll Rock), or Blomsterdalshøgda, which also takes you by the Global Seed Vault. The vault houses more than a million seeds and serves as a vital backup for the world's food supply.

Back in town, learn about the area's history, geology, and wildlife at the Svalbard Museum; put on your explorer's hat at the North Pole Expedition Museum; and sample craft beer at Svalbard Bryggeri (the world's northernmost brewery). For a fascinating experience, take a boat trip to Pyramiden, a former Russian mining town abandoned in 1998 that looks frozen in time.

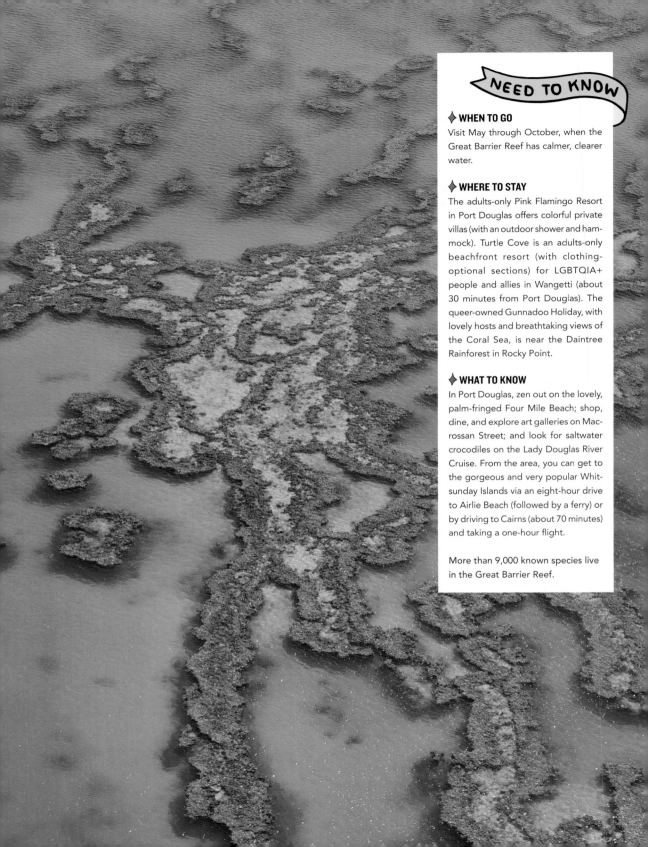

◆ WHEN TO GO

Visit May through October, when the Great Barrier Reef has calmer, clearer water.

◆ WHERE TO STAY

The adults-only Pink Flamingo Resort in Port Douglas offers colorful private villas (with an outdoor shower and hammock). Turtle Cove is an adults-only beachfront resort (with clothing-optional sections) for LGBTQIA+ people and allies in Wangetti (about 30 minutes from Port Douglas). The queer-owned Gunnadoo Holiday, with lovely hosts and breathtaking views of the Coral Sea, is near the Daintree Rainforest in Rocky Point.

◆ WHAT TO KNOW

In Port Douglas, zen out on the lovely, palm-fringed Four Mile Beach; shop, dine, and explore art galleries on Macrossan Street; and look for saltwater crocodiles on the Lady Douglas River Cruise. From the area, you can get to the gorgeous and very popular Whitsunday Islands via an eight-hour drive to Airlie Beach (followed by a ferry) or by driving to Cairns (about 70 minutes) and taking a one-hour flight.

More than 9,000 known species live in the Great Barrier Reef.

SWIM ABOVE THE WORLD'S LARGEST CORAL REEF SYSTEM.

Great Barrier Reef, Queensland, Australia

A humphead wrasse and diver share a "kiss" underwater at the Great Barrier Reef.

THE LGBTQIA+ LOWDOWN Cairns and Port Douglas, gateways to the Great Barrier Reef, are very queer friendly. We preferred Port Douglas, a laid-back seaside town and host of the Hot and Steamy Festival, an LGBTQIA+ event featuring a pool party, dance fests, luau, and drag shows.

OK, we cheated, because this is more like swimming on the wild side rather than spotting wildlife on land. But the Great Barrier Reef is such an astonishing place (it's the largest living thing in the world!) that we just had to include it.

Located off the coast of Queensland, the Great Barrier Reef is the world's largest reef system and an absolute must-see for divers and snorkelers with its 1,600 species of fish, 134 species of sharks and rays, 30 species of whales and dolphins, and 700 species of hard and soft coral.

If you're interested in snorkeling, book a day tour with Wavelength Reef Cruises, an eco-certified company that offers smaller group excursions and is owned by local marine biologists. The company visits popular reefs such as Tongue, Opal, and St. Crispin (we spotted dolphins and whales en route, via high-speed catamaran), with the skipper picking the best spot based on the day's conditions. With three opportunities to snorkel, and thanks to the incredibly friendly and helpful staff, we saw colorful coral gardens, reef sharks, rays, turtles, giant clams, and a variety of fish, including the Maori wrasse and clownfish.

Other companies, such as Quicksilver Cruises, offer excursions where you can choose between scuba diving and snorkeling. The company also has a platform on Agincourt Reef where you can view an underwater gallery, take a semisubmersible coral reef viewing tour, and do an "Ocean Walker" helmet dive—all while keeping your hair dry.

Another option is to book a shorter, half-day excursion to one of the inner reefs, which you can reach in half the time. The Low Isles, for example, are just nine miles (14 km) off the coast of Port Douglas. Tours here allow you to snorkel directly from the beach in search of sea turtles and tropical fish, so it's a good choice for families with young children, those who prefer being close to land or having beach time with their reef experience, and anyone not comfortable with a two-hour boat ride.

Back on land, don't miss a visit to the Daintree Rainforest, a 140-million-year-old gem and the world's oldest tropical rainforest (about 90 minutes from Port Douglas). Swim in Mossman Gorge, see flora and fauna on canopy walks, and continue on a scenic drive to Cape Tribulation, a stunning site where the rainforest meets the Great Barrier Reef.

CHAPTER 8

Get Your THEME ON

Destinations with one thing to focus on are fun (hello, beach vacation), but we also love a good theme to inspire a memorable trip. Whether becoming one with *Downton Abbey* on a thrilling U.K. castle tour, enjoying Gay Days and the Animal Kingdom Theme Park at Walt Disney World, two-stepping in Nashville and Dollywood, or doing some California dreaming, we're here to help. No matter how you travel or who you travel with, embracing plenty of good old-fashioned quirky fun offers something for everyone.

CELEBRATE GAY DAYS AT WALT DISNEY WORLD.
Orlando, Florida, U.S.A.

Gay Days at Walt Disney World are all about amping up Pride in the parks.

THE LGBTQIA+ LOWDOWN With annual park Gay Days and a Disney Pride Collection (100 percent of profits during Pride month are donated to charities that support the LGBTQIA+ community), Walt Disney World continues to welcome the queer community.

With so many Disney parks, it's hard to choose a favorite, but we especially love Walt Disney World's Animal Kingdom Theme Park. This zoological delight, which opened on Earth Day in 1998, sees fewer visitors than any other Disney park but deserves a top spot for its animal-themed attractions and conservation efforts.

One of the reasons we love Animal Kingdom is its accessibility benefits, which allow those who would be challenged by other natural environments (like safari destinations) to safely experience majestic animals and landscapes up close.

For rides, we love them all. Start with Avatar Flight of Passage, where you can ride atop a winged mountain banshee for a 3D-simulated flight over Pandora's otherworldly landscape. Next, hit up Maharajah Jungle Trek, where you'll cross footbridges and see rushing waterfalls in a magical jungle environment. See Asian tigers and spot water buffalo, deer, foxes, and more. And don't miss Gorilla Falls Exploration Trail, where you'll be mesmerized watching the world's largest primates eat, play, and interact in a huge habitat.

For more animal spotting, hop on an open-air vehicle for the Kilimanjaro Safaris, a guided tour through 110 acres (45 ha) of open plains, forests, and rocky wetlands on a savanna. Look out for roaming giraffes, baboons, elephants, and lions.

At the Conservation Station, you can learn all about how the animals are cared for, including seeing the Veterinary Treatment Room and maybe even catching a glimpse of a procedure in progress.

When you're ready to take in a show, don't miss the Festival of the Lion King, filled with songs, pageantry, and puppetry. For another magical experience, head to the Tree of Life (which is more than 145 towering feet tall/44 meters) for a light show where fireflies dance and flicker. Shows take place every 10 minutes after dark, and in between you can look for the more than 300 animals carved into the tree.

Our favorite meal is at the upscale (but still approachable) Tiffins, especially if you can get a seat on the porch overlooking the river. Inside, you can see original sketches by Joe Rohde (the Imagineer responsible for Animal Kingdom) and art from Africa. No matter where you sit, get the bread service.

NEED TO KNOW

◆ WHEN TO GO

The first week in June for Gay Days at Disney World, an unofficial event first organized by the LGBTQIA+ community in 1991 to increase Pride visibility in the parks. What started as a few thousand folks has now grown to hundreds of thousands of people—including couples, families, and groups of friends—all decked out in rainbows and Disney gear. In 2023, Disney made Pride an official event. The parks are less crowded in September, when kids are back in school. January and February are the quietest, but it will probably be too cool to hang by the pool.

◆ WHERE TO STAY

Stay at Disney's Animal Kingdom Lodge to see resident flamingos, relax by the pools, and be surrounded by four savannas home to hundreds of roaming animals, including zebras, giraffes, and gnu.

◆ WHAT TO KNOW

If you have time, head to EPCOT for some great dining. EPCOT's International Food & Wine Festival (July through November) lets you experience global cuisine by sampling delicacies throughout each country. One thing we love about all the parks—aside from the rides, of course—is the food, but especially the consideration of vegetarians and vegans, with plenty of plant-based options.

Embrace the rainbow in Disney's Magic Kingdom.

NEED TO KNOW

◆ WHEN TO GO
June brings Mid-South Pride and Tri-State Black Pride in Memphis and Nashville Pride.

◆ WHERE TO STAY
The Peabody Hotel (Memphis) is in the heart of the city and features an adorable duck parade. The Kimpton Aertson (Nashville) has chic interiors, an awesome rooftop pool, and a complimentary wine happy hour. Dollywood's DreamMore Resort and Spa is an award-winning hotel with exclusive park perks.

◆ WHAT TO KNOW
Dollywood does its best to accommodate people with disabilities. Its tram and many rides are wheelchair accessible, and the park offers a calming room for guests who may have sensory overload and need a quiet space.

More than 350 yards (320 m) of fabric cover the Pool Room at Elvis Presley's Graceland.

BREAK OUT YOUR COWBOY BOOTS AND RHINESTONE JACKETS ON A FUN- AND MUSIC-FILLED TRIP THROUGH TENNESSEE.

Nashville, Dollywood, and Memphis, Tennessee, U.S.A.

THE LGBTQIA+ LOWDOWN Though Tennessee is conservative, Nashville and Memphis have out-and-proud queer communities, and Dolly Parton, a beloved ally, strongly influences the inclusiveness of Dollywood (and the surrounding areas).

Tennessee, with its lively cities, historic sites, and famous southern cooking, doesn't make you work hard to find a good time.

Start in Memphis at Graceland, where you don't have to be an Elvis Presley fan to appreciate his costumes and the over-the-top decor. Then head to Mud Island to stroll along the Mississippi (and see a hydraulic model of the river) and get great views of the Memphis skyline.

At the National Civil Rights Museum, you can pay your respects at the place where Dr. Martin Luther King, Jr., was assassinated in 1968. Visit the room where he spent his last hours, and see hundreds of artifacts, films, exhibits, and interactive media.

At night, join the crowds and take in the sounds of Beale Street, one of the most iconic streets in America. For queer nightlife, check out Atomic Rose for drag shows, bingo, and dancing, and Dru's Bar in Midtown for karaoke and comedy shows.

After a few days in Memphis, make the three-hour drive to Nashville. See shows at famed music venues like the Grand Ole Opry and Ryman Auditorium. Visit the Country Music Hall of Fame and Johnny Cash Museum, and honky-tonk hop at Tootsies, Nudie's, and other bars on Lower Broadway.

Elsewhere in the city, browse boutiques and adorable eateries on 12 South, pose for photos at the "WhatLiftsYou" (Angel Wings) mural in the Gulch, and hit up Centennial Park in Midtown for a picnic near the Nashville Parthenon (a full-scale reproduction of the Athens original). Head inside to see the gold-leafed Athena. At 42 feet (13 m), she's the tallest indoor statue in the country.

When the sun sets, hop on the Big Drag Bus for hilarious drag queen performances. The ride is tons of fun in a very mixed and welcoming space. The bus starts and stops at Tribe, a queer bar that's also super straight friendly. Continue the party there, or head to the Lipstick Lounge in trendy East Nashville. One of the last remaining lesbian bars in the U.S., it's a place for "everyone that's human."

From Nashville, drive to Dollywood at the base of the Great Smoky Mountains. At this 150-acre (61 ha) "dream park" by icon and queer ally Dolly Parton, you can ride roller coasters and take a scenic train ride on the Dollywood Express. Don't leave without trying the glazed ham and mashed potatoes at Aunt Granny's Restaurant or seeing a performance like the "My People, My Music" show, where members of Dolly Parton's family take the stage.

The Nashville skyline and John Seigenthaler Pedestrian Bridge

CELEBRATE MARIA AND MOZART WHERE THE HILLS ARE ALIVE.
Salzburg, Austria

THE LGBTQIA+ LOWDOWN Austria legalized registered partnerships in 2010, and in 2015, the Constitutional Court of Austria legalized adoption by queer couples. Salzburg goes even further with the Salzburg Global LGBT Forum (est. 2013), a network of more than 75 human rights leaders that supports LGBTQIA+ people around the world.

Salzburg, the birthplace of renowned composer Wolfgang Amadeus Mozart, sits on the German border with views of the Eastern Alps. It's known for stunning baroque architecture, its historic center, cobbled streets, hidden alleys, and a picturesque bridge over the Salzach River.

Start in Old Town, a UNESCO World Heritage site, and see Mozart's birthplace by visiting the Hagenauer Haus at No. 9 Getreidegasse (Salzburg's busiest pedestrian area). Tour the home's original rooms, explore letters and portraits from Mozart's life, and see his violin and clavichord. From there, weave through the streets for more historic buildings, churches, and squares: Domplatz (Cathedral Square) for a large church with a statue of the Virgin Mary; Alter Markt with stalls for food and crafts; and Residenzplatz (Residence Square) for one of the most beautiful fountains in Salzburg and a filming location for *The Sound of Music*.

For more *The Sound of Music* love, head to Nonnberg Abbey, where you can walk through the gate and sing your own rendition of "I Have Confidence!" while taking in incredible views of the city. Next, go to Mirabell Palace and Gardens and *do-re-mi* your way through the famous fountain and garden, ending on the iconic steps where Maria and the children performed their grand finale. To get the full experience, board a big red bus on Panorama's Original Sound of Music Tour and wind through hills alive with music (they play tunes on the bus). See the house where the fictional von Trapp family lived, the gazebo where Captain von Trapp kissed Maria for the first time, and more fun movie highlights.

For a different perspective, consider the queer city tour led by Roman Forisch, a native of Salzburg and certified Austria guide. This experience highlights how those in the LGBTQIA+ community have influenced the 1,000-year history of Salzburg (summer dates only).

More sites to wander include the Fortress Hohensalzburg landmark, a preserved medieval castle (the largest in Europe); Makartsteg Bridge (Love Lock bridge), which crosses the Salzach River with thousands of locks attached by lovers from all over the world; and the Salzburg State Theatre with more than 400 shows a year, including opera, dance, theater, and LGBTQIA+ features.

For dining, go to St. Peter Stiftskeller, Europe's oldest restaurant (from A.D. 803), in St. Peter's Abbey, a monastery and former cathedral built in 696. At Restaurant Meissl & Schadn Salzburg, order the *paprikahendl* (chicken paprikash), a Hungarian dish, or *tafelspitz*, which is boiled beef with root vegetables (they have a great vegetarian version). Tucked away in an unassuming alley, you'll find the famous sausage stand, Balkan Grill Walter, serving for more than 40 years. For drinks, go to the Dark Eagle cruising bar (men only).

Declare your love at Makartsteg Bridge—also called "Love Lock Bridge."

NEED TO KNOW

◆ WHEN TO GO

The Salzburg Festival (est. 1920) celebrates drama and arts with lively programs over the summer. In January and early February, celebrate Mozart's birthday with the Salzburg Mozarteum Foundation and classical music. Jazz & the City is a music festival held over five days in October that draws people from all over the world. The Homosexual Initiative Salzburg (HOSI) hosts Pride in September with a week of parties and parades.

◆ WHERE TO STAY

Arthotel Blaue Gans, Salzburg's oldest inn, is only a few doors down from Mozart's house and is full of cool, eclectic, and quirky art; it's one of our favorite spots in the world to sleep. Or try Auersperg, a family-run boutique hotel for three generations that offers an organic breakfast, spa, and magical gardens. Outside of town, stay at Schloss Leopoldskron, a historic castle built in 1736 (and a filming location for *The Sound of Music*).

◆ WHAT TO KNOW

For a day trip, go to the tiny village of Hallstatt, a UNESCO World Heritage site known for its salt production—which began in the Bronze Age—and a fairy tale–like feel on a lake. Stroll around to see its picture-perfect homes, shops, churches, restaurants, and lovely waterfall. You'll be convinced you're in a dream.

Salzburg's cityscape and famous Salzburg Cathedral

SALZBURG

Of course it's cliche to say the hills are alive with the sound of music, but it's too true in Salzburg not to say it. Walk through Salzburg's historic Old Town with its cobbled streets and its own music history, then set out to explore the countryside. It's impossible not to be moved by the vibrant green mountains, picturesque bridges, and rivers and lakes that dot this delightful Austrian region. And for a pleasant surprise: We never knew Austrian wine was so good.

◆ WHEN TO GO

Spring and autumn bring the best weather. Time your visit for Pride Cymru in Cardiff (August), which includes family-friendly celebrations, or the Iris Prize LGBTQIA+ film festival (October).

◆ WHERE TO STAY

In Cardiff, try Ty Rosa for a quaint guesthouse that's a short walk to the city center. For Highclere Castle, stay in an on-site lodge or the nearby town of Newbury at the Vineyard Hotel & Spa or Hare & Hounds. For Warwick Castle, you're just 20 minutes away from scenic Stratford-Upon-Avon (the birthplace of William Shakespeare), where we like Hotel du Vin and Hotel Indigo. In Windsor, try Oakley Court or Fairmont Windsor Park. For Leeds Castle, stay on the estate and choose from bed-and-breakfasts, royal cottages, and glamping tents.

◆ WHAT TO KNOW

When renting a car in Europe, it's much cheaper to get a vehicle with a manual transmission. (Be sure to request an automatic if you don't know how to drive stick; manual is the default.) In Cardiff, browse unique artifacts at the National Museum, shop for vinyl at Spillers Records (the world's oldest record shop), see a rugby match at Principality Stadium, stroll the waterfront along Cardiff Bay, and shop in Victorian-era arcades. Or enjoy time in nature at Brecon Beacons National Park (about an hour away from the city). From the park, you're a quick drive from Hay-on-Wye, known for its vast and adorable bookshops.

Tour Highclere Castle, the filming location of *Downton Abbey*, in Hampshire.

FEEL LIKE ROYALTY ON A TOUR OF U.K. CASTLES AND CHARMING TOWNS.

Cardiff, Warwickshire, Hampshire, and Kent, U.K.

THE LGBTQIA+ LOWDOWN The United Kingdom celebrates queer culture with festivals, events, and inclusive spaces. Cardiff, where our tour begins, has a vibrant queer scene.

When it comes to historic sites, coastal views, and an eclectic mix of modern and traditional things to do, the U.K. is hard to beat. It has more than 4,000 castles and 43,000 towns to explore. But just like a royal secretary, we're happy to help you map out a plan.

Start in Cardiff, Wales, at the 2,000-year-old Cardiff Castle. Over the centuries, it's been a Roman fort, Norman stronghold, and Victorian palace, and you'll find blended architecture from each period. Check out its spectacular rooms, like the Arab Room (with Egyptian-inspired stained glass windows and gold-leaf ceiling) and the Chaucer Room (decorated in honor of Geoffrey Chaucer, the "father of English literature"). Just 20 minutes away from Cardiff, visit Caerphilly Castle, which is Wales's largest castle and dates back to the 13th century. Explore its lakes and huge drawbridges, and see the Great Hall and medieval weapons and armor displays.

Next, drive to Warwickshire to see Warwick Castle's photogenic turrets, tour the Great Hall and State Rooms, and check out lovely gardens, medieval vaults, and a tower built for climbing (the views are terrific).

The star of *Downton Abbey*, Highclere Castle is just over an hour from Warwick Castle in Hampshire. Relive your favorite Lady Grantham-isms on a tour, then stroll the gardens and the parkland's 1,000 bucolic acres (405 ha).

Next, visit the world-famous Windsor Castle, just another hour from Highclere Castle. Originally built in the 11th century, it's the largest and oldest inhabited castle in the world, and, more famously, Queen Elizabeth II often used it for weekend trips. Admire the view from the Great Park, visit St. George's Chapel (where Meghan married Harry), and see the Changing the Guard ceremony and lavish state apartments. Don't miss Queen Mary's Dolls' House, the world's largest dollhouse, with 1,500 pieces, running water, and electricity.

Last but not least, drive to Leeds Castle in Kent. The "loveliest castle in the world" is built on two islands, surrounded by a gorgeous lake, and set on 500 picturesque acres (202 ha). King Henry VIII and his first wife, Catherine of Aragon, famously used the site. Nicknamed the "Ladies Castle," it was also home to five other medieval queens. While you're there, check out King Henry VIII's Banqueting Hall, find a secret grotto, get lost in a hedge maze, and see the dog collar museum and falconry demonstrations.

Climb a steep staircase to the 12th-century Norman Keep inside Cardiff Castle.

DO SOME CALIFORNIA DREAMIN' ALONG THE SPARKLING COAST.
Los Angeles, California, U.S.A.

Catch some sun near the Venice Beach Pride flag lifeguard tower.

THE LGBTQIA+ LOWDOWN Home to one of the largest LGBTQIA+ communities in the world, Los Angeles hosts annual events, including a Pride parade and Halloween Costume Carnaval. The Los Angeles LGBT Center is a world leader in advocacy and health services.

Known for its mellow climate, iconic Hollywood sign, palm trees, and stretches of beach, the City of Angels is a sprawling and inclusive mecca with a diverse list of experiences.

For an incredible L.A. must-see—with crowds to prove it—visit the Griffith Observatory, which opened in 1935 and is the most visited public observatory in the world. There, you'll have epic views to the Pacific Ocean, plus get to use telescopes and venture through space in their planetarium.

Because you can't come to L.A. without seeing Hollywood, make your way there next. Visit the TCL Chinese Theatre, a movie palace dating back to 1927 that shows IMAX films and hosts celebrity-studded events. Outside, get your picture on the Hollywood Walk of Fame with 2,500 terrazzo and brass stars.

Then go to West Hollywood (or WeHo), famous for its lit-up Sunset Strip and huge queer community (more than 40 percent of its residents identify as LGBTQIA+). There, you'll find tons of bars and restaurants, including the Abbey. Explore queer history at ONE Archives, which has the largest collection of LGBTQIA+ books and magazines in the world since 1952.

Finally, head to the coast for all the best beauty L.A. offers. Have lunch at Malibu Seafood for no-frills fresh fish and clam chowder. Nearby, Zuma Beach has clean water and great surf, or drive the coast to Santa Monica's Ginger Rogers Beach,

which is L.A.'s unofficial queer beach. In Santa Monica, stroll the pier and the Third Street Promenade, home to more than 80 shops, and eat at the Misfit Bar for a moody vibe and a prime rib slider that can't be beat.

Book lovers, stop at Zibby's Bookshop with its dedicated LGBTQIA+ section, full roster of events, and themes curated by experience and emotion instead of genre.

Don't miss the famous Venice Beach Boardwalk, known for its street art, performers, souvenirs, Muscle Beach outdoor gym (built in 1963), and a string of marijuana shops. On the boardwalk, head to Hotel Erwin's rooftop bar to sip drinks with incredible panoramic views of the sea and sunset. Eat at Gjelina for seasonal dishes and wood-fired pizzas, or the Butcher's Daughter for a terrific vegetarian meal. The Rose Venice is a boho eatery with great breakfast burritos in an airy and supercool space. Five minutes from Venice, eat at Mendocino Farms, a casual spot with our favorite gourmet salads and sandwiches.

Continue south to the off-the-beaten-path Manhattan Beach, the poster child for SoCal vibes. Walk or cycle the Strand bike path on the oceanfront to marvel at mansions and cute cottages, then take a break on the sand. Go to Uncle Bill's Pancake House for all-day—you guessed it—pancakes, or grab any meal at Manhattan Beach Post (get the cheddar bacon biscuits).

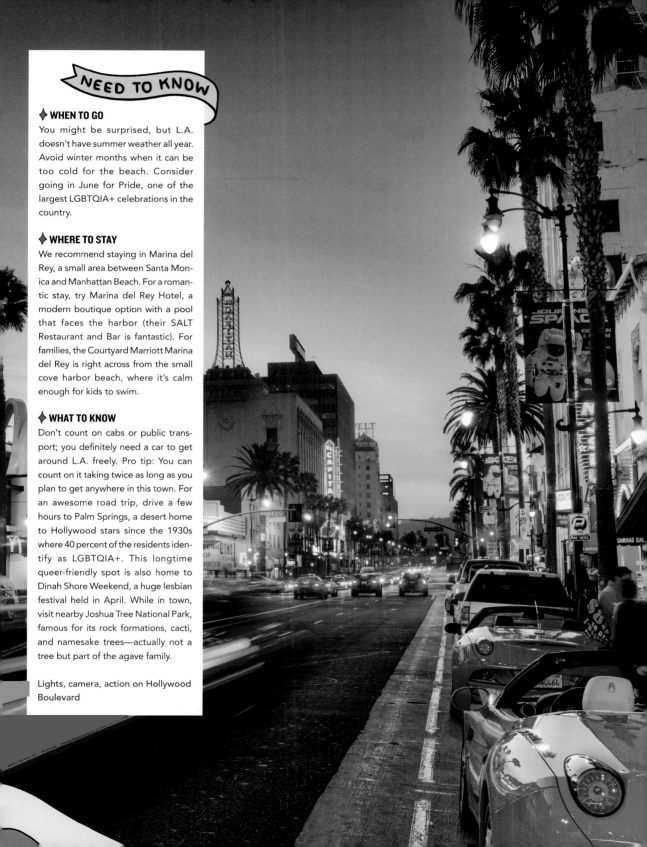

NEED TO KNOW

◆ WHEN TO GO

You might be surprised, but L.A. doesn't have summer weather all year. Avoid winter months when it can be too cold for the beach. Consider going in June for Pride, one of the largest LGBTQIA+ celebrations in the country.

◆ WHERE TO STAY

We recommend staying in Marina del Rey, a small area between Santa Monica and Manhattan Beach. For a romantic stay, try Marina del Rey Hotel, a modern boutique option with a pool that faces the harbor (their SALT Restaurant and Bar is fantastic). For families, the Courtyard Marriott Marina del Rey is right across from the small cove harbor beach, where it's calm enough for kids to swim.

◆ WHAT TO KNOW

Don't count on cabs or public transport; you definitely need a car to get around L.A. freely. Pro tip: You can count on it taking twice as long as you plan to get anywhere in this town. For an awesome road trip, drive a few hours to Palm Springs, a desert home to Hollywood stars since the 1930s where 40 percent of the residents identify as LGBTQIA+. This longtime queer-friendly spot is also home to Dinah Shore Weekend, a huge lesbian festival held in April. While in town, visit nearby Joshua Tree National Park, famous for its rock formations, cacti, and namesake trees—actually not a tree but part of the agave family.

Lights, camera, action on Hollywood Boulevard

◆ NEED TO KNOW

◆ WHEN TO GO

Summer means lobster rolls and seaside activities in Mystic (many things close after Labor Day in the coastal towns), and fall means apple picking and gorgeous fall foliage around the state.

◆ WHERE TO STAY

In Mystic, the Whaler's Inn has beachy charm, and the Mermaid Inn of Mystic is a lesbian-owned B&B in a downtown Victorian Italianate home. In Salisbury, White Hart Inn has a *Gilmore Girls* vibe—including a lobby that's become the town hangout, with a reading room, roaring fire in winter, and cozy guest rooms. If a resort feel suits you, try luxurious Troutbeck (20 minutes away in Amenia, New York) in a natural setting with hammocks by the stream, a pool, and a restaurant with dishes almost too beautiful to eat.

◆ WHAT TO KNOW

To do the whole trip from Mystic to Salisbury, allot three to four days. Add onto your trip if you want to see more of our favorite small towns in the state: Chester, Old Saybrook, Stonington, and Sharon. If you've had your fill of small towns, head to Hartford, one of America's oldest cities. Eat at Chez Est, a popular restaurant and cabaret space that's been serving the LGBTQIA+ community for more than 46 years.

Explore the Mystic Seaport Museum's *Joseph Conrad* and reconstructed coastal village.

ENJOY CHARMING TOWNS, SANDY BEACHES, AND STUNNING WATERFALLS.
Essex, Mystic, Kent, and Salisbury, Connecticut, U.S.A.

A picturesque view of the Mystic River

THE LGBTQIA+ LOWDOWN Connecticut is one of the most queer-friendly states in America. It legalized same-sex marriage in 2008, and state law bans discrimination based on sexual orientation and gender identity. It was the first state to join the LGBTQ+ Travel Association (IGLTA).

Though upstate New York and the Jersey Shore get a lot of love, Connecticut is our hidden gem. Only 70 miles (113 km) wide and just more than 100 miles (161 km) long, you can easily drive from its sparkling coastline to its rolling hills and picturesque towns.

Start in Essex, rightfully called one of the cutest small towns in America, where you'll find an adorable Main Street, historic homes and buildings, and a waterfront made for strolling. Ride the historic Essex Steam Train, along the scenic Connecticut River Valley. Stay at the Griswold Inn, dating from 1776. Eat dinner in the taproom full of Old World charm, and listen to musicians on stage. For sandwiches, soups, and the best breakfast burrito, go to Olive Oyl's, a little gourmet spot down Main Street with a small seating area outside.

Next, head to the coastline in Mystic and join the lines for a fresh slice of Mystic Pizza, famous for the 1980s movie of the same name. Nearby, visit Bank Square Books for their selection of queer titles, then spend an afternoon at Mystic Seaport Museum, the largest museum of its kind in the U.S. Wander through its re-created seaport village (with shops from the 1800s transported from other parts of New England), explore the shipyard, and take historic boats on a river cruise.

When you're hungry, head to S&P Oyster—complete with outdoor firepit tables—where you can enjoy your linguine and clams or oysters on the half shell with waterfront views. Sift Bake Shop is the perfect breakfast spot with indoor and outdoor seating and pastries to drool over.

After Mystic, head north to Kent, a fairy-tale town and home to Kent Falls State Park. Take a short walk through a red covered bridge (on an accessible path) and get up close to a series of waterfalls cascading into a pool. If you want to picnic, stop first at 109 Cheese & Wine for charcuterie.

Continue to the tiny towns of Salisbury (with nearby Lakeville), where Litchfield County and the Berkshires meet. It's small but has activities like fishing and canoeing plus a segment of the Appalachian Trail for hiking. Pride in the Hills Fund is an organization that supports, inspires, and celebrates LGBTQIA+ people in Litchfield Hills. In Salisbury, our favorite go-to for meals with locally sourced farm burgers and handcrafted cocktails is the acclaimed taproom at White Hart Inn (an original farmhouse from 1806). The inn's café, Provisions, is perfect for a gourmet sandwich and brownie to enjoy on the great lawn.

For our favorite hike, drive 30 miles (48 km) north and cross the Massachusetts border to see Bash Bish Falls, the highest waterfall in the state (it's a mild to moderate hike).

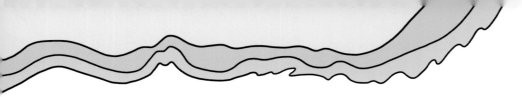

REVEL IN RELIVING *THE LORD OF THE RINGS* FILMS—AND ENJOY A REALLY GOOD SOAK.

Auckland to Tongariro National Park, New Zealand

A Progress Pride flag spans an Auckland crosswalk.

THE LGBTQIA+ LOWDOWN New Zealand is a progressive country that's ranked among the most queer friendly in the world. Discrimination based on sexual orientation and gender identity/expression has been illegal since 1993, and same-sex marriage and adoption were legalized in 2013.

Though it's been more than two decades since *The Lord of the Rings* movies first captivated audiences, people around the world still journey to New Zealand to see the iconic film locations. Even if you're not a big-time Frodo fan, the scenery is fantastic and nearby thermal baths are the perfect way to relax. So, grab your "precious" and go on an epic journey through rings and hot springs.

Start in Auckland with the must-see Sky Tower Auckland, rising more than 1,000 feet (305 m). Check out the panoramic view stretching nearly 50 miles (80 km) in every direction.

Next, learn about Maori history at the Auckland War Memorial Museum. Then head to the Auckland Art Gallery Toi o Tāmaki to browse more than 15,000 works by artists from New Zealand and around the world.

For nature, visit One Tree Hill (or Maungakiekie), a historic and sacred site atop a nearly 600-foot (183 m) volcano. Or ferry to Great Barrier Island for amazing stargazing (it's an International Dark Sky Sanctuary).

Craving some beach time? Hit our queer favorites: Mission Bay and Ladies Bay, which is swimsuit optional and, ironically, more popular with men.

At night, check out some of Auckland's cool queer spaces

such as the Eagle Bar, Caluzzi Bar & Cabaret (for deliciously over-the-top drag shows), and Family Bar and Club.

From Auckland, drive two hours for some downtime at Te Aroha Mineral Spas, a local favorite for more than 100 years. Enjoy soaking in a wooden tub and soothe your body in mineral-rich waters believed to have healing powers.

Next, make your way to Matamata, where rolling green hills give way to Middle-earth and the Hobbiton Movie Set Tour. During this unforgettable experience, you'll step into the Shire. Get a guided tour of the 12-acre (5 ha) movie set and famous sites like Hobbit Holes and the Green Dragon Inn, and learn about the moviemaking process.

After, continue your journey to Rotorua for more hot springs. The Waikite Valley Thermal Pools has six soaking areas, while the Polynesian Spa offers 30 mineral pools fed from natural springs.

After being rejuvenated, drive two hours to—gasp!— Mordor, also known as Tongariro National Park. Founded in 1887, this UNESCO World Heritage site is the oldest park in New Zealand (and one of the oldest in the world).

For some post-hike R & R, check out Wairakei Terraces and Thermal Health Spa for outdoor pools (including adults-only options) in the Wairakei geothermal valley.

NEED TO KNOW

✦ WHEN TO GO

December through March brings sunny days and ideal weather, with highs usually in the mid-70s.

✦ WHERE TO STAY

In Auckland, the Grand Mercure is minutes from the waterfront and has a rooftop bar with amazing views. In Rotorua, Regal Palms Resort has suites with individual hot spa pools, a heated outdoor pool, and a mini–golf course. In Tongariro National Park, spend the night under the stars (or stay in a chalet, if you prefer) at Discovery Lodge.

✦ WHAT TO KNOW

For more *Lord of the Rings* sites, extend your trip to Wellington, a four-hour drive from Tongariro National Park or a quick flight from Taupō or Rotorua. Visit Mount Victoria, a filming location for the Hobbiton Woods. Also go to Wētā Workshop and Wētā Cave, where you can see props and artifacts from *The Lord of the Rings* series and other movies.

Auckland's Sky Tower skims the clouds at twilight.

CHAPTER 9

Fun
HAUNTS
and Spooky
SPIRITS

We'll give you the inside scoop on DIY and professional ghost tours and other chilling experiences in some of the world's most haunted cities: must-see places such as Salem, New Orleans, and Edinburgh. We'll also share the spookiest sites, "spirited" restaurants, and hotels where things go bump in the night (and some non-haunted options for a wind-down happy hour or a good cuddle under the sheets).

◆ WHEN TO GO

Pride is held in late October and carries a Halloween theme. Outside of the spooky season, you'll find the best weather from March through June.

◆ WHERE TO STAY

Dating back to 1873, the Hamilton-Turner Inn was Savannah's first house with electricity. Nowadays, you may want to sleep with the lights on to avoid the ghost of a child who perished there. The Marshall House once served as a hospital, and guests report seeing shadowy figures and faucets running all on their own. At the historic Kehoe House, the original owners who died in the house are believed to still live there (reportedly in room 201). And at the 17Hundred90 Inn & Restaurant, a scorned lover named Anne likes to haunt couples in room 204.

◆ WHAT TO KNOW

Just 15 minutes outside of town, Bonaventure Cemetery is one of the most popular burial sites in America and is known for ornate stone monuments and massive oak trees. Take your time exploring its 100-plus acres (40 ha); it's a wonderful place for peaceful reflections under Spanish moss. Plus, you never know what you'll see, hear, or feel.

Installed in 1858, the Forsyth Park fountain is an iconic feature of Savannah's 30-acre (12 ha) park.

LOOK FOR WHAT'S LURKING UNDER THE SPANISH MOSS.

Savannah, Georgia, U.S.A.

Savannah's historic cemeteries have long contributed to the city's spookiness.

THE LGBTQIA+ LOWDOWN Savannah is an open-minded city where the LGBTQIA+ community is welcome and celebrated. You'll find an LGBTQIA+ center and weekend-long Pride (and Halloween) celebration with a masquerade ball, a parade, drag shows, and a "Downtown Takeover."

Georgia's oldest city (established in 1733) is a coastal gem. You'll find grand mansions (several turned into B&Bs), streets lined with trees that drip with Spanish moss, and lovely squares. But don't be fooled: Savannah is also filled with stories of evil deeds and lingering spirits.

As a city built over burial grounds—and the site of multiple Civil War battles, massive yellow fever outbreaks, fires, alleged murders, and unfortunate "accidents"—we're not surprised that the American Institute of Parapsychology named Savannah "America's Most Haunted City."

To learn about Savannah's ghosts, take a walking tour with Blue Orb or 6th Sense World, or drive around with family-friendly Hearse Ghost Ride. DIY your own ghost tour and visit Wright Square (also known as Hanging Square) and Factors Walk, where boutiques and galleries sit on a former Cotton Exchange, which cruelly forced enslaved people into dangerous labor.

Don't miss the Mercer Williams House, where socialite Jim Williams infamously shot his hot-tempered (and much younger) lover and assistant, Danny Hansford. According to

legend, Hansford's ghost hung around to wreak havoc on his murderer, and Williams eventually died of a heart attack in his study . . . the very same room in which he'd shot Hansford. Their story was popularized by the novel and film adaption *Midnight in the Garden of Good and Evil*, which featured appearances by Lady Chablis, a pioneer drag performer and one of the town's beloved queer residents. Both Hansford and Williams are believed to linger in the house, and unsuspecting visitors claim to feel a creepy presence in and around it.

Nearby, visit Forsyth Park and admire its flowers and gorgeous fountain from 1858. Beneath it was once a morgue tunnel where yellow fever victims were laid to rest, and it's said that some of those victims still like to call the park home.

To eat and drink with the dead, head to Moon River Brewing Company, Savannah's most haunted restaurant. A former yellow fever and Civil War hospital, the building is said to be teeming with spirits. Also try the 250-year-old Pirates' House, where you may get served by the ghost of Captain Flint.

GET BEWITCHED AND BEWILDERED (BUT HOPEFULLY NOT BOTHERED).
Salem, Massachusetts, U.S.A.

The House of the Seven Gables inspired Nathaniel Hawthorne's famous novel.

THE LGBTQIA+ LOWDOWN Salem earned a perfect score from the Human Rights Campaign's Municipal Equality Index. North Shore Pride hosts yearly events, including a Pride parade and festival, while the North Shore Alliance of GLBTQ Youth (NAGLY) empowers queer youth.

Salem, a waterfront city in northeastern Massachusetts, is believed to have gotten its name from the Hebrew word for peace. However, in 1692, Salem erupted into a devastating war against morality in the form of a literal witch hunt.

Fueled by religious insecurities and paranoia, the infamous witch trials drove Salem to mass hysteria. Trials were a circus act of far-flung accusations and little evidence, yet 19 people lost their lives.

Before visiting haunted sites, check out the Salem Witch Museum for a more in-depth look at witch trials held in Salem and around the world, then pay respects to fallen victims at the Salem Witch Trials Memorial. Just steps away, you'll find Old Burying Point, one of America's oldest cemeteries (dating back to 1637), which may be home to Martha Corey, a tragic target of the witch trials, or Jonathan Hathorne, the notorious "hanging judge" who presided over the trials and refused to apologize for it.

Next, head to Howard Street Cemetery, where the spirit of Giles Corey (husband of Martha and an accused witch who was executed) is said to roam. Don't miss Proctor's Ledge, which historians have confirmed as the site of hangings and makeshift burials and today is a place where people claim to feel dark energy or encounter a "woman in white."

Explore the Witch House, the only remaining building with a direct link to the witch trials. The house was purchased in 1675 by Judge Jonathan Corwin, another unremorseful soul who sentenced accused witches to death. Take a tour if you dare; maybe you'll hear voices or experience chills.

Don't miss House of the Seven Gables (also known as the Turner-Ingersoll Mansion), which inspired Nathaniel Hawthorne's supernatural novel of the same name published in 1851. Touring the house, you might see inexplicable flickering lights and feel the presence of spirits, especially near a secret staircase that leads to the attic. Some say they've spotted Susannah Ingersoll, who lived here in the 1800s.

When it's time for a meal, Turner's Seafood is a family-run restaurant inside Salem's historic Lyceum Hall that serves fresh New England seafood. You might even meet Bridget Bishop, the first person executed in the Salem witch trials, who is believed to visit tables.

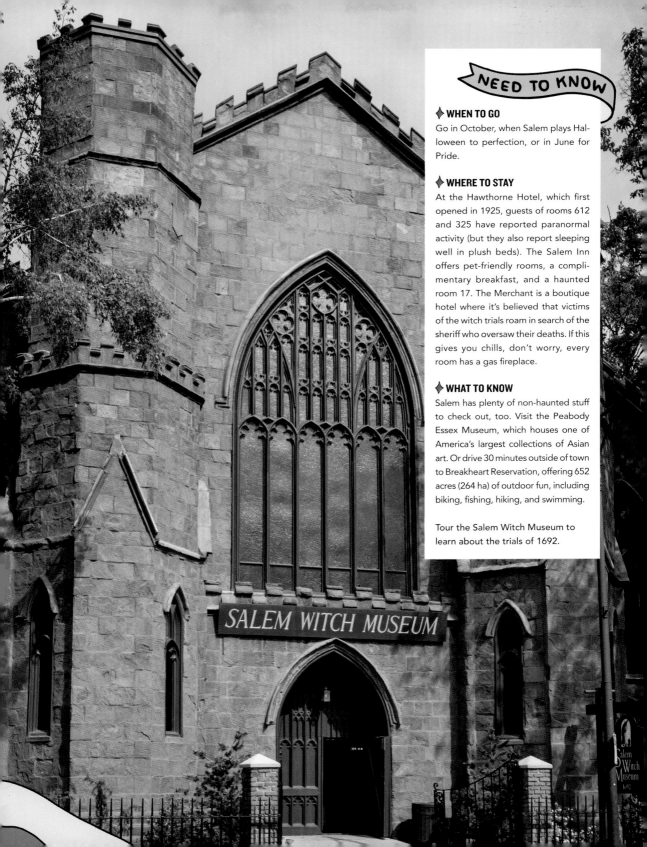

NEED TO KNOW

◆ WHEN TO GO
Go in October, when Salem plays Halloween to perfection, or in June for Pride.

◆ WHERE TO STAY
At the Hawthorne Hotel, which first opened in 1925, guests of rooms 612 and 325 have reported paranormal activity (but they also report sleeping well in plush beds). The Salem Inn offers pet-friendly rooms, a complimentary breakfast, and a haunted room 17. The Merchant is a boutique hotel where it's believed that victims of the witch trials roam in search of the sheriff who oversaw their deaths. If this gives you chills, don't worry, every room has a gas fireplace.

◆ WHAT TO KNOW
Salem has plenty of non-haunted stuff to check out, too. Visit the Peabody Essex Museum, which houses one of America's largest collections of Asian art. Or drive 30 minutes outside of town to Breakheart Reservation, offering 652 acres (264 ha) of outdoor fun, including biking, fishing, hiking, and swimming.

Tour the Salem Witch Museum to learn about the trials of 1692.

SALEM WITCH MUSEUM

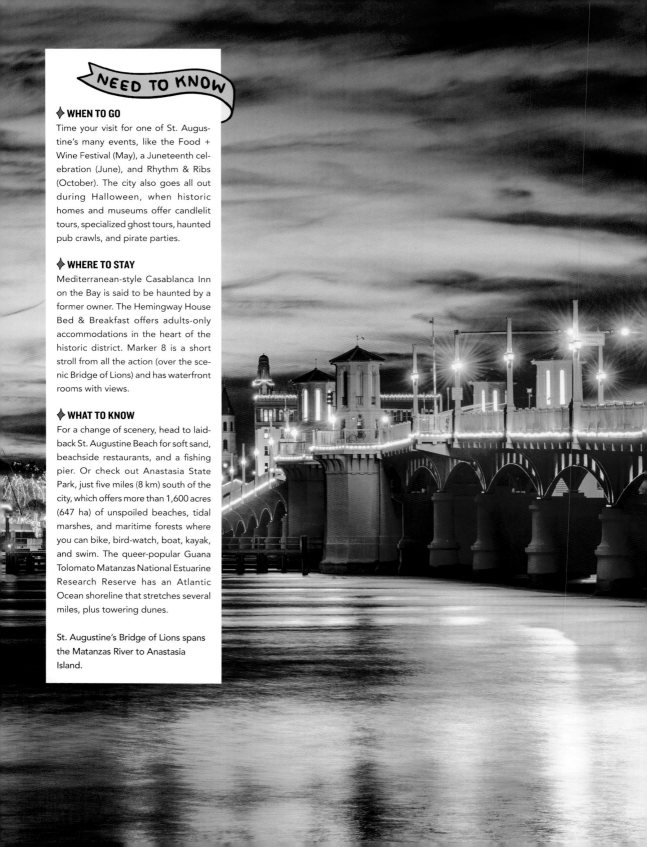

◆ WHEN TO GO

Time your visit for one of St. Augustine's many events, like the Food + Wine Festival (May), a Juneteenth celebration (June), and Rhythm & Ribs (October). The city also goes all out during Halloween, when historic homes and museums offer candlelit tours, specialized ghost tours, haunted pub crawls, and pirate parties.

◆ WHERE TO STAY

Mediterranean-style Casablanca Inn on the Bay is said to be haunted by a former owner. The Hemingway House Bed & Breakfast offers adults-only accommodations in the heart of the historic district. Marker 8 is a short stroll from all the action (over the scenic Bridge of Lions) and has waterfront rooms with views.

◆ WHAT TO KNOW

For a change of scenery, head to laid-back St. Augustine Beach for soft sand, beachside restaurants, and a fishing pier. Or check out Anastasia State Park, just five miles (8 km) south of the city, which offers more than 1,600 acres (647 ha) of unspoiled beaches, tidal marshes, and maritime forests where you can bike, bird-watch, boat, kayak, and swim. The queer-popular Guana Tolomato Matanzas National Estuarine Research Reserve has an Atlantic Ocean shoreline that stretches several miles, plus towering dunes.

St. Augustine's Bridge of Lions spans the Matanzas River to Anastasia Island.

EXPERIENCE OLD WORLD CHARM AND HISTORIC HAUNTINGS.
St. Augustine, Florida, U.S.A.

Live oak trees blanket Magnolia Avenue.

THE LGBTQIA+ LOWDOWN St. Augustine doesn't have a specific queer scene; rather, it's a place where everyone shares good times together. (Less than an hour north, Jacksonville has an LGBTQIA+ community center and other queer spaces like bars and clubs, and it hosts River City Pride in November.)

Located in northeastern Florida, St. Augustine is the United States' oldest city (or, to be more accurate, the oldest continuously occupied settlement of European and African American origin). Founded by the Spanish in 1565, St. Augustine still captures an Old World European feel with its colonial architecture and cobblestoned lanes . . . filled with spirits!

Head to the Castillo de San Marcos fort after the sun goes down. Built by the Spanish in the late 17th century, this mammoth fort is the oldest and largest masonry structure in the U.S. Widely considered one of America's most haunted sites, it's a favorite for ghost hunters. Visitors have reported seeing dead soldiers pacing about, odd shapes floating in the air, and a mysterious female ghost (believed to be a colonel's unfaithful wife who was killed by her jealous husband). If you're not too creeped out after visiting, come back during the day to take in views of the Matanzas River and the Atlantic Ocean.

Try organized ghost hunting by arresting yourself for a night tour in the Old St. Johns County Jail, which operated between 1891 and 1953. You'll explore the scariest dark corners, hear hair-raising stories, and be part of a paranormal investigation, complete with state-of-the-art equipment.

Don't miss the St. Augustine Lighthouse, which dates back to 1874. You can climb the lighthouse and learn about the city's maritime heritage—or visit its dark history. Some have reported seeing an apparition of a man believed to be Joseph Andreu (who fell to his death while painting the lighthouse) or hearing young girls laughing—attributed to Eliza and Mary, who tragically drowned here in the 1800s.

After you're done ghost hunting, wander St. George Street for shopping and visit the Lightner Museum to browse eccentric exhibits about art, architecture, and history.

When you're hungry, head to the Floridian, serving comfort food like fried green tomatoes and fish melts in a setting with tropical island vibes. Columbia Restaurant offers Cuban sandwiches made the same way since 1905. Then get drinks at the popular Scarlett O'Hara's, but be warned: You may encounter the ghost of the former owner.

IN THE BIG EASY, FINDING GHOSTS ISN'T HARD.
New Orleans, Louisiana, U.S.A.

THE LGBTQIA+ LOWDOWN As New Orleans' official website says, "Everyone's welcome here." From queer bars on Lavender Street to widespread LGBTQIA+ events like Southern Decadence, Gay Mardi Gras, and LGBTQ Halloween, NOLA is a place to feel free.

No place does southern Gothic lore better than New Orleans. Since its establishment in 1718, the city has endured tragedy after tragedy, including raging fires, brutal battles with the British, one of the largest slave markets in U.S. history, and Hurricane Katrina in 2005. Is it any wonder the Big Easy is haunted?

Start where most visitors do: the iconic French Quarter, also known as Vieux Carré. Located on the banks of the Mississippi River, it's the oldest neighborhood in the city and is known for the everlasting party that is Bourbon Street and colorful buildings with cast-iron balconies and beautiful courtyards.

After waiting in line for beignets at Café du Monde (it's a rite of passage), find a bench in Jackson Square, a historic landmark. If you'd like a palm reading, your fortune told, or a sketch of yourself, this is the place to do it. Otherwise, admire the views of St. Louis Cathedral. Dating back to the 1700s, it's the country's oldest active cathedral. Take a self-guided tour and try to find the ghost of Père Antoine, a Spanish friar who died in 1829. The square was once a site of public executions, so paranormal experts believe there's a lot of dark energy here. Walk by after 6 p.m., when the gates are closed, and you may experience a restless soul tugging on your shirt.

From Jackson Square, you're minutes away from the French Quarter's many haunted sites, including Lafitte's Blacksmith Shop Bar, one of the oldest bars in the U.S. (built between 1722 and 1732), where you might encounter the spirit of pirate Jean Lafitte. You can also visit LaLaurie Mansion, said to be a house of pure evil. Finally, don't miss St. Louis Cemetery No. 1, the Big Easy's oldest continuously operating graveyard. Its famous residents include Marie Laveau, New Orleans' "Voodoo Queen," who helped many people with financial issues or marital woes when she was alive. She's believed to still be available for consultations if you bring her flowers or alcohol.

See if your fork stands up on its own during haunted meals at restaurants such as Arnaud's, where you may be greeted by "Count" Arnaud Cazenave, the tuxedo-clad original owner who died in 1948. Or try Muriel's, a mansion turned restaurant, where a table is still set for the former owner who died in 1814 and is said to sometimes appear as a shimmering spirit. After your meal, try to contact him with a restaurant-sponsored seance. Then cap off your night at fun-filled queer spaces such as Cafe Lafitte in Exile and Napoleon's Itch.

Lafitte's Blacksmith Shop Bar is a staple of Bourbon Street's lively nightlife scene.

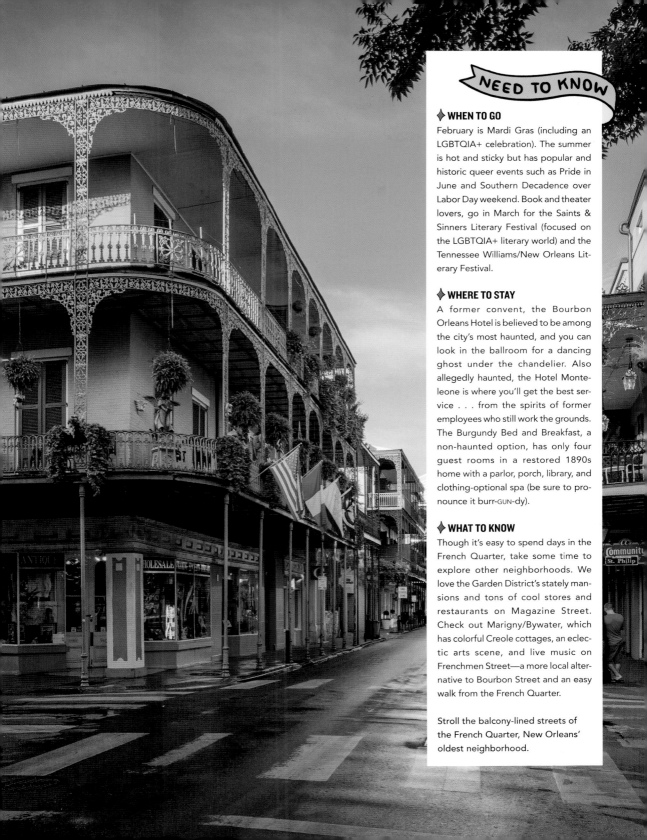

◆ WHEN TO GO

February is Mardi Gras (including an LGBTQIA+ celebration). The summer is hot and sticky but has popular and historic queer events such as Pride in June and Southern Decadence over Labor Day weekend. Book and theater lovers, go in March for the Saints & Sinners Literary Festival (focused on the LGBTQIA+ literary world) and the Tennessee Williams/New Orleans Literary Festival.

◆ WHERE TO STAY

A former convent, the Bourbon Orleans Hotel is believed to be among the city's most haunted, and you can look in the ballroom for a dancing ghost under the chandelier. Also allegedly haunted, the Hotel Monteleone is where you'll get the best service . . . from the spirits of former employees who still work the grounds. The Burgundy Bed and Breakfast, a non-haunted option, has only four guest rooms in a restored 1890s home with a parlor, porch, library, and clothing-optional spa (be sure to pronounce it burr-GUN-dy).

◆ WHAT TO KNOW

Though it's easy to spend days in the French Quarter, take some time to explore other neighborhoods. We love the Garden District's stately mansions and tons of cool stores and restaurants on Magazine Street. Check out Marigny/Bywater, which has colorful Creole cottages, an eclectic arts scene, and live music on Frenchmen Street—a more local alternative to Bourbon Street and an easy walk from the French Quarter.

Stroll the balcony-lined streets of the French Quarter, New Orleans' oldest neighborhood.

THE FRENCH QUARTER

NOLA's oldest and most famous neighborhood, the French Quarter, is always a crowd-pleaser for its colorful architecture and food and drink scene. We particularly love its buzzing queer bars and amped-up Pride during Southern Decadence and events like the Official Gay Easter Parade (pictured here). Take time to explore its deep LGBTQIA+ roots. Tour group New Orleans Secrets offers an LGBT Queer History walking tour with stories and the inside scoop on some of the first queer bars and neighborhoods in the U.S., famous queer residents like Tennessee Williams (who wrote *A Streetcar Named Desire* here), and the challenges and triumphs that made NOLA one of the world's most inclusive cities.

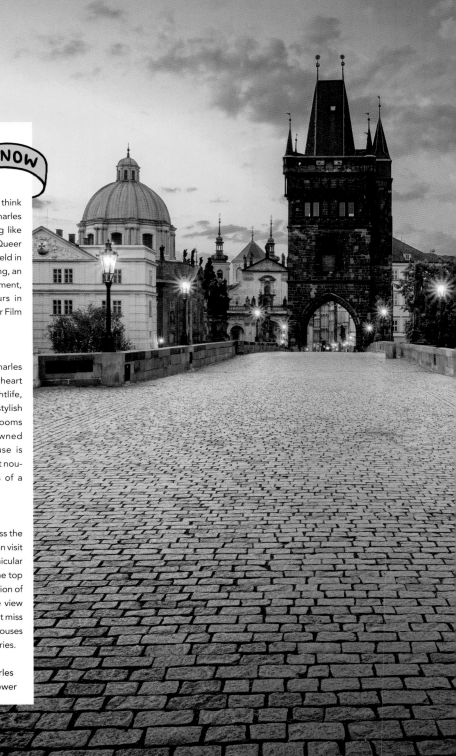

NEED TO KNOW

◆ WHEN TO GO

Some say winter is bleak, but we think it can be magical crossing the Charles Bridge in the snow while feeling like you have it all to yourself. The Queer Ball, an all-night dance party, is held in March; the Prague Rainbow Spring, an international queer sports tournament, is in May or June; Pride occurs in August; and the Mezipatra Queer Film Festival occurs in November.

◆ WHERE TO STAY

Hotel Josef offers views of the Charles Bridge and modern luxury in the heart of Old Town. Close to queer nightlife, Le Palais Art Hotel Prague is stylish and comfortable, plus some rooms come with balconies. Gay-owned Prague's Rainbow Guest House is apartment-style lodging in an art nouveau building, with the bonus of a friendly and insightful host.

◆ WHAT TO KNOW

A great day out is Petřín Hill across the river from Old Town, which you can visit either on foot or by riding a funicular to the top. Climb 299 steps to the top of the Lookout Tower, a mini version of the Eiffel Tower, for a bird's-eye view of the city. While in the area, don't miss the Strahov Monastery, which houses one of the world's prettiest libraries.

Prague's mid-14th-century Charles Bridge and Old Town Bridge Tower

STROLL ACROSS A FAIRY-TALE BRIDGE TO OLD TOWN.
Prague, Czechia

THE LGBTQIA+ LOWDOWN One of the most progressive countries in eastern Europe, Czechia (Czech Republic) decriminalized homosexuality in 1962. Prague has an open queer scene, Pride, and an LGBTQIA+ film festival. The main queer neighborhood is Vinohrady, but the entire city is very welcoming.

Lying on the banks of the Vltava River and located in the center of Europe, Prague is more than 1,000 years old but shows little signs of aging. At times, being here feels like a fairy tale, especially when visiting Prague Castle (dating back to A.D. 870) and walking across the Charles Bridge. But like most fairy tales, the city has its share of strange characters and creepy castles.

Černín Palace, a baroque castle from 1675, is a whopping 500 feet (152 m) long and thought to be a house of evil where people claim to still hear the screams of a cruel countess. Others believe in a headless Templar knight who rides through the city on horseback.

Many of the city's hauntings are said to occur in Old Town. In the light of day, Old Town Square is where you'll find the exquisitely detailed astronomical clock, built in 1410. Watch one of the world's oldest functioning clocks put on a show at the top of every hour, when the Twelve Apostles launch into a procession. But take caution on nearby Celetná Street, especially at night, as it's believed many spirits walk among you.

Just a few minutes away from Celetná Street, look for the statue of the "Iron Man." According to stories, his wife was unfaithful, and he killed her in a jealous rage. His punishment was to spend eternity trapped in a statue, coming to life every 100 years to try to break his curse with a kiss. So far, no one has stepped up.

About an hour from the city, the 13th-century Houska Castle is utterly terrifying. Referred to as the "gateway to Hell," it's built over a bottomless pit where some believe demons lurked. There are also stories of bone-chilling creatures crawling out of the hole and attacking locals. The building endured a very real dark period when the Nazis occupied it during World War II. Today, the castle is privately owned, and you can take a tour if you dare.

Back in town, shake off the spooky cobwebs at Prague's popular queer hangouts such as Q Café; the Saints, which has a cozy space and chill vibe; and Heaven to get sweaty on the dance floor. Or try the super-inclusive STORY Theatre Club & Café Bar.

Detailed figures adorn Prague's medieval astronomical clock at the Old Town Hall Tower.

EXPLORE A HAUNTED CASTLE AND GHOSTS ALONG THE ROYAL MILE.
Edinburgh, Scotland, U.K.

Victoria Street is a popular thoroughfare in Edinburgh.

THE LGBTQIA+ LOWDOWN Edinburgh is one of the most LGBTQIA+-welcoming cities in Europe. The city's "Pink Triangle" offers low-key pubs and festive bars, restaurants, coffee shops, and more.

Scotland's capital is known for its striking buildings, narrow lanes, and imposing castle. With famous arts festivals and hundreds of years' worth of history, it's a favorite destination among both theatergoers and ghost hunters.

Start at Edinburgh Castle, the literal top of the Royal Mile. At 443 feet (135 m) above sea level, the castle looms over the city and includes sites like St. Margaret's Chapel (Edinburgh's oldest building), the Great Hall, National War Museum, Stone of Destiny, and, our favorite, the Honours of Scotland (where the crown jewels are kept).

According to paranormal experts, the castle's spiritual activity is off the charts. It may have something to do with the "Black Dinner" of 1440, a murderous meal where rivals to the throne were invited to dine with King James II and were betrayed and beheaded. (*Game of Thrones* fans: This event is said to have inspired the "Red Wedding.") Some have reported seeing the spirit of soldiers, a headless drummer, and a phantom bagpiper.

Just off the Royal Mile, Mary King's Close is a former tenement where hundreds of people died during the 17th-century bubonic plague. Take a tour at night if you're feeling brave!

In the 18th century, the Niddry Street Vaults were filled with taverns, cobblers, and other businesses, but bad floods drove everyone out. After sitting abandoned, the site was used for brothels and slums—but two men, William Burke and William Hare, preyed on its residents, murdering them and selling their cadavers. Those who visit say they have heard the sounds of people screaming and bodies being dragged across the floor.

Last but not least, Greyfriars Kirkyard is a 16th-century cemetery and the final resting place of George MacKenzie. Nicknamed "Bloody MacKenzie," he was a rich lord who was charged with the torture, starvation, and death of thousands of Presbyterian Covenanters in the 17th century. Today, his poltergeist is believed to still torture those who walk the graveyard's grounds.

After the cemetery, get more twisted tales at the Palace of Holyroodhouse. Visit the bed chamber of Mary Queen of Scots, which may look pretty and elegant but was also where the queen's private secretary was brutally murdered.

Try minced meat pies at the Piemaker. The Street is a popular LGBTQIA+ bistro by day and has a party scene and cabaret performances at night. Don't miss other queer haunts like CC Blooms, the city's oldest LGBTQIA+ venue, and Habana.

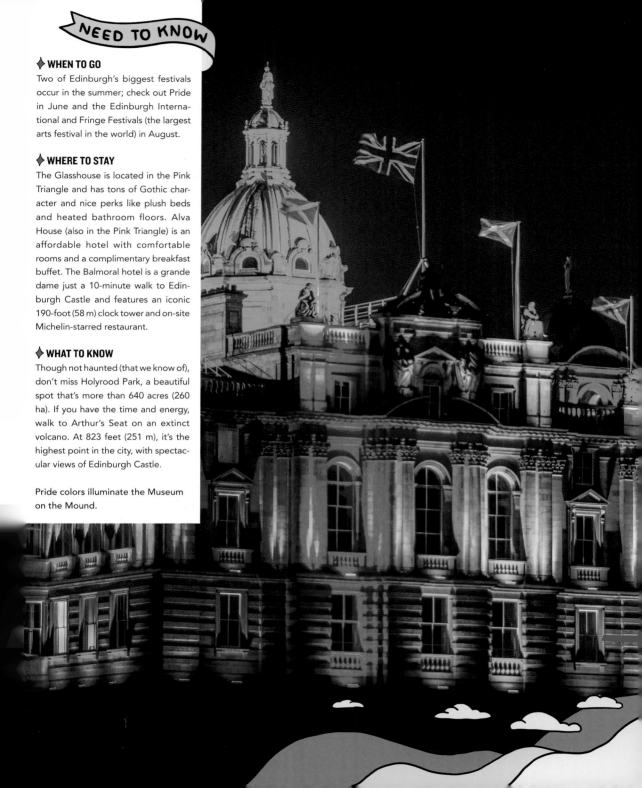

◆ WHEN TO GO

Two of Edinburgh's biggest festivals occur in the summer; check out Pride in June and the Edinburgh International and Fringe Festivals (the largest arts festival in the world) in August.

◆ WHERE TO STAY

The Glasshouse is located in the Pink Triangle and has tons of Gothic character and nice perks like plush beds and heated bathroom floors. Alva House (also in the Pink Triangle) is an affordable hotel with comfortable rooms and a complimentary breakfast buffet. The Balmoral hotel is a grande dame just a 10-minute walk to Edinburgh Castle and features an iconic 190-foot (58 m) clock tower and on-site Michelin-starred restaurant.

◆ WHAT TO KNOW

Though not haunted (that we know of), don't miss Holyrood Park, a beautiful spot that's more than 640 acres (260 ha). If you have the time and energy, walk to Arthur's Seat on an extinct volcano. At 823 feet (251 m), it's the highest point in the city, with spectacular views of Edinburgh Castle.

Pride colors illuminate the Museum on the Mound.

◆ WHEN TO GO

Visit September through November for the most pleasant weather, or check out some events held throughout the year including Pride (June), the Queer Tango Festival (November), and the LGBTQIA+-focused Asterisco film festival (November).

◆ WHERE TO STAY

The Duque Hotel Boutique & Spa in Palermo Soho has a garden, pool, and breakfast buffet. The Palacio Duhau - Park Hyatt in Recoleta is set in a neoclassical palace and is a 10-minute walk to Recoleta Cemetery. The Faena Hotel is located in trendy Puerto Madero with a European-inspired design and decadent rooms.

◆ WHAT TO KNOW

The areas of San Telmo (Argentina's historic neighborhood with a great Sunday market) and Palermo (filled with lots of green spaces and trendy bars/restaurants) are also worth exploring. While in Recoleta, check out its stately mansions and stylish boutiques. Book lovers, beeline to El Ateneo Grand Splendid, an incredible bookstore housed in a former theater—and one of our favorite places in Buenos Aires, haunted or otherwise.

At 221 feet (68 m) tall, the Obelisco de Buenos Aires towers over the city.

VISIT THE CASA ROSADA AND EVITA'S GRAVE (BUT DON'T CRY FOR HER).

Buenos Aires, Argentina

La Recoleta Cemetery is home to more than 6,400 statues, sarcophagi, crypts, and coffins.

THE LGBTQIA+ LOWDOWN Buenos Aires is among the most queer-welcoming cities in South America. In addition to a huge Pride celebration and queer-owned businesses, the city hosts Gnetwork360, an annual international conference for the LGBTQIA+ tourism industry.

More than just tango, great steak, and *Evita*, Buenos Aires is the commercial capital of Argentina with 48 distinct barrios and leafy boulevards infused with South American spirit—and *spirits*, for that matter.

Start in the famed Plaza de Mayo, where souls who were lost during the "Dirty War" still linger. Between 1976 and 1983, an estimated 10,000 to 30,000 suspected opponents of the country's dictatorship "disappeared" at the hands of the military. Traces of the country's dark period remain in the form of the Mothers of the Plaza de Mayo, an allegiance of women who lost their children and grandchildren during the Dirty War. They are credited with helping to restore democracy in Argentina. Today, the women still hold moving vigils in the plaza on Thursdays.

Despite its ghosts, the Plaza de Mayo shines brightly. One of the city's most historic sites, it dates back to the 16th century and has important landmarks. See the government house, and Casa Rosada, which is most famous for the balcony where Eva Perón delivered her speeches. Casa Rosada is officially titled Casa de Gobierno (the government house)

and is the residence of the president. Tours are available, but you must book in advance.

A 15-minute walk from the Plaza de Mayo, the Obelisco is another iconic landmark believed to be haunted. Visit at night, and you may hear the screams of a ghost, believed to be a man who fell to his death while working on the monument.

A short stroll from Obelisco is the Teatro Colón. We haven't heard of any hauntings, but this superb venue is cited as having some of the world's best acoustics and is utterly gorgeous.

Have a grand haunted finale by exploring the many Gothic mausoleums and crypts of Buenos Aires's world-famous Recoleta Cemetery. Dating back to 1822, the cemetery is like a walk of fame of the deceased, serving as a final resting place for many of Argentina's most prominent figures, including Evita herself (she's in the Duarte family tomb).

For coffee and people-watching, visit Pride Cafe. Sitges has fun drag shows and karaoke, Peuteo bar bills itself as "hetero friendly," and Amerika is one of South America's biggest queer clubs.

SEE SPOOKY PERFORMANCES, DINNERTIME HAUNTS, AND WATERFRONT GHOSTS.

Vancouver, British Columbia, Canada

A cyclist navigates through the fog at Ross Bay Cemetery, said to be one of the most haunted in British Columbia.

THE LGBTQIA+ LOWDOWN Vancouver is home to a large Two-Spirit LGBTQIA+ community. The non-profit QMUNITY provides services and safe spaces. You'll find most of the action at Davie Village.

Western Canada's biggest city, Vancouver is famous for its cosmopolitan charm, urban beaches, mild temperatures, and mountain views. But did you know it's also super haunted?

One of Vancouver's most popular spots, Stanley Park, offers nearly 1,000 acres (405 ha) of endless outdoor opportunities. Stretch your legs on the seawall, the world's longest uninterrupted waterfront path, and enjoy scenic lookouts and multiple beaches. Watch out for spirits crossing over from Deadman's Island, located just across the water. The island was ravaged by smallpox outbreaks and also saw bloody battles between Indigenous tribes. Now a navy base, some have reported creepy occurrences, such as the sound of clanking chains.

Spend your evening in Gastown, Vancouver's first commercial district (established in the late 1800s), home to Waterfront Station, the city's major transit hub. Lingering spirits include three elderly women waiting for a train who may be responsible for spooky occurrences like the sound of footsteps or furniture moving on its own.

Vancouver is a great place to take in a play or concert—but the offstage happenings may give you chills. The historic Vogue Theatre (dating back to 1941) is a former movie theater now used for live performances. Those who have performed there refer to a backstage area as the "haunted highway" due to the spirit of a man who likes to jump out and scare them. Similarly, the Stanley Theater (another historic venue, first opened in 1930) is said to be occupied by the apparitions of two men who like to sit in the orchestra, occasionally showing up in top hats and kicking the seats if they don't like the show.

For non-haunted attractions, check out the Richmond Night Market, which is North America's biggest, for Asian food stalls, as well as games and live entertainment (May through October). Or browse art made by Indigenous peoples at the Museum of Anthropology (MOA), or hit Wreck Beach, a clothing-optional spot popular with the queer community.

Gastown is the best area for eats, with numerous dining options. Built on top of an underground railroad, The Old Spaghetti Factory attracts pasta lovers and the paranormal. Check out the vintage trolley, said to house the spirit of a train conductor who still likes to steer the action.

When you're ready to have some drinks, check out LGBTQIA+ bars like Numbers and Junction. Don't miss Little Sister's Book and Art Emporium, which carries a wide selection of queer reads for all.

◆ WHEN TO GO

Halloween is the best time for the haunted stuff. Numerous other events are held throughout the year, including Whistler Pride and Ski Festival (January), Rubbout (a queer event for fans of rubber and latex), and Vancouver Pride and Vancouver Queer Film Festival (both in August).

◆ WHERE TO STAY

The Fairmont Empress Hotel is elegant, historic, and reportedly haunted by a "lady in red," who has been seen gliding through hallways (especially on the 14th floor). For something less haunted, try the West End Guest House, a Victorian-influenced B&B with a gourmet breakfast in the center of town. Or sleep in the sky at Shangri-La Hotel, Vancouver, the city's tallest building.

◆ WHAT TO KNOW

Just outside the city, Grouse Mountain has a 1.8-mile (2.9 km) trail with almost 3,000 steps to the summit, where you'll be rewarded with views of the Pacific and the city. You can also take a gondola ride to the top. Or try the Capilano Suspension Bridge, a thrilling walk 230 feet (70 m) above the Capilano River.

A monstrously decorated home awaits brave trick-or-treaters.

CHAPTER 10

NATURE

- and -

NURTURE

The great outdoors—as we see it—is the always faithful antidote to modern life, with its beautiful landscapes and fun-filled adventures. We're ready to help you experience some of the most stunning places on Earth where you can unwind and self-nurture . . . in nature and in destinations known for being especially queer welcoming. From Costa Rica's beaches and cloud forests to Iceland's waterfalls and Sedona's gorgeous red rocks and luxurious spas, you'll find just the relaxation you're seeking with plenty of LGBTQIA+-inclusive spots to explore. We also include areas like the Hudson Valley, with many queer residents, and where it's hard to resist the restorative charm of quaint villages and national parks. In addition to outlining the great fun to be had on these escapes, we provide important tips on how to explore the scenery fully while going at a pace and fitness level that ensures everyone comes away a happy camper.

♦ WHEN TO GO

Every season has its own feel here, but we recommend avoiding winter unless you're going in search of snow activities. Fall is best for apple picking and leaf peeping, and early and late summer are great for wine tastings and exploring outdoors. Note that some Hudson Valley businesses are only open on weekends in off-peak seasons, so check before you go.

♦ WHERE TO STAY

In New Paltz, outside of town, stay at Mohonk Mountain House, a historic landmark and luxury all-inclusive resort with mountain views where you can play on the lake, drink coffee on the porch, and dine your heart out. Closer to town, the Inn at Kettleboro is a renovated 19th-century family home with antique furnishings, rooms with fireplaces, and farm-to-table breakfasts over expansive views.

♦ WHAT TO KNOW

To sip through the valley, visit Robibero Winery on 42 acres (17 ha) for hand-crafted artisan wines. Or try two others, each 30 minutes from New Paltz (in different directions): Brotherhood Winery, the oldest continuously operating winery in the United States, and Benmarl Winery, with the oldest vineyard in America. For award-winning cider, go to Kettleborough Cider House, owned by the fourth generation of an apple-growing family from New Paltz.

The historic Mohonk Mountain House hotel was built in 1869.

WIND THROUGH CHARMING TOWNS WITH MOUNTAIN VIEWS.

New Paltz and Hudson Valley, New York, U.S.A.

Autumn colors take over the Hudson Valley's Shawangunk Mountains.

THE LGBTQIA+ LOWDOWN Enjoying the progress and protections of New York State, culminating from the Stonewall uprising in 1969, the Hudson Valley region is full of thriving LGBTQIA+ communities and progressive places like New Paltz, where the mayor officiated the state's first same-sex marriages in 2004.

An area that spans almost 150 miles (241 km) and both sides of the Hudson River—starting in Westchester County (northeast of New York City) and stretching up to Albany (the state's capital)—the valley is known for areas of unspoiled beauty, deep history, quaint towns, views and vineyards, artist and writer enclaves, and farm-to-table dining.

Start just 90 minutes north of New York City in New Paltz. Have outdoor fun any time of year at Wallkill Valley Rail Trail (Sojourner Park has a car lot), where you can enjoy hikes, bike rides, and cross-country skiing.

In charming downtown, head to Water Street Market, a quaint community village with art, eateries, sculptures, and a theater, all independently owned and operated. Also see Historic Huguenot Street, a 10-acre (4 ha) National Historic Landmark District that honors more than 300 years of history, including the French Huguenot settlement and the area's Indigenous and enslaved African peoples and Dutch settlers.

Another highlight of New Paltz is Mohonk Preserve, a vast stretch of more than 7,000 acres (2,835 ha) of forests, fields, lakes, and mountain ridges to explore, along with a paradise of trailheads set against Shawangunk Ridge. See the "million-dollar view" of the Catskill Mountains at Spring Farm Trailhead, which has forested paths.

Adjoining the preserve is the Mohonk Mountain House, a Victorian castle resort founded in 1869 with a world of its own to discover. Stroll along carriage roads or climb boulders and cliffs on 85 miles (137 km) of trails.

If you have more time, we have more suggestions: Go to Saratoga Springs for its mineral springs, charming downtown, and spas. Bibliophiles should take a ride north to Glens Falls to visit Black Walnut Books, an Indigenous-owned bookstore celebrating queer books and authors of color. Historic Rhinebeck is home to the Dutchess County Fair (dating back to 1919) with galleries, museums, charming tree-lined streets, hiking, and beautiful scenery. Visit Woodstock for its peace, love, and music vibes, Overlook Mountain for hiking, and shops on Tinker Street with treasures of every kind. Then drive to the Museum at Bethel Woods to see the actual site of the 1969 Woodstock festival and explore the underrated museum.

FEEL THE POWER OF THE VORTEX IN THIS FAVORITE DESERT TOWN.
Sedona, Arizona, U.S.A.

Uptown Mall on Sedona's Main Street is filled with colorful sculptures and artsy shops worth browsing.

THE LGBTQIA+ LOWDOWN In Arizona, same-sex couples can legally marry and adopt. Sedona in particular is popular with LGBTQIA+ residents and visitors alike, especially for queer weddings and friend or family retreats.

Only two hours from the capital of Phoenix, you'll find an enclave that hundreds of artists call home set against the backdrop of towering red rocks. This is the home of numerous galleries, Native American art and jewelry, expansive nature trails, and those famous vortices—places of unique abundances of energy—believed to cause local juniper trees to twist and bend as they grow.

Experience the vortices' mystical energy (believed to promote healing) at four main sites: Airport Mesa, Boynton Canyon vortex, Bell Rock vortex, and Cathedral Rock. Of all the sites, Cathedral Rock is the most popular (and arguably the prettiest). Formed from natural sandstone and accompanied by a reflecting pool, it's one of the most photographed spots in Sedona. To take your time and enjoy the views, allow at least 90 minutes to reach the top. If you're not feeling a hike, try an off-roading adventure to some of the vortices and red rocks with Pink Jeep Tours.

Vortices aside, Sedona is known for other great landmarks. Bell Rock, which is almost 5,000 feet (1,524 m) above sea level at its summit, is one of the first rock formations you'll spot coming into town. To get up close, take the 3.6-mile (5.8 km) Bell Rock Pathway. From there, you'll also get great views of Courthouse Butte, another geological formation with hues of red, sand, and orange.

Next, wander through Tlaquepaque Arts & Shopping Village, an outdoor market and landmark (since the 1970s) built around a sycamore grove with cobbled paths and stucco walls.

Enjoy a day of vino tasting on the Verde Valley Wine Trail, including a stop at Chateau Tumbleweed Winery & Tasting Room, which offers a dozen daily sampling options and a dog-friendly patio. Cellar 433 has an unconventional tasting room with esoteric-themed wines like the Bitter Creek Winery Tarot Collection and the Sultry Cellars Reserve Collection.

For restaurants, go to the beloved Casa Sedona Restaurant (located at Casa Sedona Inn), a local favorite with a garden patio. Or try family-owned and health-centric Picazzo's Healthy Italian Kitchen, with modern Italian cuisine and a full plant-based menu. Mariposa Latin Inspired Grill has Argentinian dishes with mesmerizing red rock views. Vino di Sedona has wines and craft beers on a charming patio.

◆ WHEN TO GO

Avoid the desert summer heat, which gets into the 100s, and winter, which can be too cold for some.

◆ WHERE TO STAY

Try Amara Resort and Spa for a luxury experience surrounded by red rocks and a zero-edge infinity pool. Sedona Cathedral Hideaway B&B and Casita has stunning 360-degree views and multiple decks to relax on. And Canyon Villa B&B is a charming spot with killer cinnamon rolls within walking distance to Bell and Cathedral Rocks.

◆ WHAT TO KNOW

Just a two-hour drive from Sedona, visit Grand Canyon National Park, located on the ancestral land of 11 associated tribes and one of the most dramatic examples of arid-land erosion in the world. You need a few days to do it right. Two of our favorite viewpoints include Mather Point (for capturing the vastness of the canyon) and Hopi Point (for incredible sunsets).

Magnificent Cathedral Rock is one of the most photographed sites in Sedona.

NEED TO KNOW

◆ WHEN TO GO

The best weather is April through October typically, but in winter months, you'll get a chance to see the humpback whales that migrate from Alaska to mate and birth their young right off the shores of the island (just be prepared for crowds).

◆ WHERE TO STAY

Try Kane Plantation Guesthouse, a 27-acre (11 ha) working avocado farm at the foothills of Mauna Loa with sweeping views of the Kona coast. Or the Hilo Bay Hale Bed & Breakfast, a historic building from 1914 that was saved from demolition in 2008 and restored as an inn. The eco-friendly Honu Kai is set on a lush tropical 1.3-acre (0.5 ha) estate with fruit trees and a restaurant. On the other side of the island, the Volcano House hotel is a historical retreat with vintage rooms, cozy cabins, and campsites, originally built in 1846 and located in Hawai'i Volcanoes National Park.

◆ WHAT TO KNOW

The island has two weather patterns; the dry side is on the west coast of the island (Kona side) and the wet side is on the east coast (the Hilo side). Though each has its pros and cons, do your research to plan activities—and where you want to stay—accordingly.

Lava continuously flows into the Pacific Ocean at Hawai'i Volcanoes National Park.

FROM BLACK SAND BEACHES TO VOLCANOES, THIS ISLAND'S FUN IS BIGGER THAN LIFE.

Big Island (Hawaii), Hawaii, U.S.A.

Outrigger canoe teams race across Kailua Bay.

THE LGBTQIA+ LOWDOWN Hawaii was the first U.S. state to legalize same-sex marriage (in 2013). As a longtime inclusive destination, the Big Island has a large LGBTQIA+ population, especially in communities along the scenic Red Road (Route 137).

Almost twice as big as all the other Hawaiian islands combined, the Big Island is a paradise with diverse ecosystems like lava-spewing volcanoes, splashing waterfalls, lush rainforests, and stretches of sandy coastline.

With beaches all over, the Big Island doesn't disappoint. Visit Punalu'u Black Sand Beach, where you may spot protected large *honu* (Hawaiian green sea turtles). Also see Papakōlea, one of only four green sand beaches in the world. It's more than 50,000 years old and is colored by olivine crystals. You have to hike to get there, but for those able to make the five-mile (8 km) round-trip trek, it's a site and experience you'll never forget. Hāpuna Beach is another must-visit and great for lazing, playing, and snorkeling.

Make sure to visit Hawai'i Volcanoes National Park with 123,000 acres (49,776 ha) of wilderness. A designated international biosphere reserve and UNESCO World Heritage site, it encompasses the summits of two of the world's most active volcanoes (Kīlauea and Mauna Loa). The park also offers the chance to explore sacred landscapes, including Pu'uloa, the largest petroglyph fields in Hawaii; the Footprints area to honor steps that native Hawaiians left long ago; and a scenic drive around the summit of Kīlauea to see craters.

Next, tour the Kona Coffee Living History Farm, where you'll discover the story of Kona's coffee pioneers in the early 20th century, stroll through the coffee trees, meet a Kona Nightingale (a breed of free-roaming donkey specific to this region), and visit the original 1920s farmhouse.

Don't miss the chance to stargaze at Mauna Kea, a dormant volcano and the world's tallest mountain when measured from the ocean floor. Because Mauna Kea has almost no light pollution, you can see the constellations, and even the Milky Way, with just the naked eye. (Keep in mind Mauna Kea is sacred to Hawaiians, so visit respectfully.)

Dining options abound on the island. Try Merriman's Big Island, owned by one of the founders of Hawaii Regional Cuisine. My Bar Kona is the island's largest LGBTQIA+-friendly hangout with great drinks and drag bingo.

DRIVE THE GOLDEN CIRCLE AND CHASE THE NORTHERN LIGHTS.
Iceland

THE LGBTQIA+ LOWDOWN One of the most queer-friendly countries in the world, Iceland has made more progress than most, having made same-sex marriage legal by unanimous vote in 2010. Iceland has also had multiple LGBTQIA+ leaders in government.

Iceland, part of the Nordic region, is an area settled by Vikings and known as the "land of fire and ice" for its dramatic and diverse landscapes. The capital city of Reykjavík is a jumping-off point for seeing volcanoes, geothermal springs, geysers, waterfalls, and, of course, the northern lights.

Spend one night in Reykjavík and visit Rainbow Street downtown, a long, painted road that honors the LGBTQIA+ community and is lined with little shops and restaurants. Walk up the steady incline to Hallgrimskirkja, the largest church in the country, and go to the top of its 240-foot-tall (73 m) tower for panoramic views of the city to the coast.

Between October and February, keep your eyes open for the aurora borealis—an explosive and colorful light show in the sky. Don't miss the Icelandic Punk Museum, where you can learn about the country's music history, including artists Björk and Sigur Rós, both natives of the country.

For food and drinks, try Reykjavík Kitchen, a family-owned institution with fresh Icelandic fish and meat. Kiki Queer Bar has great music, and Gaukurinn offers LGBTQIA+ events.

Next, head out of the city to have a hot soak at the Blue Lagoon (the popular geothermal spa), or go farther from town to the Secret Lagoon, which is the oldest swimming pool in Iceland (built in 1891) and much less crowded.

Then tour the Golden Circle, a drivable tourist route in southern Iceland where you'll see a waterfall, geysers, and Thingvellir National Park, a UNESCO World Heritage site. The Geysir geothermal area is where you can watch boiling pools and explosive water shows. Gullfoss is Iceland's most iconic waterfall, with a massive double-tiered cascading falls that crash into the canyon below.

After the Golden Circle, head to Reynisfjara black sand beach off Ring Road, an 825-mile (1,328 km) road that circles the entire country. Then visit the tiny village of Vik, which dates back to the ninth century.

Iceland is fairly easy to drive yourself, but if you're here in the winter or prefer to be shown around by a local, book with Hidden Iceland tours, a carbon-negative company with LGBTQIA+ guides, to see waterfalls, beaches, and secret spots. For those with mobility concerns, private tours can be personalized.

Wade in geothermal hot springs at the popular Blue Lagoon.

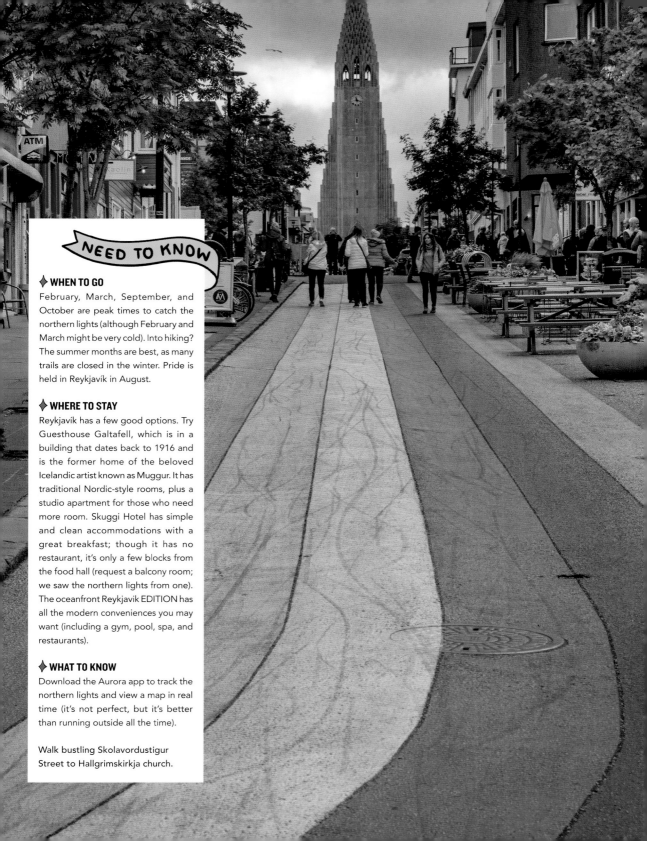

NEED TO KNOW

♦ WHEN TO GO

February, March, September, and October are peak times to catch the northern lights (although February and March might be very cold). Into hiking? The summer months are best, as many trails are closed in the winter. Pride is held in Reykjavík in August.

♦ WHERE TO STAY

Reykjavík has a few good options. Try Guesthouse Galtafell, which is in a building that dates back to 1916 and is the former home of the beloved Icelandic artist known as Muggur. It has traditional Nordic-style rooms, plus a studio apartment for those who need more room. Skuggi Hotel has simple and clean accommodations with a great breakfast; though it has no restaurant, it's only a few blocks from the food hall (request a balcony room; we saw the northern lights from one). The oceanfront Reykjavik EDITION has all the modern conveniences you may want (including a gym, pool, spa, and restaurants).

♦ WHAT TO KNOW

Download the Aurora app to track the northern lights and view a map in real time (it's not perfect, but it's better than running outside all the time).

Walk bustling Skolavordustigur Street to Hallgrimskirkja church.

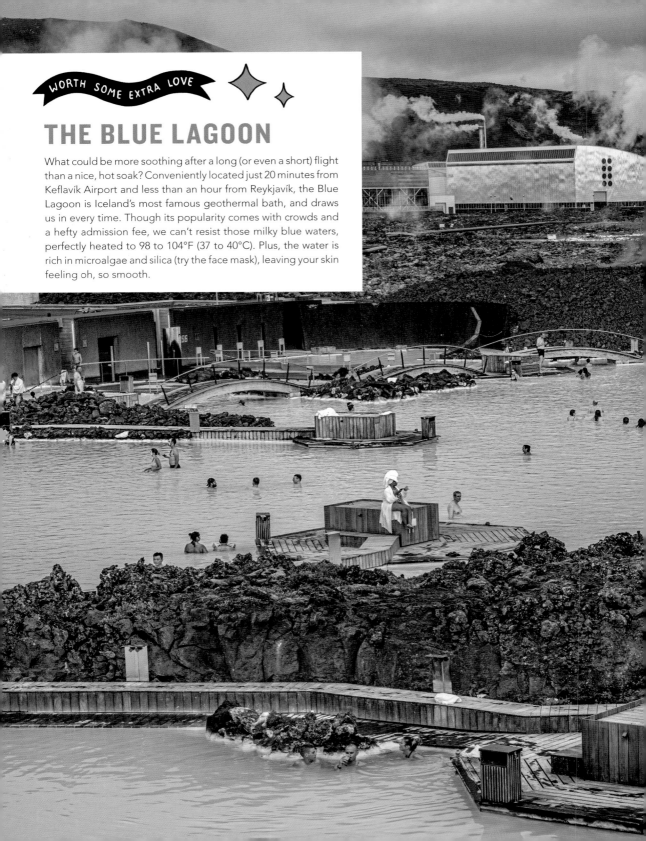

THE BLUE LAGOON

What could be more soothing after a long (or even a short) flight than a nice, hot soak? Conveniently located just 20 minutes from Keflavík Airport and less than an hour from Reykjavík, the Blue Lagoon is Iceland's most famous geothermal bath, and draws us in every time. Though its popularity comes with crowds and a hefty admission fee, we can't resist those milky blue waters, perfectly heated to 98 to 104°F (37 to 40°C). Plus, the water is rich in microalgae and silica (try the face mask), leaving your skin feeling oh, so smooth.

NEED TO KNOW

✦ WHEN TO GO

Peak times are between November and April. May through August is the wet season. If you go in June, you can celebrate Pride, a huge event that takes place in San José and includes the Diversity March.

✦ WHERE TO STAY

Hotel Villa Roca is an eco-friendly and adults-only resort with an infinity pool and rainforest garden near Manuel Antonio National Park. Tico Tico Villas in Quepos is an adults-only destination with a pool, brightly decorated rooms, and fully equipped kitchens. Parador Nature Resort & Spa is an eco-luxury resort on the outskirts of the national park with expansive views of the ocean, surrounded by 12 acres (5 ha) of tropical rainforest.

✦ WHAT TO KNOW

After Manuel Antonio, consider the three- to four-hour road trip to Monteverde (meaning "green mountain"), an area in the Puntarenas Province known for its cloud forests. You can explore several parks, but the most family friendly is Sky Walk Monteverde, with six hanging bridges, including the longest in Costa Rica (984 feet/300 meters), above the trees for views of wildlife.

Embrace the sun from a rocky viewpoint in Manuel Antonio National Park.

HERE, CLOUD FOREST AND BEACH DREAMS COME TRUE.

Quepos and Manuel Antonio National Park, Costa Rica

THE LGBTQIA+ LOWDOWN LGBTQIA+ rights in Costa Rica have evolved in the past years, with Manuel Antonio recognized as the queer center of the country, although it's more geared toward gay men.

About 50 miles (80 km) southwest of San José on the Central Pacific coast, you'll find the area of Manuel Antonio, best known for its national park. The region's access to both beautiful beaches and exotic jungles within such close proximity to each other makes it one of the most popular tourist destinations in the country.

Quepos is a gateway town to Manuel Antonio National Park and is famous for its year-round fishing—from the sand or via kayaks, traditional panga fishing boats, or large charters. Try a different kind of experience at the family-run Manuel Antonio Bee Farm, dedicated to protecting the native stingless bees, where you'll learn about the different types of bees, tour the hives (with protective suits), and have a traditional Costa Rican lunch with honeycomb for dessert.

In Manuel Antonio National Park (est. 1972), embark on rainforest adventures, relax on the sand, hike, and check out white-faced monkeys, three-toed sloths, and toucans. Hiking trails will take you from the coast through mountainous areas. Cathedral Point is a piece of land that divides two of the park's most popular beaches: Playa Espadilla Sur (a big beach with a children's playground) and Playa Manuel Antonio (a crescent-shaped stretch of sand with lots of greenery). For hiking in the park, take the Mangrove Trail from the main entrance via elevated bridges through the jungle. Or try the Sloth Trail, connected to the Mangrove Trail, where—as the name suggests—you might spot some sloths. Finally, Cathedral Point Trail is a loop between Playa Manuel Antonio and Playa Espadilla.

Want more time in the sand? Head to Biesanz Beach for calm, clear waters. Often called the "secret beach," it's a scenic cove that can only be reached from a steep trail (near Parador Resort & Spa). For a clothing-optional experience, go to Playa La Macha via a hike to the rocky oasis. Or drift through Damas Island's biodiversity (near Quepos) with Damas Mangrove Boat Tours, which take you through the canals. You'll learn about and experience the saltwater habitat and the wildlife and plants living there, including green herons, mangrove hawks, boa constrictors, tiger crabs, white-faced monkeys, anteaters, and sloths.

Sample local and other Latin cuisines at El Arado Restaurante, which has happy hour and live music in a ranch-style building with a cozy patio. La Cocina boasts authentic Costa Rican food at affordable prices. Café Milagro is a good spot for breakfast and world-famous roasted coffee. Rafaeles Las Terrazas has fresh seafood with ocean views (great at sunset) and a bar. Drunken Monkey bar caters to an LGBTQIA+-friendly crowd.

The Quepos sign makes for a perfect photo op on the seawall.

FROM THE FAMOUS CABOT TRAIL TO 100 WILD ISLANDS, THE CANADIAN COAST DELIVERS.
Nova Scotia, Canada

A ferry boasts Pride as it cruises through Halifax Harbour.

THE LGBTQIA+ LOWDOWN Nova Scotia is a queer-welcoming destination with Canada's largest population of trans and nonbinary people and extensive protections for queer people. It also has a wide array of services, including First Love Yourself, Gender Creative Kids Canada, and Nova Scotia Rainbow Action Project.

One of only three Canadian Maritime Provinces on the coast of North America, Nova Scotia is known for its rugged coastline, rolling hills, world-famous lobster, outdoor hiking and cycling, lighthouses, and the world's highest tides. In 2023, it hosted the North American Indigenous Games, bringing together 756 nations to compete and connect through sports across 21 venues.

Start between the southern coast of New Brunswick and the province of Nova Scotia to see the Bay of Fundy, home to the world's highest (and lowest) tides. The best spot to view the tides is from Hopewell Rocks Provincial Park, where you can appreciate the massive height of the tides. The bay's shoreline cliffs, the Cliffs of Fundy, are a UNESCO World Heritage site and Global Geopark and are the site of fossil records from more than 300 million years ago.

On the Cabot Trail, a famous five-hour drive, you'll have lots to see. Look for whales at Pleasant Bay, explore Cape Breton Highlands National Park, and hike from Louisbourg Lighthouse along the coastline with views of the 18th-century Fortress of Louisbourg National Historic Site. Stay on the trail to visit the Alexander Graham Bell National Historic Site, where you can explore the gardens with views of Bras d'Or Lake, tour the exhibits (or take a virtual walk via the Presentation Hall), and make a tetrahedral kite with the whole family.

On the South Shore, Lunenburg's Old Town (founded in 1753) is a UNESCO World Heritage site and one of the most beautiful towns in Canada, with the harbor at its heart.

Art and culture lovers, check out Bus Stop Theatre, which provides a space for artists—BIPOC female, trans, and nonbinary included—to showcase their art, drag, improv, and more. And the Museum of Natural History features fossils, gold, Mi'kmaq artifacts, and an eagle's nest. Or check out the Maritime Museum of the Atlantic in Halifax's historic waterfront to learn the story of the R.M.S. *Titanic*'s creation—and its demise after it struck an iceberg off the coast of Nova Scotia.

For dining well in Halifax, the Press Gang is one of the city's oldest historic stone structures (from 1759) known for formal dining, oyster selection, and signature cocktails. Stories Casual Fine Dining partners with Indigenous farmers, foragers, and fishermen and serves regional cuisine.

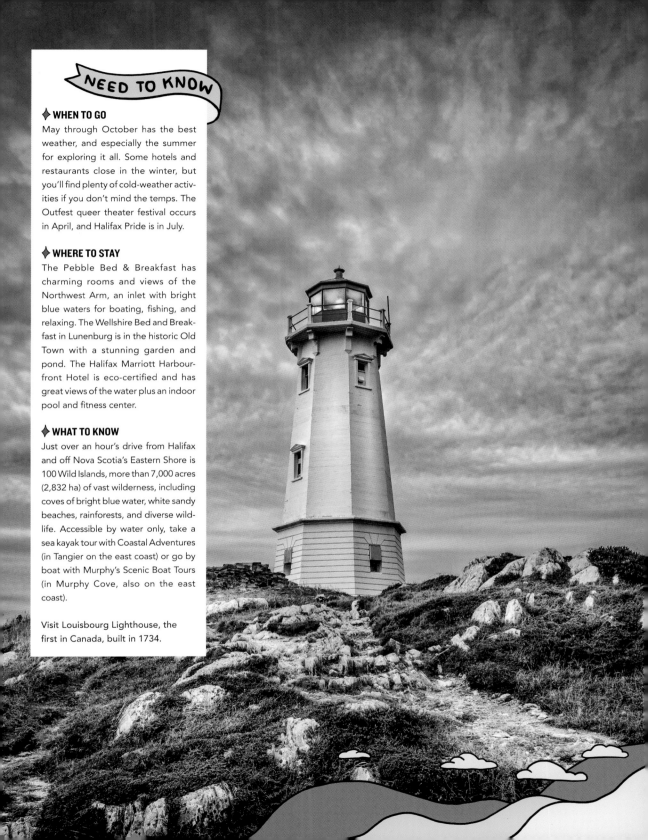

NEED TO KNOW

◆ WHEN TO GO

May through October has the best weather, and especially the summer for exploring it all. Some hotels and restaurants close in the winter, but you'll find plenty of cold-weather activities if you don't mind the temps. The Outfest queer theater festival occurs in April, and Halifax Pride is in July.

◆ WHERE TO STAY

The Pebble Bed & Breakfast has charming rooms and views of the Northwest Arm, an inlet with bright blue waters for boating, fishing, and relaxing. The Wellshire Bed and Breakfast in Lunenburg is in the historic Old Town with a stunning garden and pond. The Halifax Marriott Harbourfront Hotel is eco-certified and has great views of the water plus an indoor pool and fitness center.

◆ WHAT TO KNOW

Just over an hour's drive from Halifax and off Nova Scotia's Eastern Shore is 100 Wild Islands, more than 7,000 acres (2,832 ha) of vast wilderness, including coves of bright blue water, white sandy beaches, rainforests, and diverse wildlife. Accessible by water only, take a sea kayak tour with Coastal Adventures (in Tangier on the east coast) or go by boat with Murphy's Scenic Boat Tours (in Murphy Cove, also on the east coast).

Visit Louisbourg Lighthouse, the first in Canada, built in 1734.

◆ WHEN TO GO

Visit between September and March for the most comfortable climate. March also has the Holi festival, an ancient Hindu tradition where people throw colored powder to celebrate spring and the triumph of good over evil. September is also Queer Pride in Kerala.

◆ WHERE TO STAY

In Alappuzha, try Kalappura Homestay in a peaceful and quiet residential neighborhood with garden views and home-cooked Kerala cuisine (they also offer houseboat stays). In Munnar, stay at the Leaf Munnar with valley views, an infinity pool, family cottages, and a honeymoon pool villa. By the national park, try Niraamaya Retreats Cardamom Club Thekkady for luxury in a lush setting with an on-site Ayurvedic spa (Ayurveda is an ancient health care approach that dates back thousands of years in India).

◆ WHAT TO KNOW

Though legal and social taboos are improving in Kerala (and many other parts of India in general), there is still misunderstanding and homophobia here, in part due to campaigns by certain groups. So as in any area, be aware of your surroundings to stay safe and comfortable.

Palm tree–lined beaches make Kerala a perfect destination for sand and sun lovers.

CRUISE THROUGH THE BACKWATER CANALS AND WATCH THE COCO PALMS SWAY.

Kerala, India

Pattumala Matha Church is surrounded by the tea plantations of Peermade.

THE LGBTQIA+ LOWDOWN In 2018, the Supreme Court of India decriminalized homosexuality across the country. Kerala was one of the first states in India to create a welfare policy for transgender people (in 2016) and is the most progressive. The Queerala organization (est. 2013) works to promote the rights of Malayali people who belong to sexual and gender minorities.

Located on the Malabar Coast, Kerala, nicknamed "God's Own Country," is a small state that stretches only a few hundred miles but is well known for its beautiful backwater canals, coconut palms, beaches, spice farms, tea plantations, and ecotourism efforts.

Start in Alappuzha (Alleppey)—perhaps the most visited destination in Kerala, and for good reason. Referred to as the "Venice of the East," it has a network of streams, lush paddy fields, tropical greenery, and turtles, crabs, and waterbirds like kingfishers and terns. Board a houseboat for a day tour or stay a few nights for a longer trip. Try Marvel Cruise, one of Kerala Tourism Department's officially recognized houseboats, or Alleppey Backwater Tour Company, which has been certified as Gold Star and Green Palm (an eco rating given by the Tourism Department of Kerala). Both will show you the magic of the countryside during a multi-night tour. When you're back on land, visit Alappuzha Beach for swimming, relaxing, and a historic pier and lighthouse. Eat at Halais Restaurant for their authentic biryani and snacks, or try Cassia Restaurant, which serves Chinese and Indian cuisine. The Chai Wallah is a must-stop for traditional chai.

Next, travel to romantic Munnar (four hours inland) to experience the lush greenery of its famous tea plantations and wildlife sanctuaries. Kolukkumalai Tea Estate is the highest-elevation tea plantation in the world at almost 8,000 feet (2,438 m) above sea level. To see *kalaripayattu* (the traditional martial art of Kerala dating back thousands of years), go to Kalari Kshethra, a center that features shows of the ancient art form plus classical dance and other performances. For food, try Al Buhari for Arabic and seafood dishes. Tea Tales Cafe is great for coffee and tea tastings.

A few hours south, near the town of Thekkady, visit Periyar National Park and Wildlife Sanctuary, India's largest and oldest tiger reserve, home to 35 species of animals, including a large population of elephants. Take a jeep safari to spot the animals in their natural habitat, or tour a spice plantation. Next, visit Yodha Cultural Village in Thekkady to see dance, martial arts, and magic. At mealtime, head to Tusker Café, a family-owned restaurant with authentic Kerala cuisine. Periyar Tiger Cafe Restaurant near the entrance of the reserve is popular for South and North Indian dishes.

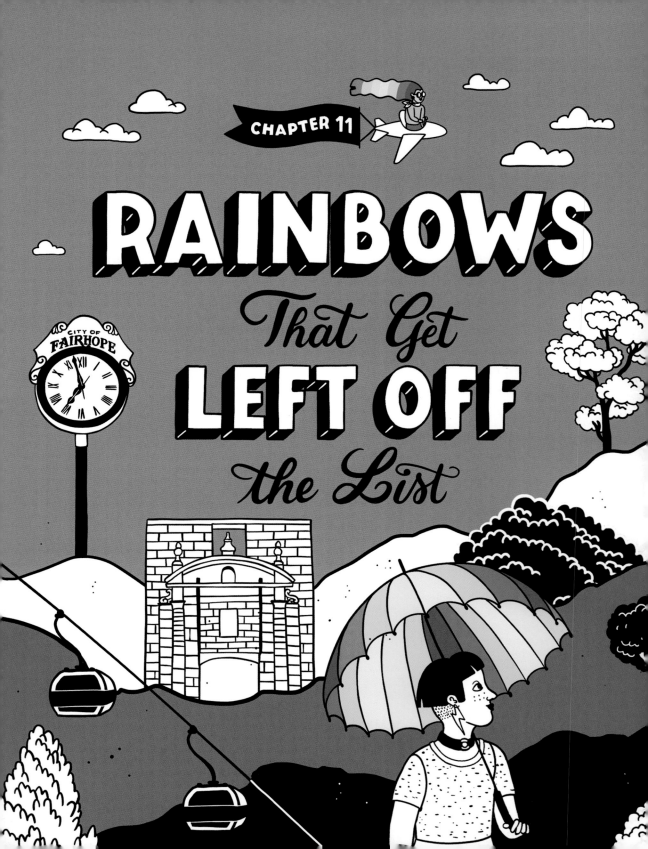

CHAPTER 11

RAINBOWS
That Get
LEFT OFF
the List

CITY OF
FAIRHOPE

As we've discussed, the LGBTQIA+ community has so many options for enjoying a vacation beyond major cities or traditional hot spots. In this chapter, we'll share some of our favorite gems in places that are often left off the list—including the beaches and historical sites of Montevideo, Uruguay; the drag shows of Phnom Penh, Cambodia; the literary charm of Fairhope, Alabama; and the thriving LGBTQIA+ scene of Salt Lake City, Utah.

HERE, YOU CAN GET YOUR MUSEUMS, PARKS, AND FRESH-AIR FIX.
Salt Lake City, Utah, U.S.A.

Pride celebrations cover parts of Salt Lake City in rainbows.

THE LGBTQIA+ LOWDOWN Salt Lake City is among the queerest cities in the U.S., and nearly 5 percent of its residents identify as LGBTQIA+ (a bigger per capita community than L.A. or New York City). The queer community and a large Mormon community manage to coexist.

It's easy to see why Utah's capital is one of the fastest-growing cities in the U.S., with its amazing views of the Wasatch and Oquirrh Mountains, easy access to outdoor adventures, and a downtown that includes everything from cultural institutions to craft breweries.

Before setting out for Salt Lake City's main sites, get to know the city and its residents by supporting some LGBTQIA+-owned and queer-inclusive businesses, including Under the Umbrella Bookstore, which caters specifically to the queer community (including providing a safe space to "congregate and celebrate"); Pantry Products, 100 percent female- and LGBTQIA-owned, for all-natural health and wellness products; and Sugarhouse Coffee, serving eats and locally roasted Rimini Coffee. It also hosts art shows, open mic nights, and events such as Queer Mingles Night.

Tour more of the city at Temple Square, a 35-acre (14 ha) Mormon complex and centerpiece of the city that is, in fact, open to everyone. See the architecture of the Assembly Hall and Mormon Temple (which dates back to 1893), hear the Tabernacle Choir sing or the famous pipe organs play, or sit by the fountain and people-watch.

Save plenty of time to explore Salt Lake City's fantastic museums: the Utah Museum of Fine Arts, featuring more than 21,000 pieces from around the world, and the Natural History Museum of Utah, housed in a stunning LEED-certified building.

Just next to the Natural History Museum is Red Butte Garden with more than 21 acres (8.5 ha) of themed spaces focusing on fragrance, herbs, and medicinal plants. It also has five miles (8 km) of hiking trails. Then head across town to Liberty Park, an 80-acre (32 ha) green space and the city's largest park.

For some of Salt Lake City's best restaurants, try queer-owned Laziz Kitchen, featuring classic Lebanese dishes, and Chanon Thai, known for its flavorful dishes. Or book a table at Valter's Osteria for Italian classics.

After dinner, see a touring Broadway show at the grand Eccles Theater. Or check out cool queer hot spots like the Sun Trapp (which has a fantastic patio), Club Try-Angles (for fun cocktails and theme nights), and Metro Music Hall (great for drag shows).

NEED TO KNOW

◆ WHEN TO GO

Fans of winter sports, go for Elevation
Utah, an LGBTQIA+ ski weekend in the
Park City area (January), which also
hosts the famous Sundance Film Fes-
tival (January through early February).
The LOVELOUD Festival is a music
event that raises money for human
rights groups while celebrating Utah's
LGBTQIA+ community (May). Salt
Lake Pride's multiday extravaganza is
in June. And October offers Damn
These Heels, a queer film festival.

◆ WHERE TO STAY

Try Ellerbeck Mansion Bed and Breakfast for a well-located and cozy stay.
The Kimpton Hotel Monaco is a cool
space with modern rooms and an
on-site restaurant and bar. The Peery
Hotel is a boutique historic landmark
hotel dating back to 1910.

◆ WHAT TO KNOW

Salt Lake City is also a gateway to
Utah's "Mighty Five" national parks:
Arches, Bryce Canyon, Canyonlands,
Capitol Reef, and Zion.

SLC has plenty of green spaces,
from parks to the mountains just
outside the city.

NEED TO KNOW

◆ WHEN TO GO

The best weather is from April through October. In June, Stonewall Columbus (an organization working to uplift LGBTQIA+ identities) hosts a huge Pride celebration with a march, festival, and resource fair.

◆ WHERE TO STAY

The Timbrook Guesthouse is a luxury B&B on tropical grounds with breakfast that gets all the raves. Or try Graduate Columbus, a trendy spot with an art collection and rooms inspired by Olympic icon Jesse Owens and astronaut John Glenn, plus its own restaurant. The Hotel LeVeque, Autograph Collection, has a sophisticated bar and lounge downtown with views of the river.

◆ WHAT TO KNOW

Just under two hours from Columbus is the largest Amish community in the world (Holmes County). Consider visiting to learn about its rich history and experience the culture that remains strong today. Check out Schrock's Amish Farm and Village to shop, take an Amish buggy tour, and interact with farm animals. To stay in the country, go to White Oak Inn, which has 14 wooded private acres (6 ha) surrounded by farms. Stay in the main inn, guesthouse, or luxury cabin—all complete with a bountiful breakfast.

The Scioto River reflects the 47-story LeVeque Tower and downtown Columbus.

FIND PERFORMING ARTS, GERMAN BREWS, AND QUEER-FRIENDLY VIBES IN THIS UNIVERSITY TOWN.

Columbus, Ohio, U.S.A.

Columbus's Ohio Theatre, opened in 1928, rivals Broadway with dance shows, classical music, and plays.

THE LGBTQIA+ LOWDOWN In Ohio, almost 5 percent of adults identify as LGBTQIA+. Columbus has several particularly LGBTQIA+-friendly neighborhoods, while Campus Pride named Ohio State one of the "Best of the Best Colleges and Universities for LGBTQ+ Students" in the U.S.

The state capital of Ohio, Columbus has one of the biggest college campuses in the U.S., fantastic museums (from arts to science), and plenty of places to enjoy the riverfront, bike, hike, and hit the walking trails.

Start at the Columbus Museum of Art, where you can see late 19th- and early 20th-century American and European pieces and photography exhibits.

Also visit the Franklin Park Conservatory and Botanical Gardens to explore greenhouses, gardens, and a huge collection of glass artwork by Dale Chihuly.

Experience the great outdoors at Topiary Park, a 10-acre (4 ha) garden that is a living re-creation of Georges Seurat's famous Postimpressionist painting, "A Sunday Afternoon on the Island of La Grande Jatte."

Short North Stage is LGBTQIA+ owned, housed in a 1920s building downtown, and the jewel of the Short North Arts District. The neighborhood is home to several LGBTQIA+-owned businesses (stop at Mouton for a fun cocktail like Not Your Grandmother's G&T plus a cheese plate, and visit W*nder for CBD-infused sparkling beverages).

Just north, head to Ohio State University's Wexner Center for the Arts, a "multidisciplinary, international laboratory for the exploration and advancement of contemporary art" that often features special exhibits on queer culture and Black artists.

The German Village & Brewery District, built by 19th-century immigrants, is another LGBTQIA+-welcoming neighborhood with charming brick buildings, pubs, shops, and a bustling craft beer scene. Barcelona is a decades-old LGBTQIA+-owned Spanish restaurant that's extremely popular and has a nice outdoor patio. Also in this area is Goodfellow's Tonsorial Parlor, an LGBTQIA+-owned classic barbershop known for giving great cuts.

For restaurants, go to Budd Dairy Food Hall with eight pop-up kitchens; Tremont Lounge, an LGBTQIA+ hangout since 1987; or Club Diversity, a fun spot in a circa-1880 house with karaoke, theme nights, and happy hours. Slammers Bar & Pizza Kitchen is Ohio's only remaining lesbian bar and one of the few left in the U.S.

TURN A FUN-FILLED PAGE IN THIS CREATIVE SOUTHERN CITY.
Fairhope, Alabama, U.S.A.

Charming shops, cafés, and art galleries line Section Street in downtown Fairhope.

THE LGBTQIA+ LOWDOWN Alabama is conservative, but the artists' enclave of Fairhope is widely accepting with a creative soul and welcoming spirit. If you're seeking queer nightlife, you'll find bars, drag shows, and more in Mobile, just 30 minutes away.

On a bluff overlooking Mobile Bay, Fairhope is a haven for those seeking some southern charm. Start downtown at the Fairhope Museum of History, housed in a pretty Spanish mission–style building from 1928, where you can learn about the people who shaped this special place. Then stay in the area and stroll flower-lined Fairhope Avenue to take selfies at the Fairhope Clock, an iconic city landmark; hunt for vintage treasures at Crown and Colony Antiques; and browse books and greeting cards at Page & Palette. You'll find a wide selection of titles and author events in this family-owned bookstore that's been a community gathering place since 1968. Plus, it has an on-site café (Latte Da, perfect to refuel) and a bar in the basement (the Book Cellar). Have a beer, a glass of wine, or try cleverly named craft cocktails like the Last of the Mojitos.

Continue downtown to find more great reads at the Book Inn (est. 1979). More into listening than reading? Dr. Music Records sells new and used vinyl, turntables, and handmade suitcase boom boxes, also known as the Sonic Suitcase (invented by Dr. Music himself).

Beyond shopping, see works by local and national artists at the Eastern Shore Art Center, which also hosts the popular First Friday Art Walks. When you need a rest, there's no better place than Fairhope Municipal Pier overlooking Mobile Bay. Chill on the beach, look for shorebirds, or simply find a bench and enjoy the view. The pier is also a place to catch a spectacular natural phenomenon: the jubilee. Occurring in Mobile Bay, mostly during the summer months, crab, shrimp, flounder, and more swarm the water in droves. This kind of occurrence only happens in two places in the world: Fairhope and Tokyo Bay.

After working up an appetite, head to Panini Pete's in the cute French Quarter and try a stacked sandwich (like the muffuletta, and don't skip the beignets). Or dine at the Hope Farm, a family-run restaurant with ingredients from sustainable farming methods. Then sample locally made beers at Fairhope Brewing Company, or head to Bucky's Lounge for cocktails next to firepits or in a cozy piano lounge. Fancy something sweet? Get ice cream or a Fairhope Float (coffee, frozen yogurt, and whipped cream) at Mr. Gene's Beans.

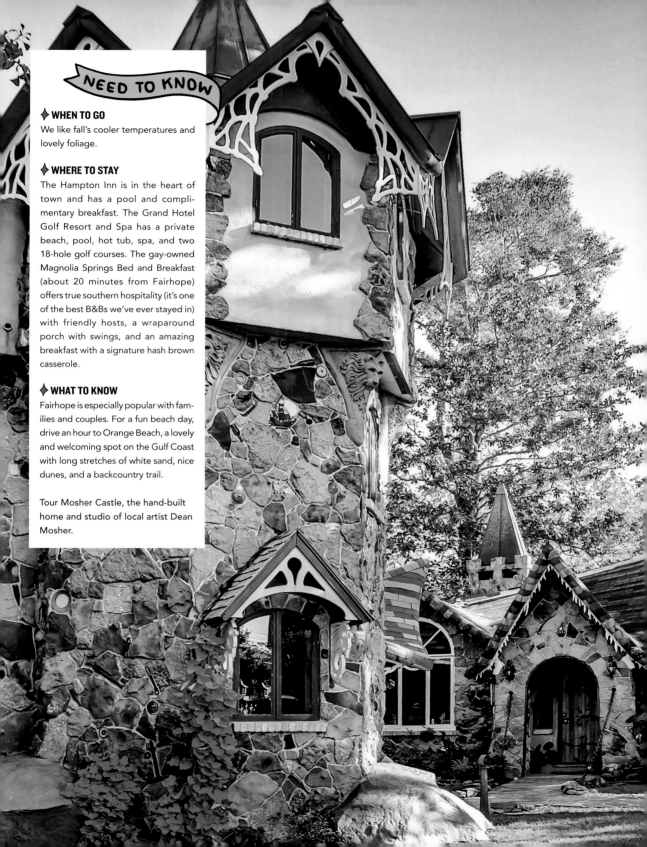

✦ WHEN TO GO

We like fall's cooler temperatures and lovely foliage.

✦ WHERE TO STAY

The Hampton Inn is in the heart of town and has a pool and complimentary breakfast. The Grand Hotel Golf Resort and Spa has a private beach, pool, hot tub, spa, and two 18-hole golf courses. The gay-owned Magnolia Springs Bed and Breakfast (about 20 minutes from Fairhope) offers true southern hospitality (it's one of the best B&Bs we've ever stayed in) with friendly hosts, a wraparound porch with swings, and an amazing breakfast with a signature hash brown casserole.

✦ WHAT TO KNOW

Fairhope is especially popular with families and couples. For a fun beach day, drive an hour to Orange Beach, a lovely and welcoming spot on the Gulf Coast with long stretches of white sand, nice dunes, and a backcountry trail.

Tour Mosher Castle, the hand-built home and studio of local artist Dean Mosher.

◆ WHEN TO GO

Bloomington does Pride right with Pridefest (in August), including a three-day Pride Film Festival, which has been running for more than a decade. The Lotus World Music & Arts Festival is one of the oldest world music festivals in the U.S. and happens in September. The Kiwanis Indiana Balloon Fest also takes place in September.

◆ WHERE TO STAY

Grant Street Inn is a historic boutique hotel with 40 one-of-a-kind rooms— from Victorian chic to modern Old World elegance—spread across five buildings. Close to downtown, stay at Fourwinds Lakeside Inn & Marina with a pool overlooking Monroe Lake. Or try the pet-friendly Hyatt Place Bloomington with a pool and bar (downtown and within walking distance to Indiana University).

◆ WHAT TO KNOW

Hoosier National Forest, 30 minutes from downtown Bloomington, is Indiana's only national forest and is a popular spot to hike, bike, horseback ride, and search for geodes.

Bloomington Pridefest has been held since 2014.

CULTURE AND PRIDE BLOOM BRIGHTLY IN THIS COOL SPOT.
Bloomington, Indiana, U.S.A.

The Courthouse Square Historic District in Bloomington

THE LGBTQIA+ LOWDOWN Bloomington has scored 100 points or more on the Human Rights Campaign's Municipal Equality Index every year since 2015 and even has its own dedicated LGBTQIA+ police liaison to better support members of the community.

This idyllic and progressive college town is well known for its culture, bikeable downtown, farm-to-table dining, shop-local mentality, and nearby wine country. It's also home to the world-renowned Kinsey Institute for Research in Sex, Gender, and Reproduction at Indiana University.

Start at the Eskenazi Museum of Art (est. 1941), in the heart of the Indiana University campus, to see treasures from antiquity and sub-Saharan Africa, paintings by Monet and Picasso, and work from contemporary artists. Then see what's playing at the historic Buskirk-Chumley Theater. Built in 1922 as a cinema, it's now home to the Lotus World Music & Arts Festival, the PRIDE Film Festival, and Indiana University's African American Arts Institute. On the first Friday of every month, a collection of downtown art galleries (all within walking distance of one another on Arts Mile) stay open later for Gallery Walk Bloomington. Just outside of town, visit the Tibetan Mongolian Buddhist Cultural Center, where you can view the structures and iconography, and learn the meaning behind the Wheel of Life.

Vino lovers, Indiana's wine country is a must-do, with more than 100 wineries, such as Oliver Winery, the oldest in the state and one of the largest in the country (their summer spritzers are on point). Sip award-winning Apple Pie and Cherry Moscato and enjoy the hilltop views. Then head to Butler Winery and Country Heritage Winery for Seyval Blanc and rosé. Skip the driving with a tour that includes transportation, such as deTours or Beyond the Vine wine tours. If wine isn't your thing, try Cardinal Spirits, Bloomington's first craft distillery and makers of a special Pride Vodka (10 percent of proceeds go to LGBTQIA+ organizations, year-round).

At FARMbloomington, you'll find vintage vibes and great garlic fries (and a club downstairs). The Owlery is the spot for vegan and vegetarian dishes, craft beer, and baked goods. After dinner, go to the Back Door for drag, burlesque, and cabaret shows, live music, dance parties, and karaoke. Orbit Room is a fun spot with pinball machines, food, drinks, and shows (for all ages until 8 p.m.).

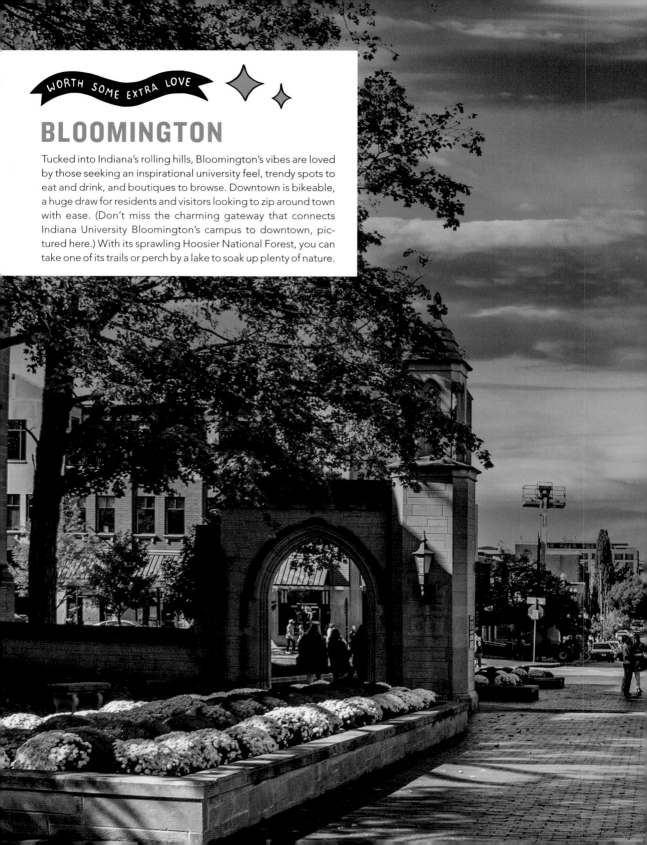

BLOOMINGTON

Tucked into Indiana's rolling hills, Bloomington's vibes are loved by those seeking an inspirational university feel, trendy spots to eat and drink, and boutiques to browse. Downtown is bikeable, a huge draw for residents and visitors looking to zip around town with ease. (Don't miss the charming gateway that connects Indiana University Bloomington's campus to downtown, pictured here.) With its sprawling Hoosier National Forest, you can take one of its trails or perch by a lake to soak up plenty of nature.

ENJOY STRETCHES OF BEACH AND CLIFFS HIGH ABOVE THE SEA.
Tirana, Albania

THE LGBTQIA+ LOWDOWN Though many parts of Albania are still conservative in terms of LGBTQIA+ rights, the Parliament of Albania passed a law in 2010 banning discrimination based on sexual orientation and gender identity. Conversion therapy is also banned. Since 2012, Tirana has hosted an annual Pride parade.

Founded in 1614, Tirana, the small capital city of Albania, has pastel buildings, museums, and monuments, and is the future home to what will be one of the world's largest buildings—a vertical forest to honor Skanderbeg, an Albanian national hero.

Start with tours of two Bunk'Art locations (massive antinuclear bunkers from the Cold War), where you can explore underground tunnels and rooms in which government officials would conduct business and hide out to stay safe.

Back aboveground, take the Austrian-built Dajti Ekspres cable car 15 minutes to the peak of Dajti Mountain, where you can play mini golf or go hiking, biking, and in-line skating. Stay for a meal at the cliffside restaurant, Ballkoni Dajtit, with traditional stews and other authentic dishes paired with views of the city from more than 3,281 feet (1,000 m) above sea level.

Peruse history at the Museum of Secret Surveillance, originally built in 1931 as an obstetric clinic. The museum is dedicated to teaching visitors about the activities conducted during the Communist regime.

Don't miss Pazari i Ri (the New Bazaar), set in one of the oldest parts of the city. Open 24 hours a day, you'll find shops, a green market, a fishmonger, and a butcher. You'll also find bars and restaurants, including Art and the City for food, literature, and music; Reka Patisserie for delicious pastries made from nearly 100-year-old recipes; and Restorant Tradita, serving traditional dishes.

Gaily Tours, a company with LGBTQIA+-friendly guides, conducts day and night excursions to explore the city, its history, and attractions with a local guide and in a group—which may provide an extra level of comfort for some.

Spend some time on the Adriatic Sea with a visit to Durrës, one of the oldest cities in Albania that dates back to 627 B.C. Head to the Beach of Durrës, the most popular stretch of sand in Albania, and then go see the ruins of the Durrës Roman amphitheater. For another Durrës adventure, head to the hills to Duka Winery and Vineyard, which makes Merlot, Tempranillo, and Cabernet Sauvignon, and offers tastings (reserve in advance).

To visit another ancient place, drive south to Berat and see the "City of a Thousand Windows," a UNESCO-listed city known for its Osum River location. You'll also see Ottoman houses stacked on the cliffs, plus the Berat Castle, a fortress that encompasses Byzantine churches, the Red Mosque, and the Onufri Iconographic Museum.

Explore more than 5,000 artifacts spanning from the Bronze Age to the modern era at the National Historical Museum.

◆ WHEN TO GO

Visit spring to early summer to avoid extreme weather. Tirana Pride is typically held in May.

◆ WHERE TO STAY

Maritim Hotel Plaza Tirana is a new and modern spot next to the city's main square and has a rooftop restaurant and bar. Hotel Mondial has deluxe suites with balconies and an on-site restaurant.

◆ WHAT TO KNOW

The Albanian Riviera (about three hours from Tirana in southwest Albania) makes a great overnight trip. Vlorë is known for its beaches and stunning bay. It's also less than an hour to Llogara National Park, one of the most visited national parks in Albania (located in the Ceraunian Mountains). Enjoy long hiking trails and views of the Ionian Sea.

Bunk'Art 2, a former nuclear bunker in Tirana, is now a museum and artists' space.

Fireworks burst above downtown Montevideo during a Pride parade.

SEE A HISTORIC DOWNTOWN AND CRUISE A REALLY LONG WATERFRONT SIDEWALK.

Montevideo, Uruguay

THE LGBTQIA+ LOWDOWN Uruguay is a South American trendsetter for LGBTQIA+ rights. Homosexuality has been legal since 1934, same-sex adoption and marriage rights were approved in 2013, and numerous antidiscrimination measures have been established.

Though often eclipsed by next-door neighbors Buenos Aires and Rio de Janeiro, Montevideo is a laid-back yet cosmopolitan city with an interesting historic center and plenty of beaches to explore.

Start your day in Ciudad Vieja (Montevideo's Old Town), with its narrow lanes lined with colorful buildings and cool street art. You'll also find the city's main square, Plaza Independencia. Built in 1937, the plaza connects Montevideo's old and new areas via the impressive Puerta de la Ciudadela (City Gate).

Just off the square is Teatro Solís, a treasured cultural institution that dates back to the 1850s. With its striking columns, a lavish auditorium, and excellent acoustics, it's a terrific place to see an opera, play, or concert. From the theater, stroll along the pedestrian-only Calle Sarandí and take your pick of cafés and boutiques. Then check out Plaza Constitución, a leafy park with a nice fountain; the Montevideo Cabildo history museum; and the Catedral Metropolitana de Montevideo, which dates back to the 18th century.

Next, explore the world-famous Rambla. Bring your favorite walking shoes (or grab a bike, scooter, or in-line skates), because this waterfront sidewalk stretches a whopping 14 miles (23 km)—the longest continuous sidewalk in the world. One of our favorite walks along the Rambla is between Ciudad Vieja and Playa de Los Pocitos. It's about five miles (8 km), but you'll find plenty of spots to rest and hydrate with some maté (Uruguay's national drink). During the walk, you'll also pass Playa Ramirez and Pittamiglio Castle, the former home of architect Humberto Pittamiglio. Inside, you'll find an eccentric maze of 23 towers and 54 rooms, random staircases, and hidden symbols. Once you reach Playa Pocitos, stay for the afternoon to sunbathe or enjoy a seaside cocktail. The water here is a mix of river and ocean, so don't expect Caribbean-like beaches, but it's worth hanging out to experience the fun and local flavor.

Other great highlights include browsing locally made crafts at the Mercado Agrícola de Montevideo (MAM) or catching a soccer game at the Estadio Centenario (built in 1930), the site of the first ever FIFA World Cup.

Of course, you can't come to Montevideo without sampling some of its terrific food like *chivito* (Uruguay's national sandwich, typically piled high with beef, cheese, and tomato, and served over a ton of fries) and *morcilla* (blood sausage). Try it all at the popular Mercado del Puerto. For drinks, check out some of the city's queer bars like Chains Pub or Il Tempo. Don't leave town without perfecting your moves at Tango Queer Uruguay.

Play on the sand or in the surf at one of Montevideo's many beaches.

SOUK YOURSELF IN THE RED CITY.
Marrakech, Morocco

Dusk falls over the lively Jemaa el-Fna square in Marrakech.

THE LGBTQIA+ LOWDOWN With a strong French influence, Marrakech is among Morocco's most open-minded cities, with friendly, welcoming people. Though homosexual acts are illegal, it's rarely enforced for foreigners. Still, avoid PDA and be respectful of local customs and you'll have a great vacation.

Located in northern Africa, in the foothills of the Atlas Mountains, Marrakech is unquestionably alluring. From the frenetic energy of its souks (traditional markets) to relaxing gardens, the "Red City" always shines bright.

Base yourself in the medina (the older, historic section) and get lost in the twisting alleyways. Don't fight it; you'll get turned around 10 times and that's part of the fun. Wander the souks to browse spices, carpets, ceramics, robes, and babouche (Moroccan slippers) among dazzling lights. If you need a break, take your pick of cafés and enjoy a world-famous Moroccan mint tea. Eventually, make your way to Jemaa el-Fna square (go in the morning for fewer crowds, although also fewer street performers). Try to get a good look at the Kutubīyah Mosque, which dates back to the 12th century and has a 253-foot-high (77 m) minaret (note: Only Muslims are allowed inside).

Continue exploring Marrakech's Old Town with a stop at the Saadian Tombs, a 16th-century burial ground for the rich featuring elaborate marble tombs, and El Badi Palace, the ruins of a 16th-century megabuilding that had more than 300 rooms. Don't miss the 19th-century Bahia Palace, which has lavishly decorated rooms and gardens.

Then venture to Ville Nouvelle (New Town) and the trendy neighborhood of Gueliz. In contrast to the medina, there are wide boulevards, designer stores, and cafés with spacious patios. The star attraction is Jardin Majorelle, a 40-year passion project by French painter Jacques Majorelle that gay fashion designer Yves Saint Laurent later bought and restored. Wander the garden and check out an eclectic (and slightly psychedelic) collection of cacti and plants from around the world. Crisscrossing walkways and an electric blue building (popular on Instagram feeds) blend art deco and Moorish styles. Saint Laurent loved the garden so much that his ashes are spread here. To learn more about him, visit the Musée Yves Saint Laurent next door.

As the sun begins to set, head back to the medina and revisit the Jemaa el-Fna, now bustling with storytellers, street performers, and musicians. Take in the energy, then head to the north section with a wide selection of food stalls serving classic Moroccan dishes like lamb and beef tagines, couscous, and harira soup.

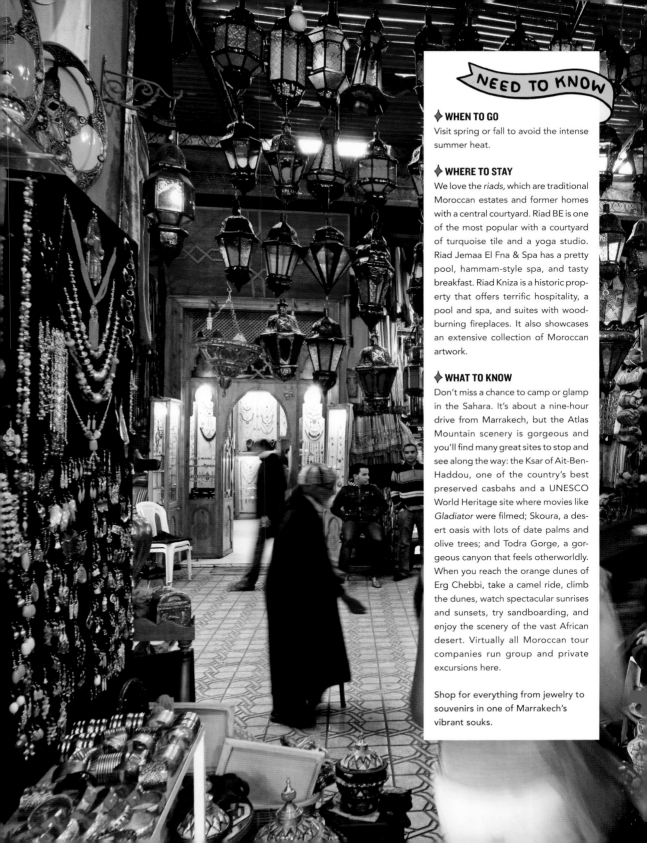

NEED TO KNOW

◆ WHEN TO GO
Visit spring or fall to avoid the intense summer heat.

◆ WHERE TO STAY
We love the *riads*, which are traditional Moroccan estates and former homes with a central courtyard. Riad BE is one of the most popular with a courtyard of turquoise tile and a yoga studio. Riad Jemaa El Fna & Spa has a pretty pool, hammam-style spa, and tasty breakfast. Riad Kniza is a historic property that offers terrific hospitality, a pool and spa, and suites with wood-burning fireplaces. It also showcases an extensive collection of Moroccan artwork.

◆ WHAT TO KNOW
Don't miss a chance to camp or glamp in the Sahara. It's about a nine-hour drive from Marrakech, but the Atlas Mountain scenery is gorgeous and you'll find many great sites to stop and see along the way: the Ksar of Ait-Ben-Haddou, one of the country's best preserved casbahs and a UNESCO World Heritage site where movies like *Gladiator* were filmed; Skoura, a desert oasis with lots of date palms and olive trees; and Todra Gorge, a gorgeous canyon that feels otherworldly. When you reach the orange dunes of Erg Chebbi, take a camel ride, climb the dunes, watch spectacular sunrises and sunsets, try sandboarding, and enjoy the scenery of the vast African desert. Virtually all Moroccan tour companies run group and private excursions here.

Shop for everything from jewelry to souvenirs in one of Marrakech's vibrant souks.

Buddhist monks walk past the Royal Palace.

TOUR THE TEMPLES AND MARKETS, THEN JUMP FOR JOY.
Phnom Penh, Cambodia

The National Museum of Cambodia is dedicated to preserving and showcasing the ancient Khmer culture.

THE LGBTQIA+ LOWDOWN In Cambodia, same-sex activity is legal and same-sex relationships are widely accepted, especially in major cities. Cambodia holds an annual weeklong Pride celebration. Phnom Penh has a small LGBTQIA+ scene with a few bars and restaurants central to the community.

The bustling capital of Phnom Penh was founded in 1372. From its Riverfront Park and busy side streets with temples, monuments, great dining, and shopping, you'll find plenty to explore.

Start at Riverfront Park, one of the most important places in the city as the home of the Royal Palace, residence to the king. Though you can't go inside, it's worth getting up close for photos and to see the Silver Pagoda, named for the five tons (4.5 t) of silver tiles inside. Next to the palace, visit the National Museum of Cambodia. The country's largest museum was inaugurated in 1920 and houses artifacts related to art, history, and religion. Close by, see Wat Ounalom, one of the oldest pagodas in the country, with more than 40 buildings, including a main temple and multiple statues. It's also famous as a center of Cambodian Buddhist education and for its stupa, containing an eyebrow hair of the Buddha.

Experience something totally different at Fly Phnom Penh, the first ever trampoline park in Cambodia, where you can do the ninja course and play on a Velcro wall.

Don't miss learning how to make Khmer cuisine with Banana Cooking Class. Choose from a half- or full-day experience to explore a local market, meet the vendors, and discover the secrets of preparing traditional dishes with an experienced Cambodian chef. Or catch a ferry for a day tour of Silk Island (Koh Dach) to see the silk-weaving communities keeping this ancient tradition alive.

When cravings hit, go to 2Pangea, a hugely popular buffet featuring seafood, homemade pizza and pasta, dim sum, sushi, noodles, and dessert. Namaste India Restaurant BKK has fine authentic dining with food cooked in a tandoor (clay oven) imported from India. Curry Pot TTP is a beloved restaurant serving Indian and Nepali cuisine. For drinks, go to Blue Chilli, the longest-running LGBTQIA+ bar in the country, with drag shows, dancing, and cocktails. At Space Hair Salon and Bar, you can get your hair done and your drinks poured in one place; the Pride of Phnom Penh is a bijou music bar with LGBTQIA+ crowds; and the Toolbox is "geared" toward gay men.

CLASSIC CITIES
— With —
SOMETHING
for Everyone

What a wonderful journey around the world we've taken. Are you a traveler who likes to keep busy on vacation yet gets overwhelmed by a ton of choices? We want to help you simplify things—and give you a list of what to do in these well-known queer-friendly cities. From museum-hopping to theater and great restaurants, you really can have it all with some of this chapter's destinations. And for those of you who want a great getaway with fewer crowds, we suggest alternative destinations that often play second fiddle but are well worth their own trip. So, let's get started to help you make the most of major destinations and off-the-beaten-path experiences, while also sharing day trips to help you soak up even more of the scenery.

FIND BEAUTY AND BRIGHT LIGHTS IN THESE TWO BELOVED CITIES.

New York, New York, and Philadelphia, Pennsylvania, U.S.A.

Philadelphia's Market Street is home to a number of queer-friendly and queer-owned shops and restaurants.

THE LGBTQIA+ LOWDOWN NYC has the largest queer population in the U.S. and is an iconic location of the LGBTQIA+ rights movement in the country. Philly also has a large queer population and its own history as the host of the first major demonstration for LGBTQIA+ rights in the U.S.

New York City has wowed tourists since the first ones started arriving in the 1820s, and as a lifelong New Yorker (Mark) and a six-year resident (Amy), we can understand why. But it's better to say goodbye to the crowds to find what is truly the best of New York.

The city's history, especially in Greenwich Village, can be explored via Christopher Street Tours, which gives the inside scoop on historic sites and LGBTQIA+ pioneers. We could spend all day people-watching in Washington Square Park, but so many other great sites are nearby: the Stonewall Inn, a historic landmark where the 1969 riots further launched the gay rights movement; Marie's Crisis Café, an iconic LGBTQIA+ piano bar (dating back to 1929), where you can belt out show tunes; and Henrietta Hudson for lesbian karaoke and dancing.

New York has so many great museums, too. Of course, there are famous ones, but don't overlook the Museum of the City of New York, which details the city's history and has a moving exhibit on progress for LGBTQIA+ rights.

Just a two-hour train ride away, Philly holds so much of our country's history—it's where the Declaration of Independence was signed and the Constitution was written—plus, it's easy to get around and has plenty of parks and culture to explore.

The African American Museum in Philadelphia, which opened in 1976 as part of the city's bicentennial celebration, was the first museum in the U.S. dedicated to Black American history, traditions, and culture.

For additional important history, Giovanni's Room is the oldest LGBTQIA+ and feminist bookstore in the country, and Beyond the Bell Tours offers a trans history tour of Philadelphia, which we think is really awesome.

In 2007, Philly's mayor John Street dedicated 36 rainbow street signs around the blocks between 11th and Broad Streets and Pine and Chestnut Streets, an area that was nicknamed the "Gayborhood" in the '90s for being the heart of the city's LGBTQIA+ community and culture. You can now find more than 70 rainbow street signs decorating homes and businesses in the area.

And finally, visit the famous red-lettered "LOVE" statue in LOVE Park, which was created by Robert Indiana in 1970 and always captures our hearts.

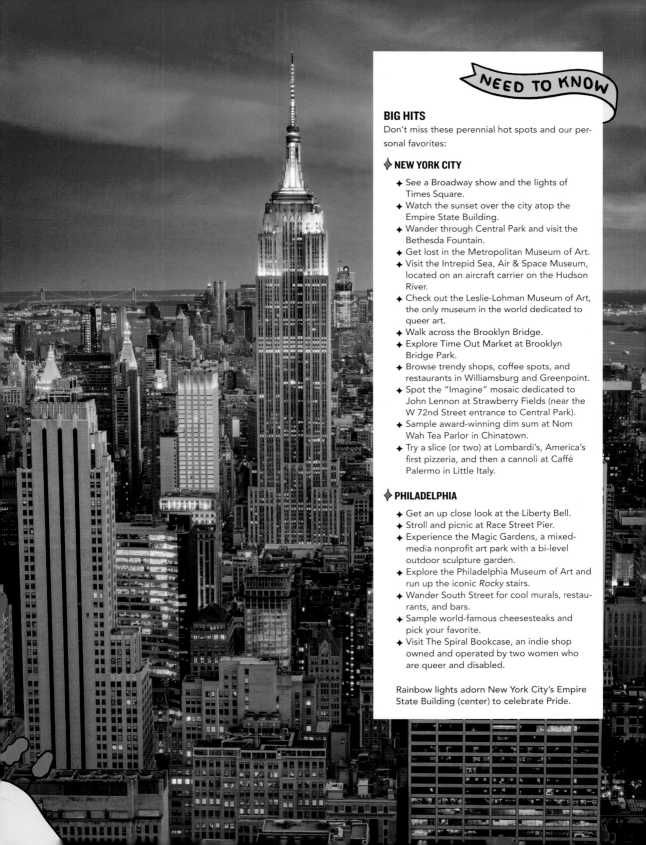

BIG HITS

Don't miss these perennial hot spots and our personal favorites:

◆ NEW YORK CITY

- ◆ See a Broadway show and the lights of Times Square.
- ◆ Watch the sunset over the city atop the Empire State Building.
- ◆ Wander through Central Park and visit the Bethesda Fountain.
- ◆ Get lost in the Metropolitan Museum of Art.
- ◆ Visit the Intrepid Sea, Air & Space Museum, located on an aircraft carrier on the Hudson River.
- ◆ Check out the Leslie-Lohman Museum of Art, the only museum in the world dedicated to queer art.
- ◆ Walk across the Brooklyn Bridge.
- ◆ Explore Time Out Market at Brooklyn Bridge Park.
- ◆ Browse trendy shops, coffee spots, and restaurants in Williamsburg and Greenpoint.
- ◆ Spot the "Imagine" mosaic dedicated to John Lennon at Strawberry Fields (near the W 72nd Street entrance to Central Park).
- ◆ Sample award-winning dim sum at Nom Wah Tea Parlor in Chinatown.
- ◆ Try a slice (or two) at Lombardi's, America's first pizzeria, and then a cannoli at Caffé Palermo in Little Italy.

◆ PHILADELPHIA

- ◆ Get an up close look at the Liberty Bell.
- ◆ Stroll and picnic at Race Street Pier.
- ◆ Experience the Magic Gardens, a mixed-media nonprofit art park with a bi-level outdoor sculpture garden.
- ◆ Explore the Philadelphia Museum of Art and run up the iconic *Rocky* stairs.
- ◆ Wander South Street for cool murals, restaurants, and bars.
- ◆ Sample world-famous cheesesteaks and pick your favorite.
- ◆ Visit The Spiral Bookcase, an indie shop owned and operated by two women who are queer and disabled.

Rainbow lights adorn New York City's Empire State Building (center) to celebrate Pride.

BIG HITS

Don't miss these perennial hot spots and our personal favorites:

◆ WASHINGTON, D.C.

- ✦ Explore the National Mall (especially the Washington Monument and Lincoln Memorial) at night when the monuments are illuminated.
- ✦ Stroll Georgetown's shops, restaurants, and cafés.
- ✦ See the cherry blossoms in the spring, which always live up to the hype (and are worth battling the crowds).

◆ BALTIMORE

- ✦ Hit up the Walters Art Museum for artifacts from Egypt and Rome, and the Baltimore Museum of Art for the world's largest Matisse collection.
- ✦ Spend the day at Chesapeake Beach.
- ✦ Visit Fort McHenry, just outside the city.
- ✦ See Edgar Allan Poe's former home and museum and his grave. Run into his ghost at the Horse You Came In On Saloon.
- ✦ Eat your way through the 200-plus-year-old Lexington Market with 100 vendors selling everything from Maryland crab cakes to vegan dishes.

The Washington Monument peeks through the famous cherry blossoms along D.C.'s Tidal Basin.

EXPLORE U.S. HISTORY, SOME OF THE WORLD'S BEST MUSEUMS, AND TWO WASHINGTON MONUMENTS.

Washington, D.C., and Baltimore, Maryland, U.S.A.

Atomic Books, an independent bookstore in Baltimore, specializes in indie comics and small-press publications.

THE LGBTQIA+ LOWDOWN Washington, D.C., is home to one of the United States' largest queer communities. In equally welcoming Baltimore, you'll find many LGBTQIA+-owned and queer-friendly stores, restaurants, and bars in the historic Mount Vernon Square area and sprinkled throughout the city.

In D.C., history is literally everywhere—from Capitol Hill to Cedar Hill (Frederick Douglass's former home). And don't miss the Smithsonian museums (they're free!), including the National Air and Space Museum, the National Museum of African American History and Culture, and the hidden gem of the National Museum of Women in the Arts.

The District is also a fun outdoor city. Stroll around a less frequented green space like Tregaron Conservancy with trails, wild gardens, meadows, and a lily pond that's a real oasis in the city.

You'll also find a strong literary and theatrical spirit, especially catching up on queer reads at Kramers Bookstore, Bar & Restaurant, Politics and Prose, Loyalty Bookstore, and Little District Books. And going to Busboys and Poets, a café and bookstore named after Langston Hughes, never fails to inspire.

Of course, one of the best things about D.C. is its many queer-owned and super-welcoming places such as Republic Restoratives (distilled spirits like vodka and brandy, anyone?); Red Bear Brewing, serving craft brews; Three Fifty Bakery & Coffee Bar for fresh pastries and a tasty caffeine fix; Miss Pixie's, where you can shop eclectic "furnishings

and whatnot"; and tons of classic community bars, including JR's Bar & Grill, Nellie's (famous for its drag brunches), Pitchers (a gay sports bar), and its next-door neighbor A League of Her Own (popular with queer women).

Just like D.C., Baltimore is filled with a lot of history and features 19th- and 20th-century row houses. Mount Vernon Square is home to the original Washington Monument, and the George Peabody Library is an incredible house of books with lots of natural light.

Great bookshops include Atomic Books (it's so cool that John Waters gets his fan mail here). Red Emma's is a worker-owned queer bookstore and café.

As for being on the water, it doesn't get much better than the Inner Harbor, where you'll find the Maryland Science Center and the National Aquarium.

In the theater scene, Center Stage is dedicated to making theater accessible to everyone, while Artscape is an annual outdoor festival (held every summer).

And for queer nightlife, having a drink at historic Leon's, which has been open since 1957, never gets old. Other great options include the Drinkery, Rowan Tree, and Factory 17 for dancing.

DISCOVER BEAUTY AND HISTORY IN THE BAY AND BEYOND.

San Francisco and Sacramento, California, U.S.A.

Drivers navigate one of San Francisco's famously steep hills in the Castro District.

THE LGBTQIA+ LOWDOWN San Francisco's LGBTQIA+ culture dates all the way back to the 1848 gold rush and has only gotten stronger. It's one of the largest and most prominent queer communities in the U.S. Ninety minutes away, Sacramento has a perfect Human Rights Campaign score of 100 and has been a longtime destination attracting queer visitors.

San Francisco steals hearts with its picturesque bay, hills, and historic neighborhoods, plus its iconic cable car system. It's also the site of some of the most important queer history in the U.S.

There's always something fun playing at the Castro Theatre, a landmark since 1976, and a beloved queer community space for film, music, comedy, and more—we can't visit San Fran without a stop here. Castro Walking Tours shares its queer history while on a great trek through the neighborhood.

We could spend an hour—or the whole day—at Golden Gate Park, a bucolic wonderland with lakes, meadows, and redwood groves.

The City by the Bay should be called the City by the Books because there are so many great bookstores here. Fabulosa Books is a jackpot of queer lit, along with reads on witchcraft, poetry, politics, and more.

In the heart of Chinatown—one of the oldest in the U.S.— Golden Gate Fortune Cookie Factory has been making the treats by hand since 1962 (sometimes up to 10,000 a day). It's always cool to see the cookie-making process in person and explore the rest of Chinatown's narrow alleys.

Sacramento's gold rush history is a throwback to the 1800s, but the city has so much more: the Sacramento Waterfront, a National Historic Landmark District; the Sacramento History Museum, a reproduction of the 1854 City Hall and Waterworks building; and the Crocker Art Museum, founded in 1885, with an incredible collection of California pieces.

The midtown Lavender Heights neighborhood is Sac's official LGBTQIA+ area (on par with SF's Castro District). It's home to the Sacramento LGBT Community Center and is a landmark of Sacramento's vibrant LGBTQIA+ community. Sac also has a rainbow crosswalk and boutiques, galleries, restaurants, and bars.

For a fun road trip, we love the charming and LGBTQIA+- friendly gold rush town of Nevada City and nearby Grass Valley, tucked in the heart of the Sierra Nevada mountains.

BIG HITS

Don't miss these perennial hot spots and our personal favorites:

◆ SAN FRANCISCO

- ✦ See the windmills, Japanese Tea House and Garden, and Queen Wilhelmina Tulip Garden at Golden Gate Park.
- ✦ Go to City Lights bookstore.
- ✦ Wander the Haight-Ashbury neighborhood, home to the flower power movement of the '60s. Spot the former residences of icons like the Grateful Dead and Janis Joplin.
- ✦ Shop new vinyl, books, and vintage posters at Amoeba Music.
- ✦ Check out Chinatown's dim sum restaurants, herbalists, and shops.
- ✦ Admire artifacts at the Chinese Historical Society of America Museum.
- ✦ Visit Tin How Temple, one of the oldest Chinese temples in the country.
- ✦ Don't miss the Mission District, vibrant Japantown, or Berkeley and Oakland across the San Francisco Bay.

◆ SACRAMENTO

- ✦ Tour underneath the city with the Sacramento History Museum and learn how Sacramento dealt with the floodwaters of the 1800s.
- ✦ Ride along the Sacramento River via the California State Railroad Museum.
- ✦ Take a scenic and historic river cruise, bike, or walk along the Sacramento River National Recreation Trail.
- ✦ Visit William Land Regional Park for lakes, a golf course, and a rock garden.
- ✦ Check out California State Capitol Park's walking paths, roses, and unforgettable views.
- ✦ Have drinks on the patio at Mercantile Saloon.
- ✦ Go to nearby Grass Valley for Empire Mine State Historic Park, one of the oldest gold mines in California.

Spend a tranquil morning at the Sacramento River watching the sun rise over Tower Bridge.

BIG HITS

Don't miss these perennial hot spots and our personal favorites:

◆ CHICAGO

- ◆ Visit the American Writers Museum, where you can use a typewriter that once belonged to Truman Capote.
- ◆ Check out the Field Museum of Natural History—its "Inside Ancient Egypt" collection is outstanding.
- ◆ Browse the Art Institute of Chicago for O'Keeffe, van Gogh, Monet, and Renoir all in one place.
- ◆ Enjoy Garfield Park Conservatory and Alfred Caldwell Lily Pool in the Lincoln Park Conservancy.
- ◆ Stroll and shop the Magnificent Mile.
- ◆ Sample deep-dish pizza.

◆ DETROIT

- ◆ Spot the murals and graffiti art at the Dequindre Cut Greenway.
- ◆ Wander the revitalized RiverWalk.
- ◆ Ride the People Mover transit.
- ◆ Get a famed Coney dog and Detroit-style pizza.
- ◆ Peruse Eastern Market, one of the largest and oldest in the United States.
- ◆ Chill out at Belle Isle Park on the Detroit River.

Rowers on the Chicago River get an epic view of the city's skyline.

EXPERIENCE A MIDWEST RENAISSANCE IN THE WINDY AND MOTOR CITIES.

Chicago, Illinois, and Detroit, Michigan, U.S.A.

Eclectic art installations adorn the yards and facades of abandoned houses in Detroit's Brightmoor neighborhood.

THE LGBTQIA+ LOWDOWN Both Chicago and Detroit have lively queer scenes and many LGBTQIA+-owned and queer-supported businesses.

Where else in the world besides Chicago can you see the shadows of skyscrapers on the shores of Lake Michigan (from the 360 Chicago observation deck) or view towering buildings from the water while on an architecture river cruise?

When you want outside time, Chicago has the Lakefront Trail and the Riverwalk right in the city. Kathy Osterman Beach, also known as Hollywood Beach, is popular with the queer community.

In Grant Park, you could stare at Buckingham Fountain (one of the world's biggest) for hours. Its choreographed presentation of lights, music, and water shooting 150 feet (46 m) in the air will get you every time.

Chicago is home to great theater at companies such as Victory Gardens, which designs its seasonal showings with inclusive stories about people of varying cultures, races, and genders. And Second City, where Tina Fey and Amy Poehler once took the stage, rakes in the laughs.

For queer life, Sidetrack and Roscoe's Tavern in Northalsted are always fun, and we love browsing the LGBTQIA+ literary selections at nearby Unabridged Bookstore and Women & Children First in Andersonville.

It's hard not to appreciate a city like Detroit, which demonstrates both heart and character in spades. Though it's experienced some turbulent times, Motor City is now refreshed and revitalized.

Detroit has an amazing arts and culture scene with lots of reimagined spaces. In the Heidelberg Project, artist Tyree Guyton used recycled materials to transform disheveled buildings and crumbling streets in the McDougall-Hunt neighborhood (where he grew up) into art installations. The Belt is an alley turned into a hip art space with creative cocktail bars. And the Dequindre Cut Greenway is a former rail line that's now a paved trail with murals and graffiti art.

Midtown is known as Detroit's cultural center. The Detroit Institute of Arts is widely hailed as one of America's top museums. We also highly recommend the Charles H. Wright Museum of African American History, which offers exhibits, education, and research opportunities related to the contributions and culture of African Americans. And visiting the Motown Museum is practically mandatory.

There are also great queer spaces, like Menjo's Entertainment Complex (where Madonna once danced), Gigi's Gay Bar, and Woodward.

EXPLORE THE BRITISH CHARMS OF OLD AND NEW IN TWO OF THE WORLD'S MOST QUEER-FRIENDLY CITIES.

London and Manchester, England, U.K.

THE LGBTQIA+ LOWDOWN London has one of the biggest Pride celebrations on the planet. You'll find queer-owned and LGBTQIA+-welcoming places all around. Manchester is home to the Gay Village (along Canal Street) and also hosts a large Pride festival.

Obviously, London has certain must-dos like seeing blockbuster theater in the West End, Big Ben, Buckingham Palace, and the Tower of London. But you could also spend days exploring East London. Victoria Park's lakes and gardens are lovely, Shoreditch and Hackney Wick have cool street art, and Las Vegas has nothing on the retro neon signs at Gods Own Junkyard. At Columbia Road Flower Market, you'll always find the brightest bulbs. Also worth your time are awesome queer spaces like Dalston Superstore (great drag brunches) and the Glory, a bar and performance space owned by local drag queens.

The neighborhood of Bloomsbury is where Virginia Woolf, T. S. Eliot, Charles Dickens, and other literary powerhouses lived. It's home to a special LGBTQIA+ tour called "Desire, Love, and Identity." Bloomsbury is also home to Gay's the Word, the U.K.'s oldest LGBTQIA+ bookstore (est. 1979), a true gem.

When we first came up with the concept of this book, cities like Manchester immediately came to mind, specifically for the Gay Village (on Canal Street), where the LGBTQIA+ community and allies come together to eat, drink, socialize, and enjoy fun times.

At Richmond Tea Rooms, go down the rabbit hole with drag queens at *Alice in Wonderland*–themed Mad Hatter's Tea Parties and late-night sing-alongs. Churchills is a great pub to watch cabaret and drag shows, and to toast a pint with your friends. The Eagle is a long-standing sanctuary for men, while Vanilla is a popular lesbian bar that's considered one of the best in the U.K.

It's hard not to get swept up in the football energy, but cheering on Manchester United at Old Trafford (called the "Theatre of Dreams") is practically required.

Because Manchester was the world's first "industrial city," a visit to the Science and Industry Museum feels especially befitting. It's housed in a former railroad station (one of the world's oldest) and has the popular air and space collections, among other exhibits. The Manchester Art Gallery has one of the largest collections in the U.K. in a 200-year-old building.

If you're a bookworm like us, Chetham's Library is the oldest public library in England and has been in continuous use for more than 370 years. For history and fun, visit the Victoria Baths, a lavish bathhouse with lovely stained glass and brickwork; it dates back to 1906 and has undergone a major renovation.

Canal Street and the surrounding neighborhood have been dubbed the Gay Village of Manchester.

BIG HITS

Don't miss these perennial hot spots and our personal favorites:

◆ LONDON

- ✦ Shop Old Spitalfields Market, one of London's oldest public markets.
- ✦ Spend hours at the British Museum, which holds the Rosetta Stone, Parthenon sculptures, and a bust of Ramses the Great.
- ✦ Explore Brick Lane for vintage stores and more than 20 curry houses, coffee shops, bars and pubs, and food stalls.
- ✦ See the Temperate House, the world's largest Victorian glasshouse.
- ✦ Check out the Hive, a 55-foot (17 m) art installation depicting life in a beehive.
- ✦ Enjoy the lovely afternoon tea at the Royal Botanic Kew Gardens, a UNESCO World Heritage site in Richmond.

◆ MANCHESTER

- ✦ Get your sports fix at the National Football Museum.
- ✦ Visit the Manchester Museum for natural history, archaeology, and anthropology.
- ✦ Browse the Whitworth Art Gallery, including works by Renoir and Cézanne.
- ✦ Explore the John Rylands Library for its Gothic architecture, archways, vaulted ceilings, and impressive collection of books.

Pride revelers are pretty in (retro) pink as they parade through London.

LONDON

With its spectacular theater scene, literary pedigree, and never-ending choices of things to do, London always tops our list of favorite getaways. Full disclosure: We have a particular fondness for the city because Mark spontaneously proposed to his boyfriend there over Christmas dinner; thank goodness, he said yes. Like millions of others, we love walking along the Thames and taking in the iconic view of Parliament and Elizabeth Tower (both pictured here). Did you think we meant Big Ben? Fun fact: That's actually the name of the massive bell hanging within the tower.

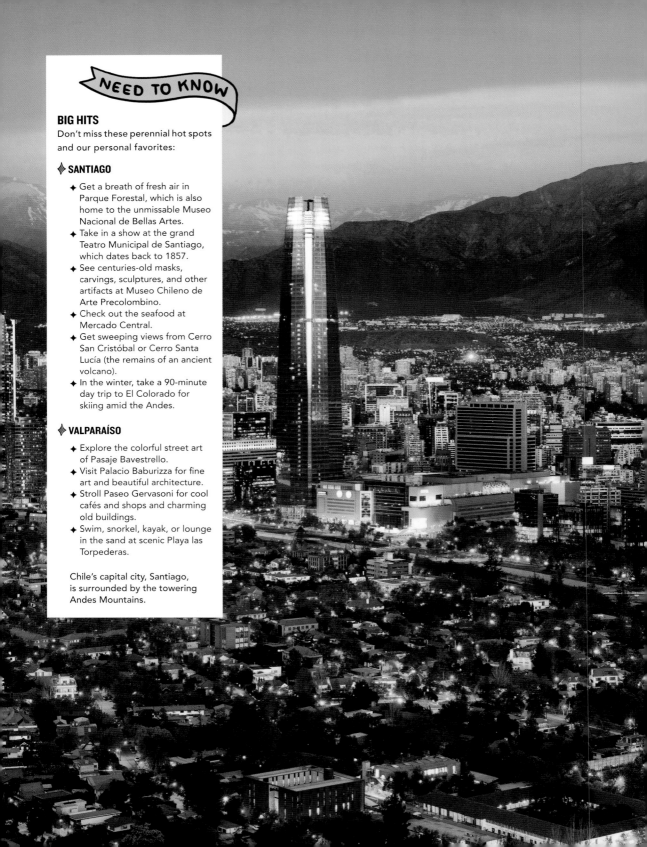

NEED TO KNOW

BIG HITS

Don't miss these perennial hot spots and our personal favorites:

◆ SANTIAGO

- ◆ Get a breath of fresh air in Parque Forestal, which is also home to the unmissable Museo Nacional de Bellas Artes.
- ◆ Take in a show at the grand Teatro Municipal de Santiago, which dates back to 1857.
- ◆ See centuries-old masks, carvings, sculptures, and other artifacts at Museo Chileno de Arte Precolombino.
- ◆ Check out the seafood at Mercado Central.
- ◆ Get sweeping views from Cerro San Cristóbal or Cerro Santa Lucía (the remains of an ancient volcano).
- ◆ In the winter, take a 90-minute day trip to El Colorado for skiing amid the Andes.

◆ VALPARAÍSO

- ◆ Explore the colorful street art of Pasaje Bavestrello.
- ◆ Visit Palacio Baburizza for fine art and beautiful architecture.
- ◆ Stroll Paseo Gervasoni for cool cafés and shops and charming old buildings.
- ◆ Swim, snorkel, kayak, or lounge in the sand at scenic Playa las Torpederas.

Chile's capital city, Santiago, is surrounded by the towering Andes Mountains.

FIND AMAZING STREET ART, COLORFUL BUILDINGS, AND RICH HISTORY IN THESE SOUTH AMERICAN GEMS.

Santiago and Valparaíso, Chile

THE LGBTQIA+ LOWDOWN With same-sex marriage recently legalized, and queer residents allowed to openly serve in the armed forces and give blood, Chile's progress surpasses many of its South American neighbors. Santiago's vibrant queer scene is one of the largest in the country.

Santiago offers amazing views of the Andes, colonial architecture, a historic center, museums, and so much more. Plus, it's a gateway to Patagonia—famous around the world for its glaciers, wildlife, national parks, and spirit of true adventure.

Plaza de Armas, the city's heart, has the can't-miss neoclassical Metropolitan Cathedral (the seat of the archbishop of Santiago). It also has great museums like the Chilean National History Museum (one of the oldest in South America, housed in the historic Palacio de la Real Audiencia, built in 1808) and the Museum of Memory and Human Rights, which memorializes the victims of violations of human rights committed during the Chilean military dictatorship between 1973 and 1990. There's also the National Museum of Fine Arts and the Museum of Contemporary Art in Parque Forestal, a fantastic urban park. Love a great view? Sky Costanera, a glass-wall observation deck with panoramic views of the entire city and the Andes Mountains stretching below—including the peak of Cerro Aconcagua, the tallest point in South America—never disappoints.

Take some time to walk around the Bellavista neighborhood, which is a lively queer district. Don't miss Patio Bellavista, a cool urban space that has more than 20 theaters, sidewalk mosaics and original works by Chilean artists, and tons of stores and restaurants. For drinks, Ex Femme is a great queer bar and nightclub, and Contramano Restopub has drag and burlesque.

About an hour from Santiago, Valparaíso has brightly colored houses and some amazing street art. Riding the funicular is pure joy. The oldest (of 15 currently operating ones) is Ascensor Concepción. Dating back to 1883, it brings you to Paseo Gervasoni for great shops and restaurants.

As fans of the great Chilean and Nobel Prize–winning poet Pablo Neruda, we found it especially meaningful to visit his former home, La Sebastiana. It's an uphill climb to get there, but it rewards with incredible views of the Pacific and a museum with detailed stories of Neruda's life and work.

For scenic squares, they don't come much better than Plaza Sotomayor, where you can stare at the majestic Armada de Chile (a naval command building) all day long. Nearby, the waterfront promenade at Muelle Prat makes for a nice stroll. From here, you can catch scenic harbor cruises and take in city views—and maybe even spot a sea lion or two.

Discover creative street art and rainbow paths in Valparaíso's brightly colored neighborhoods.

EXPLORE RUINS, ENJOY MARIACHI BANDS, AND DRINK TEQUILA.

Mexico City and Guadalajara, Mexico

Teatro Degollado, a neoclassical theater in Guadalajara, holds ballets, operas, and concerts.

THE LGBTQIA+ LOWDOWN Mexico City is one of the most progressive places in Mexico for LGBTQIA+ rights (transgender people have been able to change their legal gender and name here since 2008). Guadalajara is home to one of the largest Prides in Latin America and played host to the 2023 Gay Games.

As one of the oldest cities in the Americas, Mexico City wows with its architectural diversity—from colonial buildings to Aztec ruins—and lively neighborhoods, world-class museums, and terrific gastronomy scene.

Mexico City has so many museums you can't miss. Museo Frida Kahlo (known as the Blue House, Casa Azul) is a museum in the Coyoacán neighborhood where the famous artist lived and created art with painter Diego Rivera by her side. After learning about all things Frida, it's fun to stay in this historic and colonial area to roam Mercado de Coyoacán (est. 1921), a market where you can eat at traditional food stalls or shop for spices, textiles, produce, souvenirs, and more. The Museo de la Mujer aims to review the history of Mexico with a gender approach to raise the visibility of the historical work of women—including painting, sculpture, and lost wax bronze—starting in prehistoric times. The "Zona Rosa" (Pink Zone) is Mexico City's LGBTQIA+ district, worth visiting for shopping, discos, mariachi, and more.

At Embarcadero Nuevo Nativitas, you can experience the UNESCO World Heritage site Floating Gardens of Xochimilco. Board brightly painted, flat-bottom boats (*trajineras*) and cruise through the canals where Aztec people used to grow food on "floating" plant beds constructed in the water.

The capital of the Jalisco state in western Mexico, Guadalajara is the birthplace of tequila and mariachi. It's also renowned for its ceramics, cultural sites, and architectural wonders.

In Centro Histórico, wander through the plaza and see the double-spired Metropolitan Cathedral, which took 50 years to complete. Catch ballet and performances by the Jalisco Philharmonic Orchestra at Teatro Degollado.

Guadalajara has its own Zona Rosa, with Avenida Chapultepec being the heart of the area, full of great restaurants, trendy bars, and nightclubs (many focus on or welcome the LGBTQIA+ community).

Book lovers like us should know about the Guadalajara International Book Fair (FIL), the most important event in Spanish-language publishing, with a devoted LGBTQIA+ literature section.

BIG HITS

Don't miss these perennial hot spots and our personal favorites:

◆ MEXICO CITY

- ✦ Visit Museo Nacional de Antropología, the most popular museum in the country.
- ✦ Explore Museo Soumaya, with the biggest collection of pre-Hispanic and colonial-era coins in the world.
- ✦ Stroll through the Centro Histórico neighborhood, a UNESCO World Heritage site.
- ✦ Bike or walk El Zócalo pedestrian zone.
- ✦ Admire the Metropolitan Cathedral.
- ✦ Take in the National Palace in the city's main square.
- ✦ Discover the Great Temple archaeological museum.
- ✦ Wander San Jacinto Plaza on Saturdays for crafts, street food, live music, and buzzy vibes.

◆ GUADALAJARA

- ✦ Shop at Mercado San Juan de Dios, the largest indoor market in Latin America.
- ✦ See the work of famous Mexican caricaturist and painter José Clemente Orozco at Instituto Cultural Cabañas, which was one of the largest orphanages and hospitals in the Americas and is now a museum and UNESCO World Heritage site.
- ✦ Chill out at Mirador Independencia Park's outdoor amphitheater.
- ✦ Hike Barranca de Huentitán National Park's trails.
- ✦ See the Guachimontones archaeological site's 2,000-plus-year-old moss-covered pyramid structures in the Tequila Valley region.

The sun rises over Metropolitan Cathedral and Palacio Nacional in Zócalo, Mexico City's main square.

BIG HITS

Don't miss these perennial hot spots and our personal favorites:

◆ BERLIN

- ◆ Walk around the famed Brandenburg Gate.
- ◆ Visit the Schwules Museum, the world's first museum dedicated to LGBTQIA+ history.
- ◆ Tour the Reichstag building, home of Germany's parliament.
- ◆ Take in the views from the Berlin TV Tower.
- ◆ Feel like royalty at Charlottenburg Palace.

◆ HAMBURG

- ◆ Walk or bike through the art deco Old Elbe Tunnel, built in 1911.
- ◆ Take a breath at Planten un Blomen with more than 110 acres (45 ha) of gardens, ponds, and lawns.
- ◆ Stroll along Alster Lakes.
- ◆ Take in the sights of Hamburg-Altstadt (old town), including Hamburg City Hall.
- ◆ See fine art at Hamburger Kunsthalle and historic ships at the International Maritime Museum.

Berlin has a number of LGBTQIA+-friendly nightclubs and discotheques.

FROM THE BRANDENBURG GATE TO FUN ALONG THE WATER, DEUTSCHLAND'S LARGEST CITIES DON'T DISAPPOINT.

Berlin and Hamburg, Germany

Enjoy a riverside meal with views of City Hall in downtown Hamburg.

THE LGBTQIA+ LOWDOWN Berlin has a long history as a queer-welcoming city, from legendary cabaret and drag shows to the world's first museum dedicated to LGBTQIA+ history. Hamburg is also very queer friendly, with a thriving LGBTQIA+ scene around the areas of St. Georg and St. Pauli.

Berlin is one of our favorite European capitals, thanks to its come-as-you-are vibe coupled with its fantastic options for art, history, eating, nightlife, green spaces, and thriving queer scene.

Berlin also addresses the horrific events of World War II. The Memorial to Homosexuals Persecuted Under Nazism, located in the Tiergarten near the Brandenburg Gate, is one of several sites of remembrance.

A short walk away are two traveler favorites: the Gendarmenmarkt, a gorgeous square with a concert house and cathedrals, and Museum Island, a UNESCO World Heritage site that's home to five of the country's most historic museums. You can spend an entire vacation here, but the most popular on the island (and in all of Berlin) is the Pergamon Museum, known for its Museum of Islamic Art and impressive Ishtar Gate, among other exhibits.

We'd be remiss if we didn't mention some of our favorite LGBTQIA+ stops. They include bookshops Another Country and Prinz Eisenherz; cafés and restaurants Café Berio,

Romeo & Romeo, and Sissi; and bars/clubs SchwuZ, Heile Welt, Prinzknecht, Tom's Bar (for men), and Silverfuture. Berlin also has amazing drag shows: Some of the best can be found at Bar Zum Schmutzigen.

Germany's second largest city, Hamburg has more canals than Amsterdam and Venice combined. It also has at least 2,500 bridges, more than any other city in the world.

Because 75 percent of Hamburg was destroyed in WWII, the city has constantly tried to rebuild and has completed great areas such as HafenCity, the biggest waterfront development in Europe, with the stunning Elbphilharmonie.

Adjacent to HafenCity is Speicherstadt, the world's largest complex of warehouses. It's a UNESCO World Heritage site with neo-Gothic brick buildings home to Miniatur Wunderland (voted Germany's top tourist attraction).

For queer-friendly spaces, eat at Café Gnosa and Café Uhrlaub, and shop at Bruno's (for Pride supplies and adult toys, mostly for men) and Männerschwarm queer bookstore. For drinks, try M&V Bar, Kyti Voo, Wunderbar, and Bellini Bar.

GET YOUR FIX OF COSMOPOLITAN FUN AND GREAT FOOD.

Hong Kong, China, and Taipei, Taiwan

Tour the elaborately decorated interior of Man Mo Temple in Hong Kong.

THE LGBTQIA+ LOWDOWN Though there are thriving queer communities throughout Asia, there are still not adequate protections for LGBTQIA+ people. Rights in Taiwan are considered the most progressive on the continent. Every year, Pink Dot Hong Kong hosts a local LGBTQIA+ carnival and concert (typically in October).

Hong Kong strikes a great balance between a cosmopolitan city full of skyscrapers, hustle, great dim sum restaurants, and glitz, and green spaces—including beaches and hiking trails.

We appreciate the city's opportunities to learn about its LGBTQIA+ history with companies such as Walk in Hong Kong, which offers private tours that share the history, activism, and culture of Hong Kong's queer community. They also created Hong Kong's first wheelchair-friendly tour of the city.

Marvel at Hong Kong's skyline—the view from Victoria Peak is simply incredible. Getting to the top—at 1,811 feet (552 m)—via the Peak Tram is also really fun. Elsewhere in the city, the Man Mo Temple is always worth visiting.

Hong Kong also has bustling markets, especially the Temple Street Night Market. Shop for antiques, jade, electronics, Buddha figurines, and more. Or try Cat Street Market, which has more than 100 years of history, art, and antiques.

No trip to this city is complete without plenty of dim sum and great Chinese food. Tai Ping Koon Restaurant is one of the world's oldest Chinese restaurants, originally opened in 1860. Tim Ho Wan is a dim sum chain that's one of the world's cheapest Michelin-starred restaurants.

For LGBTQIA+ nightlife, most is centered around the Central District zone (SoHo) and on Hong Kong Island, where you'll find FLM, one of the most popular queer bars in Hong Kong (on Jervois Street in the Sheung Wan district).

Taipei is a special city with an abundance of night markets, ancient temples, parks, and restaurant culture (it's such a common practice to eat out that many apartments don't even have kitchens). It also hosts one of the biggest Pride celebrations in Asia.

Raohe Street Night Market is the most popular night market with tourists and offers a variety of Taiwanese street food. Tonghua Night Market is also full of food stalls, a handful of which are Michelin listed. Shilin Night Market is the largest, known all over Taiwan for its incredible selection of snacks.

The Ximending district is a lively LGBTQIA+ hangout with many queer bars and nightclubs, and the Red House in Wanhua District is a historical theater packed with LGBTQIA+ nightlife.

BIG HITS

Don't miss these perennial hot spots and our personal favorites:

◆ HONG KONG

- ◆ Join Hong Kong's Ghosts & Food Tour or Chinese Wellness & Old Shops Food Journey.
- ◆ Ride Asia's oldest funicular, the Peak Tram, which began running in 1888.
- ◆ Wander through Flower Market for tons of blooms, seeds, and plants.
- ◆ Take the Central–Mid-Levels escalator and walkway system, the longest out-door covered escalator in the world.
- ◆ Admire Lantau Island's bronze "Tian Tan Buddha" statue.
- ◆ Hang out at Repulse Bay, one of Hong Kong's most popular beaches.
- ◆ Hike Tai Long Wan, a daylong route that leads through volcanic rocks and four bays.
- ◆ Try local favorite restaurants Ho Lee Fook, Dim Sum Library, and Under Bridge Spicy Crab.

◆ TAIPEI

- ◆ See the Buddhist Longshan Temple, built in 1738.
- ◆ Walk Bopiliao Historic Block with Qing dynasty architecture.
- ◆ Peruse the National Palace Museum with a collection of more than 700,000 pieces of Chinese artifacts and art.
- ◆ Visit Taipei 101, one of the world's tallest buildings, with an 89th-floor observation platform.
- ◆ Take a trip to Beitou Hot Springs, a popular, mixed-gender complex in Beitou, a small town 30 minutes outside the city.
- ◆ Marvel at the mountainous Yangming-shan National Park.
- ◆ Road trip to Houtong Cat Village, Houtong Coal Mine Ecological Park, and Houtong Miner's Culture & History Museum, all an easy hour-long train ride away.

Take a tram up Victoria Peak, Hong Kong Island's tallest point, for exquisite skyscraper views.

To our spouses, Michael and Charlotte, the best travel partners anyone could ask for.

ACKNOWLEDGMENTS

Thank you to our dynamic publishing team: Steven Harris at CSG Literary, agent extraordinaire, for his support in every way on this project; Allyson Johnson and Ashley Leath, for their belief in this project from the start; and the entire National Geographic team who helped bring this book to life, including art director Sanáa Akkach, illustrator Laurène Boglio, director of photography Adrian Coakley, and associate production editor Becca Saltzman. And thank you to Susan Shapiro, an incredible writing teacher, mentor, and literary matchmaker. We met in her class in 2018 and have been friends and collaborators with each other ever since!

To friends around the globe who shared local recs and showed us around: Andrew Wasserstein, Jessica Rodriguez, Emily Francis, Amy Micallef Decesare, Jagdish Bijlani, Alison Meersschaert, Kirsten Meersschaert, Nick Rutigliano, Monica Stoddard, Susie Wilkins, Sharon Maloney, Eric Holm, Kate Kerr-Clemenson, Vanessa Lawrence, Tatiana Scher, Valerie and Alan Keelan, Angie Ramos Galvan, Michael Golden, Heather Swallow, Beth Eubanks, and Amy Wetsch.

And to the LGBTQIA+ community and our allies, with whom we are always proud to be Out in the World.

From Mark: Thank you to everyone who has supported my journeys and writing by reading my essays and travel stories, seeing one of my plays, giving me journals, and asking my favorite question, "Where are you going next?" To Betty, the best mom and cheerleader I could have. To my siblings, nieces, nephews, and my extended and chosen families for a lifetime of encouragement. Also grateful to my "aunties," writing groups, teachers, and fellow artists who helped me find both the right words and confidence in myself, and to great editors, including Lisa Bonos, Nikki Gloudeman, Jessie Fetterling, Jerry Portwood, Noah Michelson, Dan Jones, and Miya Lee, for publishing my work and helping me grow as a writer. And to those who are no longer with us but whom I will always carry with me around the world: Dad, Nanny, and Grampie.

From Amy: Thank you to my friends and family who have cheered me on, enthusiastically asked me how the writing was going (to which there's always a different answer), and almost never complained about how much time I spend at my desk. I always say it takes a village to write a book, and I feel like I hit the jackpot with mine. And infinite gratitude to my mom, Ellen Scher. My thanks for you could fill its own book.

ILLUSTRATIONS CREDITS

2-3, David/Adobe Stock; 4-5, zoompics/Alamy Stock Photo; 6-7, Neil McAllister/Alamy Stock Photo; 8-9, Francois Roux/Adobe Stock; 12, eye35.pix/Alamy Stock Photo; 18, Mariana Schulze, courtesy of Beato Chocolates; 19, David Litschel/Alamy Stock Photo; 20, Susan Pease/Alamy Stock Photo; 21, Tom Croke/Alamy Stock Photo; 22, Terra Fondriest; 23, courtesy of Eureka Springs, Arkansas CAPC; 24, George Oze/Alamy Stock Photo; 25, JWCohen/Shutterstock; 26, Ann Moore/Alamy Stock Photo; 27, Susan Candelario/Alamy Stock Photo; 28-9, Jerry Fornarotto/Alamy Stock Photo; 30, Janet Horton/Alamy Stock Photo; 31, Victahh1/Wirestock Creators/Adobe Stock; 32, Ayotunde Ogunsakin/Shutterstock; 33, Roy Johnson/Alamy Stock Photo; 34, Ingo Oeland/Alamy Stock Photo; 35, Philip Game/Alamy Stock Photo; 36, ververidis/Adobe Stock; 37, Georgios Tsichlis/Shutterstock; 38, Jean Frizelle/Alamy Stock Photo; 39, Simon Holdcroft/Alamy Stock Photo; 42, James Schwabel/Alamy Stock Photo; 43, Jon Bilous/Adobe Stock; 44, Efrain Padro/Alamy Stock Photo; 45, jjwithers/Getty Images; 46, Maciej Bledowski/Alamy Stock Photo; 47, Jen Lobo/Adobe Stock; 48, Thomas Kelley/Alamy Stock Photo; 49, 4kclips/Adobe Stock; 50, Krista Rossow/Alamy Stock Photo; 51, Panoramic Images/Leo L. Larson/Alamy Stock Photo; 52, Inge Johnsson/Alamy Stock Photo; 53, Bob Daemmrich/Alamy Stock Photo; 54, Chris Thigpen, Ace Studios, Courtesy of Out in the Vineyard; 55, Alexandra Latypova/Alamy Stock Photo; 56-7, Matt May/Alamy Stock Photo; 58, courtesy of Steenberg Farm; 59, bildundmeer/Shutterstock; 60, David Noton Photography/Alamy Stock Photo; 61, 3Fotografia/LatinContent via Getty Images; 62, ITPhoto/Alamy Stock Photo; 63, Nathaniel Noir/Alamy Stock Photo; 64, SAKhanPhotography/Shutterstock; 65, Martin Thomas Photography/Alamy Stock Photo; 66, eye35.pix/Alamy Stock Photo; 67, John Bracegirdle/Alamy Stock Photo; 68, Jim Engelbrecht/DanitaDelimont/Alamy Stock Photo; 69, Beatrice Prève/Adobe Stock; 72, ZUMA Press/Alamy Stock Photo; 73, NeonJellyfish/Getty Images; 74, David Roossien Photography/Alamy Stock Photo; 75, William Reagan/Getty Images; 76, Mira/Alamy Stock Photo; 77, Douglas Peebles Photography/Alamy Stock Photo; 78, rabbitti/Adobe Stock; 79, DigitalVues/Alamy Stock Photo; 80, Henry Beeker/Alamy Stock Photo; 81, Fikander82/Getty Images; 82, Katja Kreder/imageBROKER/Alamy Stock Photo; 83, luchschenF/Adobe Stock; 84-5, ZGPhotography/Adobe Stock; 86, Katja Kreder/imageBROKER/Alamy Stock Photo; 87, davidionut/Adobe Stock; 88, Nino Marcutti/Alamy Stock Photo; 89, Martin Strmiska/Alamy Stock Photo; 90, Pilar Olivares/Reuters/Redux; 91, Wirestock/Getty Images; 92, Sean3810/Getty Images; 93, Jack Malipan Travel Photography/Alamy Stock Photo; 94, Marco Simoni/robertharding; 95, Agenzia Sintesi/Fabio Fiorani/Alamy Stock Photo; 96, Roman Belogorodov/Shutterstock; 97, Alex Hinds/Alamy Stock Photo; 100, Steve Bly/Alamy Stock Photo; 101, christiannafzger/Getty Images; 102, darekm101/RooM the Agency/Alamy Stock Photo; 103, Philip Scalia/Alamy Stock Photo; 104, Randy Duchaine/Alamy Stock Photo; 105, Joseph Creamer/Alamy Stock Photo; 106, Antonio Gravante/Shutterstock; 107, Kevin Britland/Alamy Stock Photo; 108, Stockbym/Adobe Stock; 109, Stockbym/Adobe Stock; 110-1, SCStock/Adobe Stock; 112, Hercules Milas/Alamy Stock Photo; 113, SvetlanaSF/Adobe Stock; 114, Urban Photography TLV/Alamy Stock Photo; 115, Nick Brundle Photography/Shutterstock; 116, Patrick Batchelder/Alamy Stock Photo; 117, Peter Adams/Jon Arnold Images/Alamy Stock Photo; 118, Maridav/Adobe Stock; 119, Yadid Levy/Alamy Stock Photo; 120, Jon Arnold Images/Alamy Stock Photo; 121, Rubens Alarcon/Alamy Stock Photo; 124, H. Mark Weidman Photography/Alamy Stock Photo; 125, Earth Pixel LLC/Alamy Stock Photo; 126, Ian Dagnall/Alamy Stock Photo; 127, Pat & Chuck Blackley/Alamy Stock Photo; 128, Jamie Pham/Alamy Stock Photo; 129, JFL Photography/Adobe Stock; 130, Greg Vaughn/Alamy Stock Photo; 131, Reinhard Dirscherl/Alamy Stock Photo; 132, Angelo Cavalli/robertharding; 133, John Kellerman/Alamy Stock Photo; 134-5, Beatrice Prève/Adobe Stock; 136, Travelpixs/Shutterstock; 137, tawatchai1990/Adobe Stock; 138, Cindy Hopkins/Alamy Stock Photo; 139, Sergey/Adobe Stock; 140 and 141, Sean Pavone Photo/Adobe Stock; 142, Mark Payne-Gill/Nature Picture Library/Alamy Stock Photo; 143, Frederick Millett/Shutterstock; 144, Luke Farmer/Alamy Stock Photo; 145, Laura Grier/robertharding; 148, Inge Johnsson/Alamy Stock Photo; 149, Tegra Stone Nuess/Getty Images; 150, Hilda DeSanctis/Alamy Stock Photo; 151, Allen Creative/Steve Allen/Alamy Stock Photo; 152, Ellen Rooney/

robertharding; 153, Felix Lipov/Alamy Stock Photo; 154, Efrain Padro/Alamy Stock Photo; 155, Ricardo Arduengo/AFP via Getty Images; 156, Megapress/Alamy Stock Photo; 157, Schoening/Alamy Stock Photo; 158, Earth Pixel LLC/Alamy Stock Photo; 159, Pierre-Jean Durieu/Shutterstock; 160-1, Kristina Blokhin/Adobe Stock; 162, Brigitte Merz/Image Professionals GmbH/Alamy Stock Photo; 163, Joern Sackermann/Alamy Stock Photo; 164, napa74/Adobe Stock; 165, Ton Koene/Alamy Stock Photo; 166, Joana Kruse/Alamy Stock Photo; 167, iWebbstock/Alamy Stock Photo; 168, Prisma by Dukas/Alamy Stock Photo; 169, Bill Perry/Adobe Stock; 170, Leonid Andronov/Adobe Stock; 171, Zheng Hui Ng/Alamy Stock Photo; 174, Dave Hutchison/All Canada Photos/Alamy Stock Photo; 175, Ed Callaert/Alamy Stock Photo; 176, Amit Satiya/Alamy Stock Photo; 177, Henk Meijer/Alamy Stock Photo; 178, Doug Lindstrand/Design Pics/Alamy Stock Photo; 179, Steven Miley/Design Pics/ Alamy Stock Photo; 180, Michael Melford/National Geographic Image Collection; 181, Michael Nolan/robertharding; 182, travelstock44/Juergen Held/Alamy Stock Photo; 183, Eric Nathan/Alamy Stock Photo; 184-5, Alain Evrard/robertharding; 186, NicoElNino/Adobe Stock; 187, nickolya/Adobe Stock; 188, Kipperpig/Alamy Stock Photo; 189, Noppasinw/Adobe Stock; 190, Alexander Lutsenko/Alamy Stock Photo; 191, G&M Therin-Weise/robertharding; 192, Chad Copeland/National Geographic Image Collection; 193, Steffen Binke/Alamy Stock Photo; 196 and 197, Lawren Simmons/The New York Times/ Redux; 198, Patrick Frilet/hemis/Alamy Stock Photo; 199, Sean Pavone Photo/Adobe Stock; 200, Mark Phillips/Alamy Stock Photo; 201, rudi1976/Adobe Stock; 202-3, Jan Wlodarczyk/Alamy Stock Photo; 204, Monica Wells/Alamy Stock Photo; 205, Ian Dagnall/Alamy Stock Photo; 206, Ricardo Cohen/Shutterstock; 207, Sean Pavone/Shutterstock; 208, Ian Dagnall/Alamy Stock Photo; 209, Bill Heinsohn/Alamy Stock Photo; 210, Brian Scantlebury/Shutterstock; 211, rudi1976/Adobe Stock; 214, Inge Johnsson/Alamy Stock Photo; 215, XiFotos/Getty Images; 216, Philippe Renault/hemis/Alamy Stock Photo; 217, Ian Dagnall/Alamy Stock Photo; 218, Sean Pavone Photo/Adobe Stock; 219, Dennis MacDonald/Alamy Stock Photo; 220, Charles O. Cecil/Alamy Stock Photo; 221, Inge Johnsson/Alamy Stock Photo; 222-3, Laura Prieto/Alamy Stock Photo; 224, rudi1976/ Adobe Stock; 225, castenoid/Getty Images; 226, Richie Chan/Adobe Stock; 227, Phil Wilkinson/Alamy Stock Photo; 228, R.M. Nunes/Shutterstock; 229, Sean O. S. Barley/Alamy Stock Photo; 230, Bill Gozansky/Alamy Stock Photo; 231, quitthistown/ Stockimo/Alamy Stock Photo; 234, Walter Bibikow/DanitaDelimont/Alamy Stock Photo; 235, Susan Candelario/Alamy Stock Photo; 236, Ian Dagnall/Alamy Stock Photo; 237, Yefim Bam/Alamy Stock Photo; 238, DirkR/Adobe Stock; 239, Debra Behr/ Alamy Stock Photo; 240, Erika Skogg/National Geographic Image Collection; 241, Robin Weaver/Alamy Stock Photo; 242-3, Luca Locatelli/National Geographic Image Collection; 244, Mostardi Photography/Alamy Stock Photo; 245, Keith Adamek/ Alamy Stock Photo; 246, Ben MacLeod/Alamy Stock Photo; 247, Mark Llewellyn/Alamy Stock Photo; 248, Roger Cracknell 01/classic/Alamy Stock Photo; 249, Joana Kruse/Alamy Stock Photo; 252, Heidi Besen/Shutterstock; 253, Jason Finn/Getty Images; 254, Paul Klein/Alamy Stock Photo; 255, SG cityscapes/Alamy Stock Photo; 256 and 257, Carmen K. Sisson/Cloudy- bright/Alamy Stock Photo; 258, Jeremy Hogan/Alamy Stock Photo; 259, Nicholas Klein/Alamy Stock Photo; 260-1, Susan Vineyard/Adobe Stock; 262, Maciej Dakowicz/Alamy Stock Photo; 263, trabantos/Shutterstock; 264, Andres Stapff/Reuters/ Redux; 265, Oliver Gerhard/imageBROKER/Alamy Stock Photo; 266, Jan Wlodarczyk/Alamy Stock Photo; 267, Gavin Hellier/ robertharding; 268, Yadid Levy/Alamy Stock Photo; 269, Luca Tettoni/robertharding/Alamy Stock Photo; 272, Ian Dagnall/ Alamy Stock Photo; 273, Inge Johnsson/Alamy Stock Photo; 274, Ellisphotos/Alamy Stock Photo; 275, Randy Duchaine/ Alamy Stock Photo; 276, Rohan Van Twest/Alamy Stock Photo; 277, Chris/Adobe Stock; 278, franckreporter/Getty Images; 279, NurPhoto SRL/Alamy Stock Photo; 280, JoeFox Liverpool/Radharc Images/Alamy Stock Photo; 281, Steve Vidler/mau- ritius images/Alamy Stock Photo; 282-3, John Michaels/Alamy Stock Photo; 284, Jose Luis Stephens/Adobe Stock; 285, Pep Roig/Alamy Stock Photo; 286, Christian Kober 1/Alamy Stock Photo; 287, Bill Perry/Adobe Stock; 288, Juergen Henkelmann Photography/Alamy Stock Photo; 289, rudi1976/Adobe Stock; 290, Sean Pavone/Alamy Stock Photo; 291, Sean Pavone Photo/Adobe Stock.

INDEX

Boldface indicates illustrations.

A

Accessible sites
   Copenhagen, Denmark 119
   Dollywood, Tennessee, U.S.A. 198
   Hong Kong, China 290
   Québec City, Québec, Canada 159
   San Sebastián, Spain 112
   Speyside, Scotland, U.K. 66
   Walt Disney World, Florida, U.S.A. 196
Alabama, U.S.A.: Fairhope **256,** 256–257, **257**
Alaska, U.S.A. **178,** 178–179, **179**
Albania: Tirana **262,** 262–263, **263**
Antarctica **186,** 186–187, **187**
Argentina
   Buenos Aires **228,** 228–229, **229,** 264
   Mendoza wine region **60,** 60–61, **61**
Arizona, U.S.A.: Sedona **236,** 236–237, **237**
Arkansas, U.S.A.: Eureka Springs **22,** 22–23, **23**
Asheville, North Carolina, U.S.A. **104,** 104–105, **105**
Atlanta, Georgia, U.S.A. **150,** 150–151, **151**
Auckland, New Zealand **210,** 210–211, **211**
Austin, Texas, U.S.A. **52,** 52–53, **53**
Australia
   Daylesford, Victoria **2–3, 34,** 34–35, **35**
   Great Barrier Reef, Queensland **192,** 192–193, **193**
   Sydney, New South Wales **94,** 94–95, **95**
Austria: Salzburg **200,** 200–203, **201, 202–203**
Autism spectrum 42

B

Baltimore, Maryland, U.S.A. 274–275, **275**
Bangkok, Thailand **4–5, 108,** 108–111, **109, 110–111**
Barcelona, Spain **96,** 96–97, **97**
Bath, England, U.K. **166,** 166–167, **167**
Beer and breweries
   Boise, Idaho, U.S.A. 100
   Boulder, Colorado, U.S.A. 46
   Columbus, Ohio, U.S.A. 255
   Dublin, Ireland 65, **65**
   Fairhope, Alabama, U.S.A. 256
   Grand Rapids, Michigan, U.S.A. 74
   Portland, Oregon, U.S.A. 102
   Spitsbergen, Norway 191
The Berkshires, Massachusetts, U.S.A. **126,** 126–127, **127**
Berlin, Germany **288,** 288–289
Big Island, Hawaii, U.S.A. **238,** 238–239, **239**
Blind travelers 132
Bloomington, Indiana, U.S.A. **258,** 258–261, **259, 260–261**
Blue Lagoon, Iceland **240,** 242, **242–243**
Boise, Idaho, U.S.A. **100,** 100–101, **101**
Boracay, Philippines **92,** 92–93, **93**
Boulder, Colorado, U.S.A. **46,** 46–47, **47**
Bourbon Trail, Kentucky 49, **49**
Brazil: Rio de Janeiro **90,** 90–91, **91**
Breweries *see* Beer and breweries
Brighton, England, U.K. **38,** 38–39, **39**
British Columbia, Canada: Vancouver **230,** 230–231, **231**
Buenos Aires, Argentina **228,** 228–229, **229,** 264

C

Los Cabos, Mexico **142,** 142–143, **143**
California, U.S.A.
   Los Angeles **206,** 206–207, **207**
   Monterey Bay **128,** 128–129, **129**

Ojai **18,** 18–19, **19**

San Francisco and Sacramento **276,** 276–277, **277**

Sonoma County and Russian River Valley **54,** 54–57, **55, 56–57**

Cambodia: Phnom Penh **268,** 268–269, **269**

Canada

Niagara-on-the-Lake, Ontario **32,** 32–33, **33**

Nova Scotia **246,** 246–247, **247**

Québec City, Québec **158,** 158–161, **159, 160–161**

Vancouver, British Columbia **230,** 230–231, **231**

Cape May, New Jersey, U.S.A. **78,** 78–79, **79**

Cape Town, South Africa **182,** 182–183, **183**

Cape Winelands, South Africa **58,** 58–59, **59**

Cardiff, Wales, U.K. **204,** 204–205, **205**

Carnival

Cologne, Germany **162,** 163

Curaçao, Dutch Antilles 81

Malta 82

Montevideo, Uruguay 264

Rio de Janeiro, Brazil 90, 91

Sitges, Spain 96

see also Mardi Gras

Cartagena, Colombia **144,** 144–145, **145**

Charleston, South Carolina, U.S.A. **124,** 124–125, **125**

Chiang Mai, Thailand **188,** 188–189, **189**

Chicago, Illinois, U.S.A. **278,** 278–279

Child-friendly spots *see* Family fun

Chile: Santiago and Valparaíso **284,** 284–285, **285**

China: Hong Kong **290,** 290–291, **291**

Cologne, Germany **162,** 162–163, **163**

Colombia: Cartagena **144,** 144–145, **145**

Colorado, U.S.A.: Boulder **46,** 46–47, **47**

Columbus, Ohio, U.S.A. **254,** 254–255, **255**

Connecticut, U.S.A.: Essex, Mystic, Kent, and Salisbury **208,** 208–209, **209**

Copenhagen, Denmark **118,** 118–119, **119**

Costa Rica: Quepos and Manuel Antonio National Park **244,** 244–245, **245**

Côte d'Or Beach, Seychelles **6–7,** 89

Curaçao, Dutch Antilles **80,** 80–81, **81**

Czechia: Prague **224,** 224–225, **225**

D

Daylesford, Victoria, Australia **2–3, 34,** 34–35, **35**

Dead Sea 115

Denmark: Copenhagen **118,** 118–119, **119**

Detroit, Michigan, U.S.A. 278–279, **279**

Disney World, Orlando, Florida, U.S.A. **196,** 196–197, **197**

Distilleries

Bloomington, Indiana, U.S.A. 259

Boulder, Colorado, U.S.A. **46**

Bourbon Trail, Kentucky 49, **49**

Dublin, Ireland 65

Speyside, Scotland, U.K. **66,** 66–67

Diving and snorkeling

Boracay, Philippines 93

Curaçao, Dutch Antilles 80

Fiji 131

Galápagos Islands, Ecuador 181

Great Barrier Reef, Queensland, Australia 193, **193**

Krabi, Thailand 86

Maldives 138

Seychelles 89, **89**

Tahiti, French Polynesia 168, 169

Dollywood, Tennessee, U.S.A. 198–199

Dublin, Ireland **64,** 64–65, **65**

Dutch Antilles: Curaçao **80,** 80–81, **81**

E

Ecuador: Galápagos Islands **180,** 180–181, **181**

Edinburgh, Scotland, U.K. **226,** 226–227, **227**

England, U.K.

Bath **166,** 166–167, **167**

Brighton **38,** 38–39, **39**

London and Manchester **280,** 280–283,
   281, 282–283
Warwickshire, Hampshire, and Kent **204,**
   204–205
Essex, Connecticut, U.S.A. 208–209
Eureka Springs, Arkansas, U.S.A. **22,** 22–23, **23**

F
Fairhope, Alabama, U.S.A. **256,** 256–257, **257**
Family fun
   Asheville, North Carolina, U.S.A. 104
   Atlanta, Georgia, U.S.A. 151
   Austin, Texas, U.S.A. 53
   Barcelona, Spain 97
   Boise, Idaho, U.S.A. 100
   Brighton, England, U.K. 38
   Cardiff, Wales, U.K. 204
   Charleston, South Carolina, U.S.A. 125
   Costa Rica 244, 245
   Fairhope, Alabama, U.S.A. 257
   Kerala, India 248
   Leavenworth, Washington, U.S.A. 149
   Los Angeles, California, U.S.A. 207
   Maldives 139
   Monterey Bay, California, U.S.A. 128
   Nova Scotia, Canada 246
   Portland, Oregon, U.S.A. 102
   Provincetown, Massachusetts, U.S.A. 20
   Rio de Janeiro, Brazil 90
   Rovaniemi, Finland 165
   Santa Fe, New Mexico, U.S.A. 45
   Savannah, Georgia, U.S.A. 215
   Singapore 170, 171
   Walt Disney World, Florida, U.S.A. **196,**
      196–197, **197**
   wildlife encounters 172–193
   Woodstock, Vermont, U.S.A. 152
Fiji **130,** 130–131, **131**
Film festivals
   Barcelona, Spain 96
   Bloomington, Indiana, U.S.A. 259
   Brighton, England, U.K. 38
   Buenos Aires, Argentina 228
   Cardiff, Wales, U.K. 204
   Copenhagen, Denmark 119
   Dublin, Ireland 64
   Kyoto, Japan 137
   Lima, Peru 120
   Portland, Oregon, U.S.A. 102
   Prague, Czechia 224
   Rochester, New York, U.S.A. 43
   Salt Lake City, Utah, U.S.A. 253
   San Juan, Puerto Rico, U.S.A. 154
   Sitges, Spain 96
   Tel Aviv, Israel 115
   Thessaloniki, Greece 36, 37
   Vancouver, British Columbia, Canada 231
   Venice, Italy 132, 133
Finger Lakes, New York, U.S.A. **42,** 42–43, **43**
Finland: Rovaniemi **164,** 164–165, **165**
Florence, Italy **106,** 106–107, **107**
Florida, U.S.A.
   St. Augustine **218,** 218–219, **219**
   St. Petersburg **72,** 72–73, **73**
   Walt Disney World **196,** 196–197, **197**
Food and drink festivals
   Asheville, North Carolina, U.S.A. 105
   Bangkok, Thailand 109
   Boulder, Colorado, U.S.A. 47
   Cape May, New Jersey, U.S.A. 78
   Mendoza region, Argentina 60, 61, **61**
   Newport, Rhode Island, U.S.A. 77
   San Sebastián, Spain 113
   Sonoma County, California, U.S.A. 54, **54,**
      55, 57
   Speyside, Scotland, U.K. 67
   St. Augustine, Florida, U.S.A. 218
   Willamette Valley, Oregon, U.S.A. 51
France: Lyon **68,** 68–69, **69**
French Polynesia: Tahiti **168,** 168–169, **169**

G

Galápagos Islands, Ecuador **180**, 180–181, **181**

Galena, Illinois, U.S.A. **30**, 30–31, **31**

Gaudí, Antoni 97

Georgia, U.S.A.
  Atlanta **150**, 150–151, **151**
  Savannah **214**, 214–215, **215**

Germany
  Berlin and Hamburg **288**, 288–289, **289**
  Cologne **162**, 162–163, **163**

Grampians National Park, Victoria, Australia **2–3**, **34**, 35

Grand Canyon National Park, Arizona 237

Grand Teton National Park, Wyoming, U.S.A. 176–177, **177**

Great Barrier Reef, Queensland, Australia **192**, 192–193, **193**

Greece: Thessaloniki **36**, 36–37, **37**

Guadalajara, Mexico **286**, 286–287

H

Hamburg, Germany 288–289, **289**

Hampshire, England, U.K. **204**, 204–205

Hawaii, U.S.A.: Big Island **238**, 238–239, **239**

Hill Country, Texas, U.S.A. 52–53

Hollywood, California, U.S.A. 206, 207, **207**

Hong Kong, China **290**, 290–291, **291**

Hudson Valley, New York, U.S.A. **234**, 234–235, **235**

I

Iceland **240**, 240–243, **241**, **242–243**

Idaho, U.S.A.: Boise **100**, 100–101, **101**

Illinois, U.S.A.
  Chicago **278**, 278–279
  Galena **30**, 30–31, **31**

India: Kerala **248**, 248–249, **249**

Indiana, U.S.A.: Bloomington **258**, 258–261, **259**, **260–261**

Ireland: Dublin **64**, 64–65, **65**

Israel: Tel Aviv **114**, 114–115, **115**

Italy
  Florence **106**, 106–107, **107**
  Venice **12**, **132**, 132–135, **133**, **134–135**

J

Japan
  Kyoto **136**, 136–137, **137**
  Tokyo **116**, 116–117, **117**

K

Kent, Connecticut, U.S.A. 208–209

Kent, England, U.K. 204–205

Kentucky, U.S.A.: Louisville **48**, 48–49, **49**

Kerala, India **248**, 248–249, **249**

Kid-friendly spots see Family fun

Krabi, Thailand **86**, 86–87, **87**

Kruger National Park, South Africa 184, **184–185**

Kyoto, Japan **136**, 136–137, **137**

L

Leavenworth, Washington, U.S.A. **148**, 148–149, **149**

Lima, Peru **120**, 120–121, **121**

Lisbon, Portugal **140**, 140–141, **141**

London, England, U.K. 280–283, **281**, **282–283**

Los Angeles, California, U.S.A. **206**, 206–207, **207**

Los Cabos, Mexico **142**, 142–143, **143**

Louisiana, U.S.A.: New Orleans **220**, 220–223, **221**, **222–223**

Louisville, Kentucky, U.S.A. **48**, 48–49, **49**

Lyon, France **68**, 68–69, **69**

M

Maine, U.S.A.: Ogunquit **26**, 26–29, **27**, **28–29**

Maldives **138**, 138–139, **139**

Malta **82**, 82–85, **83**, **84–85**

Manchester, England, U.K. **280**, 280–281

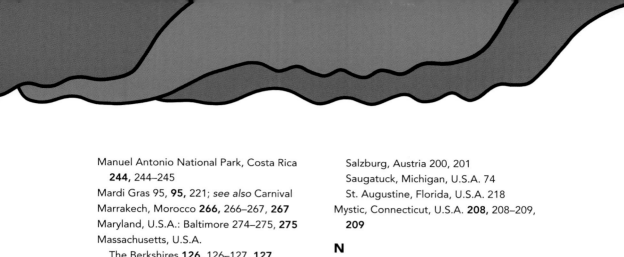

Manuel Antonio National Park, Costa Rica **244**, 244–245
Mardi Gras 95, **95**, 221; *see also* Carnival
Marrakech, Morocco **266**, 266–267, **267**
Maryland, U.S.A.: Baltimore 274–275, **275**
Massachusetts, U.S.A.
    The Berkshires **126**, 126–127, **127**
    Provincetown **20**, 20–21, **21**
    Salem **216**, 216–217, **217**
Memphis, Tennessee, U.S.A. **198**, 198–199
Mendoza region, Argentina **60**, 60–61, **61**
Mérida, Mexico **156**, 156–157, **157**
Mexico
    Los Cabos **142**, 142–143, **143**
    Mérida **156**, 156–157, **157**
    Mexico City and Guadalajara **286**, 286–287, **287**
Michigan, U.S.A.
    Detroit 278–279, **279**
    Saugatuck **74**, 74–75, **75**
Mobility issues *see* Accessible sites
Montana, U.S.A.: Yellowstone National Park **176**, 176–177, **177**
Monterey Bay, California, U.S.A. **128**, 128–129, **129**
Montevideo, Uruguay **264**, 264–265, **265**
Morocco: Marrakech **266**, 266–267, **267**
Music festivals and venues
    Austin, Texas, U.S.A. 52
    The Berkshires, Massachusetts, U.S.A. 126, 127
    Bloomington, Indiana, U.S.A. 258, 259
    Boise, Idaho, U.S.A. 101
    Cape May, New Jersey, U.S.A. 78
    Curaçao, Dutch Antilles 81
    Florence, Italy 106
    Lyon, France 68
    Monterey Bay, California, U.S.A. 129
    Newport, Rhode Island, U.S.A. 77
    Ojai, California, U.S.A. 19
    Salt Lake City, Utah, U.S.A. 253

Salzburg, Austria 200, 201
Saugatuck, Michigan, U.S.A. 74
St. Augustine, Florida, U.S.A. 218
Mystic, Connecticut, U.S.A. **208**, 208–209, **209**

N
Nashville, Tennessee, U.S.A. 198–199, **199**
New Hope, Pennsylvania, U.S.A. **24**, 24–25, **25**
New Jersey, U.S.A.: Cape May **78**, 78–79, **79**
New Mexico, U.S.A.: Santa Fe **44**, 44–45, **45**
New Orleans, Louisiana, U.S.A. **220**, 220–223, **221**, **222–223**
New Paltz, New York, U.S.A. **234**, 234–235
New York, U.S.A.
    Finger Lakes **42**, 42–43, **43**
    New Paltz and Hudson Valley **234**, 234–235, **235**
    New York City **8–9**, 272–273, **273**
New Zealand
    Auckland to Tongariro National Park **210**, 210–211, **211**
    Waiheke Island **62**, 62–63, **63**
Newport, Rhode Island, U.S.A. **76**, 76–77, **77**
Niagara-on-the-Lake, Ontario, Canada **32**, 32–33, **33**
North Carolina, U.S.A.: Asheville **104**, 104–105, **105**
Norway: Spitsbergen **190**, 190–191, **191**
Nova Scotia, Canada **246**, 246–247, **247**

O
Ogunquit, Maine, U.S.A. **26**, 26–29, **27**, **28–29**
Ohio, U.S.A.: Columbus **254**, 254–255, **255**
Ojai, California, U.S.A. **18**, 18–19, **19**
Ontario, Canada: Niagara-on-the-Lake **32**, 32–33, **33**
Oregon, U.S.A.
    Portland **102**, 102–103, **103**
    Willamette Valley **50**, 50–51, **51**
Orlando, Florida, U.S.A. **196**, 196–197, **197**

P

Pennsylvania, U.S.A.
New Hope **24,** 24–25, **25**
Philadelphia **272,** 272–273
Peru: Lima **120,** 120–121, **121**
Philadelphia, Pennsylvania, U.S.A. **272,** 272–273
Philippines: Boracay **92,** 92–93, **93**
Phnom Penh, Cambodia **268,** 268–269, **269**
Portland, Oregon, U.S.A. **102,** 102–103, **103**
Portugal: Lisbon **140,** 140–141, **141**
Prague, Czechia **224,** 224–225, **225**
Provincetown, Massachusetts, U.S.A. **20,** 20–21, **21**
Puerto Rico, U.S.A.: San Juan **154,** 154–155, **155**

Q

Québec City, Québec, Canada **158,** 158–161, **159, 160–161**
Quepos, Costa Rica 244–245, **245**
Quito, Ecuador 180

R

Reykjavík, Iceland 240, 241, **241**
Rhode Island, U.S.A.: Newport **76,** 76–77, **77**
Rio de Janeiro, Brazil **90,** 90–91, **91**
Rovaniemi, Finland **164,** 164–165, **165**
Russian River Valley, California, U.S.A. **54,** 54–57, **55, 56–57**

S

Sacramento, California, U.S.A. 276–277, **277**
Sahara, Africa 267
Salem, Massachusetts, U.S.A. **216,** 216–217, **217**
Salisbury, Connecticut, U.S.A. 208–209
Salt Lake City, Utah, U.S.A. **252,** 252–253, **253**
Salzburg, Austria **200,** 200–203, **201, 202–203**
San Francisco, California, U.S.A. **276,** 276–277

San Juan, Puerto Rico, U.S.A. **154,** 154–155, **155**
San Juan Islands, Washington, U.S.A. **174,** 174–175, **175**
San Sebastián, Spain **112,** 112–113, **113**
Santa Fe, New Mexico, U.S.A. **44,** 44–45, **45**
Santiago, Chile **284,** 284–285
Saugatuck, Michigan, U.S.A. **74,** 74–75, **75**
Savannah, Georgia, U.S.A. **214,** 214–215, **215**
Scotland, U.K.
Edinburgh **226,** 226–227, **227**
Speyside **66,** 66–67, **67**
Scuba diving *see* Diving and snorkeling
Sedona, Arizona, U.S.A. **236,** 236–237, **237**
Seychelles: coastal spots **6–7, 88,** 88–89, **89**
Singapore **170,** 170–171, **171**
Snorkeling *see* Diving and snorkeling
Sonoma County, California, U.S.A. **54,** 54–57, **55, 56–57**
South Africa
Cape Town **182,** 182–183, **183**
Cape Winelands **58,** 58–59, **59**
Kruger National Park 182, 184, **184–185**
South Carolina, U.S.A.: Charleston **124,** 124–125, **125**
Spain
Barcelona **96,** 96–97, **97**
San Sebastián **112,** 112–113, **113**
Speyside, Scotland, U.K. **66,** 66–67, **67**
Spitsbergen, Norway **190,** 190–191, **191**
St. Augustine, Florida, U.S.A. **218,** 218–219, **219**
St. Petersburg, Florida, U.S.A. **72,** 72–73, **73**
Sydney, New South Wales, Australia **94,** 94–95, **95**

T

Tahiti, French Polynesia **168,** 168–169, **169**
Taipei, Taiwan 290–291
Tel Aviv, Israel **114,** 114–115, **115**

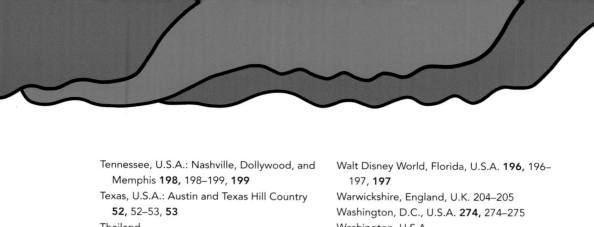

Tennessee, U.S.A.: Nashville, Dollywood, and Memphis **198,** 198–199, **199**

Texas, U.S.A.: Austin and Texas Hill Country **52,** 52–53, **53**

Thailand

Bangkok **4–5, 108,** 108–111, **109, 110–111**

Chiang Mai **188,** 188–189, **189**

Krabi **86,** 86–87, **87**

Thessaloniki, Greece **36,** 36–37, **37**

Tirana, Albania **262,** 262–263, **263**

Tokyo, Japan **116,** 116–117, **117**

Tongariro National Park, New Zealand 210–211

U

United Kingdom

Bath **166,** 166–167, **167**

Brighton **38,** 38–39, **39**

Cardiff, Warwickshire, Hampshire, and Kent **204,** 204–205, **205**

Edinburgh, Scotland **226,** 226–227, **227**

London and Manchester, England **280,** 280–283, **281, 282–283**

Speyside, Scotland **66,** 66–67, **67**

Uruguay: Montevideo **264,** 264–265, **265**

Utah, U.S.A.: Salt Lake City **252,** 252–253, **253**

V

Valparaíso, Chile 284–285, **285**

Vancouver, British Columbia, Canada **230,** 230–231, **231**

Venice, Italy **12, 132,** 132–135, **133, 134–135**

Vermont, U.S.A.: Woodstock **152,** 152–153, **153**

Vineyards *see* Wine

Visually impaired travelers 132

W

Waiheke Island, New Zealand **62,** 62–63, **63**

Wales, U.K.: Cardiff 204–205, **205**

Walt Disney World, Florida, U.S.A. **196,** 196–197, **197**

Warwickshire, England, U.K. 204–205

Washington, D.C., U.S.A. **274,** 274–275

Washington, U.S.A.

Leavenworth **148,** 148–149, **149**

San Juan Islands **174,** 174–175, **175**

Wheelchair-accessible sites *see* Accessible sites

Wildlife encounters 172–193, 249

Willamette Valley, Oregon, U.S.A. **50,** 50–51, **51**

Wine

Albania 262

Bloomington, Indiana, U.S.A. 259

Cape Winelands, South Africa **58,** 58–59, **59**

Daylesford, Victoria, Australia 35

Finger Lakes, New York, U.S.A. 42, **42**

Florence, Italy 107

Hudson Valley, New York, U.S.A. 234

Lyon, France **68,** 69

Mendoza region, Argentina **60,** 60–61

Monterey Bay, California, U.S.A. 128

Niagara Peninsula, Ontario, Canada 32

Sedona, Arizona, U.S.A. 236

Sonoma County and Russian River Valley, California, U.S.A. **54,** 54–55, **55,** 57

Waiheke Island, New Zealand **62,** 62–63

Willamette Valley, Oregon, U.S.A. **50,** 50–51, **51**

Woodstock, Vermont, U.S.A. **152,** 152–153, **153**

Wyoming, U.S.A.: Grand Teton and Yellowstone National Parks **176,** 176–177, **177**

Y

Yellowstone National Park, U.S.A. **176,** 176–177, **177**

ABOUT THE AUTHORS

Amy B. Scher is the best-selling author of five books translated into 20 languages. As a longtime traveler, she writes about how exploring our own neighborhoods and destinations around the world helps us discover who we really are. Her work has appeared in the *Washington Post, New York Daily News, Oprah Daily, Thrillist,* and more. She has also been featured on CBS and *Good Morning America.* Amy lives with her wife and bad cat in New York City.

Mark Jason Williams is an award-winning playwright, essayist, and travel writer who has visited 49 countries across all seven continents. In addition to writing for National Geographic, his work is published in newspapers and magazines in the U.S. and around the world, including the *New York Times,* the *Washington Post, HuffPost, Wired, Clarín, Courrier International, Time Out,* the *Globe and Mail, Thrillist, Salon, Out* magazine, *Insider, Far & Wide,* and *Good Housekeeping. Out in the World* is his first book. Mark lives in New York with his husband and their 15-year-old Yorkie. For more, visit *markjasonwilliams.com.*

Since 1888, the National Geographic Society has funded more than 14,000 research, conservation, education, and storytelling projects around the world. National Geographic Partners distributes a portion of the funds it receives from your purchase to National Geographic Society to support programs including the conservation of animals and their habitats.

National Geographic Partners, LLC
1145 17th Street NW
Washington, DC 20036-4688 USA

Get closer to National Geographic Explorers and photographers, and connect with our global community. Join us today at nationalgeographic.org/joinus

For rights or permissions inquiries, please contact National Geographic Books Subsidiary Rights: bookrights@natgeo.com

ISBN: 978-1-4262-2350-1

Printed in South Korea

23/QPSK/1

The information in this book has been carefully checked and to the best of our knowledge is accurate. However, details are subject to change, and the publisher cannot be responsible for such changes, or for errors or omissions. Assessments of sites, hotels, and restaurants are based on the authors' subjective opinions, which do not necessarily reflect the publisher's opinion.

SO MANY IDEAS.
SO LITTLE TIME.

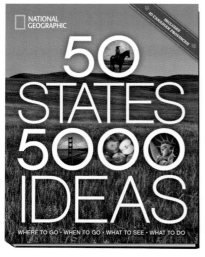

NATIONAL GEOGRAPHIC

INCLUDES 10 CANADIAN PROVINCES!

50 STATES 5000 IDEAS

WHERE TO GO · WHEN TO GO · WHAT TO SEE · WHAT TO DO

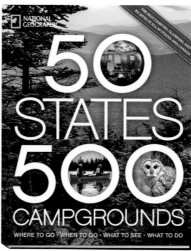

NATIONAL GEOGRAPHIC

THE BEST CAMPING, GLAMPING, AND RV SITES IN ALL 50 STATES AND CANADA

50 STATES 500 CAMPGROUNDS

WHERE TO GO · WHEN TO GO · WHAT TO SEE · WHAT TO DO

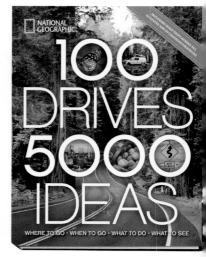

NATIONAL GEOGRAPHIC

INCLUDES ROAD TRIPS ACROSS ALL 50 STATES AND 10 CANADIAN PROVINCES

100 DRIVES 5000 IDEAS

WHERE TO GO · WHEN TO GO · WHAT TO DO · WHAT TO SEE